深圳大学学术著作出版基金资助

Subsidized by Shenzhen University Foundation for the Production of Scholarly Monographs

学术讲座中元话语的语用学研究：

顺应—关联路向

胡春华 著

中国社会科学出版社

图书在版编目（CIP）数据

学术讲座中元话语的语用学研究：顺应—关联路向：英文／胡春华著 .
—北京：中国社会科学出版社，2016.6
ISBN 978 - 7 - 5161 - 8383 - 0

Ⅰ.①学…　Ⅱ.①胡…　Ⅲ.①语用学—研究—英文　Ⅳ.①H030

中国版本图书馆 CIP 数据核字（2016）第 133856 号

出 版 人	赵剑英
选题策划	刘　艳
责任编辑	刘　艳
责任校对	陈　晨
责任印制	戴　宽

出　　版	中国社会科学出版社
社　　址	北京鼓楼西大街甲 158 号
邮　　编	100720
网　　址	http://www.csspw.cn
发 行 部	010 - 84083685
门 市 部	010 - 84029450
经　　销	新华书店及其他书店

印　　刷	北京明恒达印务有限公司
装　　订	廊坊市广阳区广增装订厂
版　　次	2016 年 6 月第 1 版
印　　次	2016 年 6 月第 1 次印刷

开　　本	710×1000　1/16
印　　张	16.75
插　　页	2
字　　数	301 千字
定　　价	62.00 元

序

　　我一直认为，究其根本，语用学是研究语言尤其是语言使用的一个视角，在 20 世纪的六七十年代是一个有别于传统语言研究的崭新的视角。20 世纪八九十年代之交欧洲大陆学界相继出现的关联论和顺应论犹如两颗原子弹爆炸，在整个语用研究领域掀起轩然大波，它的余波也震荡了中国的语言学学界。中国的研究者对国外学界的最新成果反应极快，霎时间，围绕着这两大理论的学术论文和著作大量涌现，有对这两个理论进行引介、解读、评介的，但更多的的则是以这两个理论作为框架对各种语言现象作出或重新作出解释的。胡春华的这部专著就是其中之一。不过，有别于同一范畴内其他的论文或专著的是，胡春华研究的理论框架不是关联论或顺应论，而是丰富版的顺应—关联模式，即两者的结合和互补。这在理论上的确是一个创新和进步。此外，被胡春华挑选为研究分析对象的是学术讲座的语言中的元话语。元话语置于语言的命题内容之外，它在语言交际中的作用很容易被忽视，所以在大量的话语分析的研究中对元话语的研究的确少见。胡春华的这一研究对话语分析无疑是一个重要的补缺，它的理论意义和实践价值不言自明。

　　胡春华 2005 年报考我名下的博士研究生，我在查看他的学历时不免疑虑重重：他于 1993 年至 1996 年间在江西省婺源茶叶学校读了中专的茶叶专业，后来的四年间完成了江西师范大学英语专业的自学考试本科，此后的三年在广西师范大学攻读英语专业硕士学位。我当时固然十分佩服他在四年内通过自考拿到学士学位的能力和毅力，但对他的不那么"科班"的出身总还是有几分担忧，虽然通过笔试和面试我把他录取了，但对他能不能顺利完成博士的课程和论文，我心里始终有个问号。不过事实终于打消了我的一切疑虑。我记得当年胡春华撰写论文时，他并不是一个让我感到很麻烦的学生，而如今时隔七年，再次浏览他的博士论文时我依然感觉到他文字的顺畅，阐述的清晰。所以当他请我为他的专著写序时，我欣然同意。

胡春华毕业后便受聘任教于深圳大学，我和他见面的机会不多，在他的这本专著付梓之际，首先对他表示祝贺，同时也希望他在做好一个高校教师的教学工作之余，在语言科研上再出新作。

上海外国语大学　何兆熊
2015 年元月

Abstract

Metadiscourse, an intuitively attractive concept, is often defined as the language we use to show readers how to read, react to, and evaluate what was written about the subject matter. It had been one of the hot topics in discourse analy-sis, pragmatic studies, and many other research fields even before the coinage of the term "metadiscoursé" by Harris in 1959.

So far, however, few studies on metadiscourse are pragmatic theory-driven, thus failing to offer a satisfactory account for why metadiscourse is used and how they work in utterance production as well as in utterance interpretation. And less consideration, in particular, is given to the internal mechanisms underlying the occurrence and the role of metadiscourse in academic lectures. Some baffling but significant questions still await an answer, for example:

1) Is metadiscourse pervasive in academic lectures?

2) Can the occurrence of metadiscourse in academic lectures be accounted for in the enriched Adaptation-Relevance Framework so as to advance our understanding of it? And if so, how can its occurrence be illustrated from this perspective?

3) What is the role of metadiscourse in academic lectures? Does it only function to facilitate our interpretation of lecture information?

4) Does this study have any pedagogical implications? And what are they?

Thus it is the goal of the present study to make a qualitative analysis of the occurrence and the role of metadiscourse in academic lectures within the framework of the enriched Adaptation-Relevance Model. Our analysis suggests that lecturers tend to search for relevance and make adaptations to choose the appropriate metadiscourse device while giving academic lectures. As a dynamic process, contextual adaptations of metadiscourse may be constrained by a variety of factors, such as linguistic reality, social conventions, audience's psychological motivation, etc. Meanwhile, the process of searching for relevance of metadiscourse could be measured in terms of two pairs of distinctions, namely, contextual effect/processing effort, explicit/implicit, conceptual/procedural. Our analysis within the framework of the enriched Adaptation-Relevance Model suggests that these two aspects could be integrated and a certain metadiscourse chosen is the result of searching for relevance and making adaptations. Besides, it is proposed in the study that the lecturer tends to employ metadiscourse as communicative strategies to achieve both the effective illustration of academic information and successful communication between the lecturer and the audience.

In addition, the present study has revisited the role of metadiscourse in academic lectures within the framework of the enriched Adaptation-Relevance Model, based on a brief review of traditional views on the role of metadiscourse. As a result, the role of metadiscourse in academic lectures could be regarded as the "discourse constructor" through searching for relevance and making adaptations on the part of the lecturer. And the role of metadiscourse in academic lectures is not a passive "discourse facilitator", but an active "discourse constructor". The significance of the current study lies in the fact that it has enhanced our understanding of the mechanism underlying the occurrence and the role of metadiscourse in academic lectures. In addition to the theoretical aspect, the present study also explores its pedagogical implications.

Table of Contents

List of Figures

Acknowledgements

I would like to express my sincere gratitude to all those who have helped me in the completion of my book, which is a process of both joy and torment for me. It is impossible for me to have picked up this topic and struggled to experience this process without their generous help.

First of all, I am extremely indebted to Prof. He Zhaoxiong, my supervisor, whose casual conversations, insightful ideas and thought-provoking lectures and seminars I enjoy very much. Besides, Prof. He's ever-reading help, influence and encouragement are essential to my book and my future studies. I still remember his unending patience, guidance, inspiration, and pains-taking effort in correcting and revising this book. His strict attitude towards academic research and humorous way of imparting suggestions in the process of revising my book and daily communication impressed me deeply. Without his indispensable help, this book would not have seen the light of the day.

My indebtedness also goes to Prof. Mei Deming, Prof. Xu Yulong, Prof. Su Dingfang and Prof. Yu Dongming and all the other doctoral supervisors at Shanghai International Studies University, whose wonderful lectures have impressed me and their influences will linger in my later studies and daily life.

I owe a debt of gratitude to Dr. Xu Haiming and Prof. Vande Kopple, who have provided me with many invaluable reference materials and suggestions, and other forms of help in daily communication.

I am also grateful to many of my classmates or friends, such as Zhang Jiliang, Liu Senlin, Han Geling, Liao Qiaoyun, Han Zhongqian, Tang Ruiliang, Zhu Qing, Zhu Minghai, Gao Bing, Wang Wangni, Chen Liqing, Miao Haitao, Sun Zhinong, Zhang Wei, Teng Xueming, to name just a few, who have helped me in one way or another. Besides, my thanks also go to my former classmate Fu Shuqin for printing my draft several times. Without their considerate help and concern, nothing is possible at many moments in my life.

Although so many teachers, classmates and friends have helped me, any remaining errors and misinterpretations are mine alone in this book.

Chapter One   Introduction

Metadiscourse, an intuitively attractive concept, has been one of the focuses of discourse analysis and pragmatic studies since the 1970s. Traditionally, it is often defined as the language a writer uses to show readers how to read, react to, and evaluate what was written about the subject. This definition suggests that metadiscourse may fulfill a variety of functions in the production and interpretation of discourse.

As a matter of fact, we use metadiscouse in daily communication, such as speaking, writing, etc. A huge amount of studies have been carried out to elicit the mechanism of metadiscourse in writing. For some scholars, metadiscourse is writing about our own writing. In actual writing, we tend to apply metatextual devices to catch the reader's attention or organize our text. Metadiscourse in writing serves to help the writer organize the content and signal the writer's attitude towards the content. Without metadiscourse, it is much difficult for the writer to convey ideas and positions smoothly to a certain extent. Thus, studies on metadiscourse have practical as well as theoretical significance. The emergence of a special issue on metadiscourse in *Journal of Pragmatics* in 2005 leaves us the impression that the study on metadiscourse appears to play a more and more important role in pragmatic researches and some other research fields. The charm of metadiscourse lies in the fact that it includes a wide range of specific items and could be interpreted from different perspectives. As a result, metadiscourse has triggered a flood of relevant researches despite its complicated nature. It is its complicated nature that has caught the attention of researchers and driven them to probe into the topic in order to enhance our understanding of metadiscourse.

Metadiscourse is a very complicated phenomenon which has attracted scholars in different research fields, such as semiotics, philosophy, psychology, etc. As a result, the attitudes and interpretation for metadiscourse vary across different fields due to their diversified perspectives and experiences. This is even reflected in the various terminologies for the same phenomenon with slight differences, such as "gambit", "discourse marker", "conversational cues", etc. The terminologies adopted by scholars in different fields, in a sense, convey divergent differences of their positions and interpretations. This has led to huge amount of studies of metadiscourse, which manifests the complicated nature of metadiscourse. Traditionally, many scholars tend to make a distinction between primary discourse and metadiscourse. The former is concerned with the propositional content of the discourse while the latter is related to the non-propositional content of the text. In other words, we are involved in these two aspects of discourse while constructing the discourse and these two aspects interact with each other which constitute an integrated whole. This can be regarded as the starting point of the researches on metadiscourse, although whether or not metadiscourse is concerned with propositional content of the discourse remains controversial among scholars. Just as Vande Kopple, a well-known scholar on metadiscourse, states:

> On one level we supply information about the subject of our text. On this level we expand propositional content. On the other level, the level of discourse, we do not add propositional material but help our readers organize, classify, interpret, evaluate, and react to such material. Metadiscourse, therefore, is discourse about discourse or communication about communication.
>
> (Vande Kopple, 1985: 83)

Vande Kopple is one of the pioneers in metadiscourse studiesin the west. The view on the nature of metadiscourse held by Vande Kopple echoes that of many other scholars in this research field. As one of the initiators in this field, for example, Crismore (1989) posits that two levels or planes of discourse are

2

involved in human linguistic communication, i. e. , the primary discourse level and the metadiscourse level. The primary discourse level consists of propositions and referential meanings; and the metadiscourse level consists of propositional attitudes, textual meanings, and interpersonal meanings.

Besides, Williams (1981) believes that there are two planes or levels of meaning. One of the levels deals with the propositional information of a topic, and the other one focuses its attention on the act of writing, i. e. , helping the readers interpret the writer's attitudes towards the topic. In addition, Jacobson (1960) also divides the functions of language into principal functions and secondary functions. This categorization is essentially similar to the distinction between primary discourse and metadiscourse.

To illustrate this point in detail, we can look at the following example:

Undoubtedly, there are limitations to the findings of this book.
(Hyland, K. & Polly Tse, 2004)

The above example can be regarded as an integrated discourse composed of primary discourse and metadiscourse. Accordingly, we can divide the discourse of the example into two levels. The referential meaning of the propositional message in the example is "there are limitations to the findings of this book. ", and the expression *undoubtedly* serves as a metadiscourse device to help the writer convey his/her propositional attitude towards the proposition and facilitate the interpretation of the whole discourse. Generally speaking, binary distinction makes it easier for people to interpret the meaning and functions of metadiscourse. However, it ignores the fact that it is very difficult to find out a clear boundary between primary discourse and metadiscourse, since their functions may intermingle in many cases. What the linguists can do is to try to figure out the possible separate functions of discourse at these two distinguished levels, since both primary discourse and metadiscourse are part of the whole discourse and fulfill their functions in different ways.

However, in traditional discourse studies, much attention has been attached to the propositional content or discourse level. In order to interpret the intended meanings of discourse, we are expected to take into account both the propositional content and the linguistic devices used to help us evaluate, organize, and respond to the primary discourse. And the intended meaning of an utterance depends on many aspects, among which linguistic devices (metadiscourse, e. g.) have an essential role to play. In many cases, metadiscourse may function to convey the intended meaning of the speaker or discourse constructor apart from its literal meaning.

Therefore, primary discourse and metadiscourse are the two aspects of discourse which interact with one another in human verbal communication. This also indicates the value of metadiscourse in discourse construction and interpretation. Actually, in some cases, metadiscourse plays a much more important role in the process of verbal communication with regard to its function of organizing the discourse and conveying the attitude of speaker or writer. Research shows that in human communication, oral or written, metadiscourse is pervasive, hence the significance of the studies on metadiscourse. Much importance is expected to be attached to the study of the mechanism of metadiscourse so as to improve communicative efficiency and effects in our daily communication.

Metadiscourse is a very broad concept which involves a wide range of factors and it is difficult to make a thorough study in a short time and the limited space in this book. And this book takes as its focus the occurrence and the role of metadiscourse in academic lectures, i. e. , how the lecturer monitors his/her speech to fulfill the intended communicative ends. In order to present to the readers a macro view of the book, this chapter will introduce briefly the research orientation, rationale, objective, methodology, and outline of the current study, and also remaining issues. All the introductions about the whole book will be brief, since its main purpose is to offer readers a sketchy idea of what the present book is mainly about and in what way the study will be conducted. As a general introduction of the current study, this part will not elaborate on the details of each chapter. Accordingly, six sections will be included in this part. Each part illustrates the main structure and general information of each aspect in the study, which helps the reader catch the key points in a short time. We do believe that a sketchy idea of the whole book and each chapter will help the readers better understand the concepts and interpretations mentioned in the book and a top-down way of illustrating ideas is an appropriate method in linguistic writing. Bearing this in mind, we add introduction and summary to every chapter so that the readers may have a rough impression of each chapter before reading and a solid understanding of the whole chapter after their reading. Though being a little boring sometimes, both introduction and summary of each chapter serve to illustrate the main idea in the body part of the chapter.

What is more, the language in this book is reader-friendly, since we believe that linguistic ideas should be conveyed in simple language and this maybe is the best way to make beginners in linguistics familiar with some basic concepts and theories in this area although linguistics may sound abstract and complicated in the eyes of many beginners in linguistic field. This is an obstacle for many linguistic students when they sit in linguistic classrooms at college. It is our hope that an increasing number of young scholars may join us in the near future in spreading basic ideas in linguistics and arousing the interests of ordinary people in linguistic field. In addition, a huge amount of linguistic papers in journals are written in obscure language which makes many beginners puzzled and feel confused about linguistics. We propose that papers in journals should be written in simple language since reader-friendly writing may attract more people to linguistic studies and researches. Admittedly, much effort is desired to improve current situation in this area and there is a long way to go in this respect in our linguistic circle.

1. 1   Research orientation

Much information inhuman education is conveyed through lectures in one form or another. To some extent, lectures are the main channel through which human being pass on knowledge and exchange ideas. One can imagine what the situation would be without lectures or seminars in classrooms. Academic lecture remains the main vehicle of instruction by which the lecturer imparts his/her academic knowledge to the audience and discusses with them academic issues. As an interactive communicative activity, its main purpose is to establish good academic relationship with the students so as to influence them by saying something. The significance of the study on the language used by the lecturer lies in the fact that it can tell us what linguistic devices are actually employed to empower the lecturer in his/her teaching.

It should be noted that, on the other hand, academic lectures also serve as the platform for scholars to exchange academic information. This has little business to do with teaching, but regards exchanging viewpoints and discussing about academic subjects. They may air their views on a specific topic in academic lectures or seminars in which metadiscourse has a role to play. This also constitutes an essential part of the functions of academic lectures. As a matter of fact, academic lectures in many seminars or conferences are the major channel for the communication among scholars in the world. This is an easy and convenient way of exchanging academic ideas. Metadiscourse has a role to play in facilitating the delivering of academic information and the intended meaning of the speakers.

However, our main concern in the present study is academic lectures for the purpose of teaching although we also touch upon some aspects of academic lectures for exchanging information. This is because it seems to us that academic lectures for teaching purposes constitute the major part of our academic life. And academic lectures for teaching purposes sound more important to us that other forms of academic activities. From childhood to adulthood, we mainly acquire academic information or knowledge through academic lectures, thus its significance. In order to have a better understanding of the academic information in classrooms, students need to pay attention to the metadiscourse employed by teachers since it is part of the classroom information. Less attention to metadiscourse may possibly result in the failure in grasping the academic content in classroom teaching to a certain degree.

Metadiscourse in academic lectures is a field of both theoretical significance and potential applications. Since the term "metadiscourse" was coined by Harris in 1959, a great number of studies concerning the subject have emerged (e. g., Vande Kopple, 1985; Rahman, 2004; Ifantidou, 2005; etc.). Unfortunately, on the one hand, most studies on metadiscourse in the past decades have focused their attention on written form. We were surprised to find that few of these studies deal with metadiscourse in oral communication, especially in academic lectures. As a matter of fact, metadiscourse in oral communication has its role to play in human communication. On the other hand, few studies so far are theory-driven and a theoretical interpretation of metadicourse may do its part in this area.

Most studies in this field, at least it seems to us are the explanations of the occurrence of metadiscourse in terms its functions, such as the function of engaging the readers' attention or facilitating the interpretation of the text. Many of them do not tend to make theoretical issues their primary concern, which is the essence of metadiscourse to some extent. For example, Rahman (2004) concludes that excessive use of communicative devices may be as disadvantageous as limited or no use of such expressions in the discourse. He has made a brief description of the functions of metadiscourse and the consequence of excessive metadiscourse in discourse. But what is the internal mechanism of metadiscourse in our communicative activities? This remains a question. Therefore, studies concerning theoretical support are necessary.

1. 2   Remaining issues of the existing studies

It is interesting that metadiscouse abounds in our daily communication, both written and oral. This also reflects its multifunctional nature in human communication, hence the significance of such studies. The nature of being multifunctional results in the complicated nature of similar studies. A huge amount of metadiscourse studies have been conducted to interpret the nature of metadiscourse from their own perspectives.

It seems to us that many previous studies on this topic have explained facts in terms of facts to a certain degree and few studies are conducted from pragmatic theories, thus failing to offer a satisfactory account of why metadiscourse is used and how they work in utterance production as well as in utterance interpretation. And less consideration is given to the internal mechanisms underlying the occurrence and the role of metadiscourse in academic lectures. Very often, scholars focus their attention on its taxonomies and functions in discourse and its role as devices facilitating the interpretation of utterances on the part of the audience.

So far, no systematic study has been made to explore the occurrence of metadiscourse in academic lectures from the Adaptation-Relevance perspective. As a new model, it can shed new light on the studies of metadiscourse, since it combines both the Aadptation Theory and Relevance Theory. Besides, the model examines linguistic phenomenon from a dynamic perspective. And there is also a need to revisit the role of metadiscourse in academic lectures from this framework to further our understanding of its nature.

In an effort to advance the research on metadiscourse, we propose to conduct a relatively systematic study of the role of metadiscourse as a cognitive phenomenon in academic lectures. Within the framework of the enriched Adaptation-Relevance Model, the present study reviews past studies on metadiscourse from different perspectives and attempts to further our understanding of the use and role of metadiscourse as a cognitive tool for the conveying and understanding of the message of the lecturer.

In the present study, information can be gathered about what metadiscourse features are commonly used, how they are used, and why the lecturer chooses them to achieve his/her communicative goals. And more information will also be provided regarding the way in which the audience processes the information in academic lectures. In addition, some possible pedagogical implications regarding metadiscourse will be explored. By doing so, we hope that this study will do its part in interpreting the nature of metadiscourse in academic lectures and pave the way for later studies in this area.

1. 3　Rationale of the present study

Despite the abundance of researches on metadiscourse, it is far from fully explored. Up till now, scholars have not even reached an agreement on what metadiscourse is and its working mechanism in the discourse, written or oral. What is more, scholars have not paid enough attention to the theoretical aspect of metadiscourse in academic lectures. A study of metadiscourse in academic lectures from this perspective has both theoretical significance and practical advantage. The present study aims to make a contribution to both the theoretic and application aspect of metadiscourse in academic lectures.

On the one hand, this book will provide a much deeper understanding of the occurrence and functions of metadiscourse in academic lectures. A revisit of the role of metadiscourse within the framework of the enriched Adaptation-Relevance Model will provide possible guidance for both school teachers and students. What we can do is to revisit the role of metadiscourse in academic lectures with our theoretical framework.

On the other hand, the study will shed light on teacher training and curriculum design. The significance of the current study lies in the fact that academic lectures are perhaps the genre most commonly encountered by undergraduate students and post-graduate students in their academic studies and other academic activities. One of the aims of this study is to propose a more robust model to explore how the lecturer uses metadiscourse as a means of effecting his/her academic speech. We believe that such studies can offer some implications for academic teaching in classroom and both teachers and students may benefit from a better understanding of the nature of metadiscourse in academic lectures. And a much more theoretical interpretation of metadiscourse in academic lectures may shed light on pedagogy and other teaching activities.

1. 4   Objective of the present study

The present study aims to explore the role of metadiscourse in academic lectures and provides a relatively systematic theoretic account of metadiscourse from the perspective of Adaptation Theory and Relevance Theory. Based on these two theories, an enriched Adaptation-Relevance Model will be constructed as the theoretical framework to account for the occurrence of metadiscourse in academic lectures. It will probe into how, when, and why metadiscourse occurs in academic lectures. In addition, its implications for pedagogy and course design will be explored in the book. Therefore, the research questions of the present study are as follows:

1) Is metadiscourse pervasive in academic lectures?

2) Can the occurrence of metadiscourse in academic lectures be accounted for in the enriched Adaptation-Relevance Framework so as to advance our understanding of it? And if so, how can its occurrence be illustrated from this perspective?

3) What is the role of metadiscourse in academic lectures? Does it only function to facilitate our interpretation of lecture information?

4) Does this study have any pedagogical implications? And what are they?

1.5　Methodology of the current study

The goal of the current study is to advance the researches regarding metadiscourse in academic lectures based on Adaptation Theory and Relevance Theory. Methodologically speaking, the current research is mainly qualitative and theory-driven. In this descriptive and explanatory study, qualitative contextual analysis of the occurrence of metadiscourse in academic lectures will be made and an enriched Adaptation-Relevance Model based on Adaptation Theory and Relevance Theory will be adopted as the theoretical framework for the evaluation of both the occurrence and the role of metadiscourse. Elaboration of the model will be provided in later chapters.

The present study is qualitative because we offer a description and explanation of metadiscourse in academic lectures. A number of examples are selected from many authentic lectures to illustrate the occurrence of metadiscourse in academic lectures. We do not count the frequency of metadiscourse in academic lectures, since we do not believe the frequency of metadiscourse can determine the nature of metadiscourse in academic lectures. What we focus on is interpreting the nature of the occurrence of metadiscourse in this kind of teaching activity, since our new model may possibly offer a new insight into the nature of metadiscourse.

And the present research is theory-driven, since we rely heavily on the ide-

10

as of Adaptation Theory and Relevance Theory. Basing our analysis on these two major theories, we try to revise and enrich the Relevance-Adaptation Model proposed by Yang Ping and the Adaptation-Relevance Model by Ran Yongping. In so doing, we will put forward an enriched Adaptation-Relevance Model, which we believe is much more suitable to the analysis of metadiscourse in academic lectures. Along with the theoretical framework, a working definition of metadiscourse is presented to make the research manageable and easy to operate to some extent.

Therefore, the present study is a qualitative theoretical exploration of metadiscourse with examples from academic lectures to illustrate our point of view. Besides, it has both theoretical significance and pedagogical applications. The whole book will focus on the occurrence of metadiscourse in academic lectures and we will conduct a holistic discourse analysis of two texts selected from a collection of lectures in cognitive linguistics by George Lacoff, a famous American cognitive linguist. The reason why we choose George Lacoff's academic lectures on linguistics is that he is a well-known cognitive linguist and his academic lectures are ready-made. Luckily enough, we get the video materials from one of our classmates. In other words, the former part of the book will interpret the nature of the occurrence of metadiscourse by selecting some examples from many kinds of lectures and the latter part of the book will offer a relatively complete discourse analysis of metadiscourse occurrence in two academic lectures. Both parts of the book are significant, since the former is a basis for the latter and the latter an extension of the combination of theory and practice on metadiscourse studies.

1. 6   Outline of the book

The present book consists of eight chapters, with Chapter One the introduction providing a panorama of the whole research. It describes the research orientation, rationale, remaining problems, objective, methodology, and outline of the current study.

Chapter Two reviews what has been done in the research of metadiscourse.

It looks at the diversified definitions and taxonomies of metadiscourse. By examining the earlier definitions, we put forward a working definition to meet the need of the present study. To set the current research in a larger background, five theoretical perspectives on metadiscourse are presented and evaluated, thus eliciting some remaining issues for further researches. While reviewing different perspectives on metadiscourse, we discuss the strength and weakness of these approaches.

Chapter Three describes the research methodology and data collection procedures. A description of the data and the process of collecting the data are offered. In addition, the principle of choosing data is described. The aim of this chapter is to describe the methodology adopted and data selected in this book.

Chapter Four introduces some relevant concepts in Adaptation Theory and Relevance Theory, and explores the possibility of enriching the Adaptation-Relevance Model. A general description of the theoretical framework is presented. Along with the description, we also discuss its applicative value of interpreting metadiscourse in academic lectures.

Chapter Five is devoted to a thorough discussion of the possibilities of applying the Adaptation-Relevance Model as the theoretical framework to account for the occurrence of metadiscourse in academic lectures. It is demonstrated that this framework does have the potential to provide us with a relatively satisfactory interpretation of the role of metadiscourse devices in academic lectures.

Chapter Six revisits the role of metadiscourse in academic lectures within the framework of Adaptation-Relevance Model. In addition, the new concept "metadiscourse awareness" is proposed as a result. This concept may call people's attention to the occurrence of metadiscourse in our daily communication as well as academic lectures. The new concept itself may call many scholars' attention to the studies and significance of metadiscourse in academic lectures. This is part of the motivation for coining the term for our readers.

Chapter Seven offers a systematic discourse analysis of the occurrence of metadiscourse in two complete academic lectures on cognitive linguistics by George Lakoff. It aims to get a new insight of metadiscourse from a bird-eye's view of its occurring mechanism. This is similar to a case study whose purpose is to present an example for the analysis of metadiscourse in academic lectures from the framework of the enriched Adaptation-relevance Model. Further studies may be conducted in this way.

Chapter Eight explores possible pedagogical implications, i. e. , implications for EFL teaching and learning, teacher training, and course design. This chapter focuses on the application aspect of the current study. We aim to get some insight from our analysis to do our part for EFL classroom teaching and other relevant pedagogical issues.

Chapter Nine summarizes the major findings, arguments, and some relevant basic ideas presented in earlier chapters. In this chapter, we situate the current study in a larger research context and discuss the limitations of the present study and suggestions for future researches. As the conclusion part of the book, it looks into the future by summarizing what we have done in this area. Due to limited personal capabilities and resources, there may be many mistakes and misinterpretations in the book. Please forgive us for that. We hope our readers will have a critical thinking of what we presented and carry out your own studies of metadiscourse in the near future. We do believe in the potential academic outcome in the area and more efforts are called for.

Chapter Two　Literature Review

2. 1　Introduction

This chapter is devoted to a brief review of relevant literature on metadiscourse studies. It first discusses the diversified terminologies and clarifies some confusing concepts so as to present an operational definition of metadiscourse for the present study. Then, it presents some classification systems of metadiscourse proposed by some representative scholars in this field in order to offer a much more complete picture of metadiscourse studies.

Finally, some different perspectives on metadiscourse are introduced and discussed so as to highlight some remaining issues and the significance of the current research. Besides, this will also help to clarify some misunderstandings about metadiscourse and frame our present study in a large research background. But before we embark on this, we may take a look at the existing diversified terminologies first. In this area, many scholars have carried out some similar researches with different terms. They may choose their preferred terms or perspectives to probe into the nature of metadiscourse. However, this may lead to certain confusion for researchers and followers in the area, thus the significance of clarifying terminologies.

2. 2　Terminological diversity

Since the coinage of the term by Zellig S. Harris in 1959, "Metadiscourse" has traditionally been used as an umbrella term covering a series of terms, such as "evidentials", "gambits", "cue phrases", "metacommunication" (Rossiter, 1974) , " rhetorical actions" (Colomb & Williams, 1985) , "metatext", "non-topical material", "modalities of text", "framing", " criticism" (Pierce, 1966) , " commentary" (Rabin, 1986) , " writing about writing" (Dillon, 1981) , etc. These terms reflect different focuses and understandings of metadiscourse researchers.

And sometimes the terminologies we mentioned above are usedinterchangeably in the studies of different scholars due to different views, preferences, or perspectives held by them. As a matter of fact, these terms are overlapping to a large extent and scholars may have their own concerns, focuses with regard to the functions of metadiscourse in the discourse when choosing a certain term in their studies.

Similarly, metadiscourse can take many different forms, ranging from morphemes, single words, phrases, clauses, to strings of sentences. Put it in another way, as a discourse-related concept, metadiscourse can be individual words, phrases or even some kind of sentence patterns. And the form of metadiscourse depends on the need of specific communicative situation.

This feature of metadiscourse echoes the characteristics of discourse that the length of the discourse is not certain and even a single word could form a discourse. And the length of a discourse varies from one communicative situation to another. For example, the single word " *Fire!* " in emergent situation stands as an independent discourse despite its length because it expresses a complete thought and thus forms an integrated whole. The criterion is not its length, but its function as a metadiscourse or metadiscourse. For metadiscourse or discourse, what matters is not its length but the meaning it conveys in concrete communicative situations.

What is more, there are a range of terms for metadiscourse devices. The diversified terms for metadiscourse reflect the multi-functional and fuzzy nature of metadiscourse. As a complicated concept, metadiscourse have both confused and attracted scholars to a certain degree, hence the existence of different definitions and classification systems of metadiscourse. On the one hand, metadiscourse is a fascinating area that draws attention from researchers due to its essential role in the discourse. On the other hand, the complicated nature of metadiscourse sometimes makes scholars puzzled regarding its internal mechanism.

Therefore, it seems to us that scholars have a love and hate feeling towards metadiscourse. And it is possibly this feeling that drives researchers to make further progresses in this area. As a result, metadiscourse has triggered heated discussions and a flood of researches. For the convenience of explanation, we prefer to use the term "metadiscourse" to include most such linguistic devices thought it is not complete and perfect. We hope our readers will have your own judgment on the diversified terminologies and the existing theoretical studies on metadiscourse.

2. 3   Definitions of metadiscourse

2. 3. 1   *Existing definitions of metadiscourse*

What we need to mention is that some apparent agreement reached by scholars can not veil the complicated nature of metadiscourse regarding its definition and functions. Like many other linguistic terms, "metadiscourse" since its coinage by Harris has also been interpreted in different ways. There is no doubt that there exists a problem relating to defining what is meant by metadiscourse. And there is a great variety of terms employed to refer to these special linguistic expressions. As we also mentioned above, there is no generally acknowledged definition for metadiscourse due to researchers' varied research interests and the complicated nature of the phenomenon itself.

It is believed by many scholars that the fabric of discourse falls into two components, i. e. , primary discourse and metadiscourse. Generally speaking, according to them, primary discourse focuses its attention on the generation of new propositions, based on which anideationally functioning text is complete and writers convey their ideas to the readers smoothly. In the process of constructing a primary discourse, the writers very often try to create a coherent discourse with the help of metadiscourse.

According to many scholars, primary discourse is propositional or ideational content and acts as the main part of the discourse. And metadiscourse refers to aspects of a text that explicitly organize the discourse and signal the writers' attitude, which can help to engage the readers in the interaction. Besides, primary discourse and metadiscourse in the discourse always work side by side to accomplish the task of constructing a complete text. The application of metadiscourse contributes greatly to the construction of primary discourse and the rest of the discourse as a whole.

As a matter of fact, metadiscourse in the discourse functions to establish and maintain contact between the writer and the reader. This makes it a pragmatic concept, since it is metadiscourse that supports writers' production, and readers' interpretation of the primary discourse. However, this is only one part of a writer's work of constructing a text; at this point, text generation is just writer-oriented while communication, as is known, is a bilateral interaction between writer and reader. This suggests that more researches are required to probe into the occurrence of metadiscourse in our verbal communication in order to enhance our understanding in this area.

Metadiscourse thus helps a writer to "guide, direct, and inform" (Crismore, 1989: 64) his/her readers about how he/she hopes they will respond to text content and is an important category both in the production and interpretation of the text. As a kind of comment on the running text that is usually distinguishable from the content or subject matter of the text, metadiscourse has also been labeled "non-topical material" which corresponds to the term "non-propositional content". This represents one approach of viewing metadiscourse by making a distinction between non-topical material and content matter.

A shorthand definition of it, to my knowledge, is "text about text", "discourse about the evolving discourse", "discourse about discourse", or "the writer's explicit commentary on her own ongoing text". In this narrow sense, it includes reflexive linguistic items that refer to the text itself as text or as language. This kind of definitions also takes the part of metadiscourse as secondary in the whole discourse.

In a wider sense, however, it refers to linguistic items which reveal the writer's and reader's (or speaker's and hearer's) presence in the text, either by referring to the organization of the text or by commenting on the text in other ways. Therefore, we could look at metadiscourse from different senses and achieve our own understanding of the linguistic phenomenon.

As a result, on the one hand, some scholars focus on whether or not metadiscourse provides propositional content when defining metadicourse. On the other hand, others pay attention to the functions metadiscourse fulfills in the discourse.

For the first approach, they tend to agree that metadiscourse is interpretative; it does not add propositional content but offers propositional attitudes, textual meanings, and interpersonal meanings. And it is used interpersonally to guide the reader's reaction to the propositional content. Some of the definitions can be quoted and elaborated in a chronological order below:

Zellig S. Harris, a pioneer in the studies of metadiscourse, defines metadiscourse as text segments that contain information of only secondary importance (from Skulstad, 2005). Metadiscourse and the rest of the discourse play different parts although both of them contain necessary information for the construction of the discourse. This definition echoes the distinction between primary discourse and metadiscourse, hence the minor part of metadiscourse.

Halliday (1978) defines metadiscourse as linguistic elements that do not refer to aspects of external reality but to the organization of the discourse itself and to aspects of the relationship that develop between author and writer of the texts. Here, external reality is the linguistic elements that do not constitute the propositional content of the discourse. Therefore, Halliday (1978) holds a non-propositional view of metadiscourse which treats it as the tool for organizing the discourse and establishing relationship between the interlocutors in the discourse.

Lautamatti (1978) also defines metadiscourse as one aspect of "non-topical linguistic material". According to her, there are two levels of material in any written discourse: the topical material, which is the discourse topic, and the non-topical material, which is metadiscourse. And these two kinds of materials altogether constitute an integrated whole of discourse despite their different natures.

Vande Kopple (1985) believes:

"On the level of metadiscourse, we do not add propositional material but help our readers organize, classify, interpret, evaluate, and react to such material. Metadiscourse, therefore, is discourse about discourse or communication".

(Vande Kopple, 1985: 83)

Williams (1999: 111) considers it to be "writing about writing, whatever does not refer to the subject matter being addressed. " Here, subject matter refers to the propositional content of the discourse in contrast with metadiscourse. According to him, metadiscourse does not add propositional content to the discourse and its sole function is to say something about the subject matter.

Thompson (2003: 6) echoes Williams (1999: 111) and states that metadiscourse in the discourse refers to language in a text, which talks about that text rather than the propositional content. It should be noted that many scholars use "text" and "discourse" interchangeably and here "text" equals to "discourse".

Arguments concerning whether metadiscourse adds something new to the subject matter or not exist from the very beginning. However, the functions of metadiscourse have been generally acknowledged as projecting writers themselves into texts, guiding and directing, rather than informing, readers so that it can help them achieve a better understanding of the propositional content of a text as well as the writer's attitudes or positions towards the content and their readers (Meyer, 1975; Keller, 1979; Schiffrin, 1980; Dillion, 1981; Williams, 1981; Ragan & Hopper, 1982; Vande Kopple, 1985; Crismore, 1989; etc.). As a result, we call these studies classical approach on metadiscourse since they separate metadiscourse from the subject matter of discourse.

Many scholars also define metadiscourse by focusing on the functions it fulfills in the discourse, since metadiscourse very often functions to help the listener or reader organize, interpret andevaluate the information given. We can also look at some of the definitions from this perspective:

For example, Luukka (1992) believes:

According to these definitions, metadiscourse elements are not supposed to add meanings to the propositional information of texts. Thus they could even be omitted from a text without changing its actual meaning. This definition (Vande Kopple's), however, seems problematic when a more holistic view is taken and texts are analyzed as communicative acts. The actual meaning of a text is not to be regarded as a list of propositions. . . Therefore, I do not define metadiscourse as "non-propositional" elements of texts, but instead, take a more functional approach.

(ibid. : 78)

Halliday (1973) makes a distinction between the textual andinterpersonal functions of language. He refers to textual function as "an enabling function, that of creating a text". He states:

It is this component that enables the speaker to organize what he is saying in such a way that it makes sense in the context and fulfills its function as a message.

(ibid. : 66)

As far as the interpersonal function is concerned, Halliday believes:

All that may be understood by the expression of our own personalities and personal feelings on the one hand, and forms of interaction and social interplay with other participants in the communication situation on the other hand.

(ibid.)

The distinction of textual and interpersonal function of language paves the way for the definition of metadiscourse, since many scholars propose their own definitions of metadiscourse basing themselves on Halliday's studies. Accordingly, they divide metadiscourse into two categories, i. e. , textual metadiscourse and interpersonal metadiscourse. This represents the mainstream of defining metadiscourse in academic circle.

In addition, Halliday (1994) states that metadiscourse includes linguistic elements that do not refer to aspects of internal reality but to the organization of the discourse itself and to the aspects of the relationship that develop between author and reader of the texts. Here the internal reality refers to the propositional content of the discourse, thus metadiscourse does not touch upon propositional content of the discourse and its function is textual and interpersonal.

What is more, Vande Kopple (1985: 83) refers to metadiscourse as "discourse about discourse or communication about communication". By this definition, he considers the main function of metadiscourse as helping readers in their attempts to organize, classify, interpret, evaluate and react to the propositional content of the text. Therefore, this definition focuses its attention on the functions metadiscourse fulfills in the interpretation of the discourse.

In addition, according to him, metadiscourse can help us express our personalities and our reactions to the propositional content of our texts and characterize the interaction we would like to have with our readers about that propositional content. Here, Vande Kopple also focuses on the function of metadiscourse in writing because he uses the word *text* when discussing the role of metadiscourse. Actually, many scholars adopt the term *text* when they discuss the issue of discourse. It seems to us that what matters is what they are concerned with instead of the terms they adopt. Therefore, we are expected to focus on the content under study and figure out what the scholars mean by their different terms.

What is more, any truth value that theses conveyors of interpersonal meanings carry would relate not to states of affairs in the world but to such things as our actual personalities, our true evaluations of the propositional material, our role in the situation in which the text functions, and our hopes for the kinds of responses readers might make (ibid. : 87). As a matter of fact, this is concerned with the interpersonal function of metadiscourse. The term "truth value" is widely discussed in semantics which concerns the meaning of words or sentences at the level of discourse. In pragmatic circle, we pay more attention to the situation or context in which an utterance takes place since context may exert a great influence upon its interpretation. It is admitted that semantics and pragmatics are complementary in that they look into the same linguistic facts from different perspectives.

Intaraprawat (1988 : 17) believes that metadiscourse is used to "function as interpretive framing information for the whole sets of messages so that they would create the structure which weaves the elements of the propositional content into a unified, coherent whole". His idea sounds very traditional since he regards metadiscourse as the elements that organize the discourse to deliver propositional content in a coherent way, which paves the way for later similar researches.

In Hyland (2000 : 109), "metadiscourse" is defined as the linguistic resources used to organize a discourse or the writer's stance towards either its content or the reader. This definition suggests that, on the one hand, metadiscourse is the potential resources for the writer to choose in concrete communicative situations. On the other hand, metadiscourse does not constitute the content of the discourse. As a modern scholar, he is also a traditional researcher who makes a distinction between metadicourse and discourse in writing and confines metadiscourse to the non-propositional part. His contribution lies partly in the fact that he calls our attention to the concrete communicative situations in which a writer chooses metadicourse to finish his/her writing. Hyland very often focuses on the role of metadisocurse in writing since he believes that metadiscourse plays a much more important part in writing.

And he also holds that metadiscourse is typically used as an umbrella term to include a heterogeneous array of cohesive and interpersonal features which help the understanding and values of a particular discourse community (Hyland, 1998a). Metadiscourse here refers to the linguistic devices writers employ to shape their arguments to the needs and expectations of their target readers. What we should mention is that he takes into account readers or audience in writing when writers construct a discourse, which is great progress to this field.

In addition to the definitions mentioned above, some scholars also try to probe into the nature of metadiscourse from a holistic perspective so as to get a better understanding of the term. Some of these definitions may touch upon both the distinction between propositional content and non-propositional content and the functions metadiscourse fulfills in the discourse. We can quote some of them in the following part.

As a representative scholar in the field of metadiscourse studies, Crismore has split much ink on the definition of metadiscourse in his writing. For example, Crismore (1989: 80) regards metadiscourse as the "author's overt and non-overt presence in the discourse in order to direct rather than to inform readers".

What is more, Crismore et al. (1993: 40) hold that metadiscourse is "linguistic material in texts, written or spoken, which does not add anything to the propositional content but that is intended to help the listener or reader organize, interpret and evaluate the information given". As a matter of fact, Crismore's idea echoes the stands of many traditional scholars in that he also pays more attention to the functions metadiscourse fulfils in the construction and interpretation of discourse.

Fairclough (1992) believes that metadiscourse is a kind of "manifest intertextuality" where the writer interacts with his/ her own text. As we know, intertextuality is a common term in literary criticism which refers to the phenomenon that common features may be possessed by literary works and the same writer may write similar works. In this definition, metadiscourse is regarded as the devices the writer employed to interact with his/her own text.

Geisler (1994) refers to "metadiscourse" as "rhetorical process" which concerns both the writer and the audience, contrasting these two terms with the so-called "domain content". Rhetorical processes are considered by her to be "shaped by the writer's relationship with the intended audience" (Geisler, 1994: 82).

Similarly, metadiscourse could be defined as discourse about discourse from a holistic perspective. It is considered as the discourse that calls attention either to the relationship between the author and the claims in the text or to the relationship between the author and the text's readers. Researchers in different fields may have their own understanding of metadiscourse phenomenon.

For example, speech communication theorists define metadiscourse in a much broader sense. They regard metadiscourse as metacommunication, i. e. , communication about communication, whether it is verbal or non-verbal and whether it is about communication in general or about specific communicative interactions. This actually goes too far from metadiscourse itself since a broad view of it may make it difficult to focus on the key issues in metadiscourse studies. That is to say, we are expected to narrow down the scope of the subject matter so as to have a more accurate study of metadiscourse.

In the field of rhetoric, metadiscourse is broadly defined as commentary in the discourse. For example, Rabin (1986) sees commentary as text about the text that facilitates the construction of text on the part of the writer. In order to produce a coherent text, the writer is expected to choose appropriate metadiscourse which may facilitate the process of writing.

As a famous researcher in the field of rhetoric, Conley (1983) defines metadiscourse as figures of thought, which are rhetorical strategies used for effective communication in writing rather than just for ornamentation. The definitions from this perspective very often pay attention to the functions metadiscourse fulfills in the process of writing a text. In addition, metadiscourse is also regarded as a kind of strategy adopted by the writer in order to construct coherent and effective discourse. Therefore, studies of metadiscourse in rhetoric are conducted mainly from the perspective of writing since writing is related to rhetoric to a certain extent. When we talk about rhetoric, we focus more on the role of rhetoric in effective writing instead of speaking. This reflects partly the nature of rhetoric in linguistic field. Both Rabin and Conley focus on the metadiscourse in writing.

As an expert in sociolinguistics and discourse analysis, Schriffrin (1980) uses the term "metatalk" and sees it as the talk about the ongoing talk. And metatalk, according to her, conveys the social information on the part of both the speaker and the hearer, hence a sociolinguistic view on metadiscourse. The term "metatalk" itself suggests that Schriffrin pays more attention to speaking instead of writing. And he mainly looks at metadsicourse from a social perspective since his attention is attached to the role of metadiscourse in social interaction.

Keller (1979) refers to metadiscourse as "gambits", which are psychological strategies used by participants in communication. With these strategies, participants could monitor their speech or writing so as to achieve the intended communicative ends. This reflects a psychological perspective on the nature of metadiscourse. Metadiscourse studies from this perspective make it more complicated to many people since human mind and psychology sound more mysterious to some extent. This may add to the complicated nature of metadiscourse in academic lectures.

Beauvais's speech act model (1986) offers a much more complex definition of metadiscourse, since he makes a distinction between illocutionary acts and propositional content as well as between metadiscourse and primary discourse. He defines metadiscourse as "the elements in a sentence that convey illocutionary content in either fully or partially explicit form" (ibid.: 30). Thus, metadiscourse is believed to be secondary elements that contain illocutionary content.

The functional approach to metadiscourse is based on Halliday's functional view of language. For example, Meyer (1975) uses Halliday's notion of "theme" and defines metadiscourse as "signaling", a non-content aspect of writing that gives emphasis to certain aspects of the semantic content or points out the structural organization of the content.

According to Meyer, signaling does not add new topical content but simply accents information already contained in the content structure and shows the writer's perspective on and commitment to the content. This also suggests that metadiscourse has nothing to do with the propositional content, and hence being secondary.

Williams (1981) regards metadiscourse as a stylistic variable which is discourse about discoursing. To him, we usually have to write on two levels whenever we write a few words. We write about the subject we are addressing, of course: foreign policy, falling sales, operation of a computer system. But we also directly or indirectly tell our audience how they should take our ideas.

According to him, we should use a term to distinguish this kind of writing that guides the reader from writing that informs the reader about primary topics (ibid.: 47). And metadiscourse can be such a choice. As a matter of fact, metadiscourse functions to help the reader distinguish primary discourse from metadiscourse and get the intended meaning of the writer apart from the literal meaning. Metadiscourse serves as a stylistic variable to help the writer organize the discourse.

The definitions of metadiscourse we mentioned above may vary, depending on their different perspectives and approaches. However, they all shed light on the complicated phenomenon of metadiscourse and help us gain a better understanding of it regardless of their strengths and weaknesses.

Besides, operationally, it is difficult to talk about the functions of metadiscourse without talking about its types. We must make a distinction between macro-functions and micro-functions of metadiscourse. These two aspects of functions constitute a whole of the role of metadiscourse in our communication. However, due to limited space, this book is mostly concerned with the macro-functions of metadiscourse in academic lectures.

When talking about the macro-functions of metadiscourse, Crismore (1989) holds that metadiscourse has semantic, social, psychological, communicative, and rhetorical functions. For Crismore, metadiscourse is used for rhetorical aims: informative, persuasive, or expressive. Basically, the textual function serves informative aims and the interpersonal function serves persuasive or expressive aims. His study lays a solid foundation for later macro-functional researches on metadiscourse since his general description of the functions of metadiscourse points out the directions in this field.

According to Halliday (1973), we use language to express ourexperience of the world (ideational), to interact with our audience (interpersonal), and to organize our expression into a cohesive and coherent text (textual). Each text is an integration of all these two kinds of meanings. Here "text" is similar to "discourse" because different scholars may take diversified terms to express their views from their own stands. Sometimes the theories they founded may also be based on a system of newly-coined terms.

Hyland (1998a) revises both Crismore et al.'s (1993) and Halliday's (1973) researches, and defines two categories of metadiscourse: textual metadiscourse and interpersonal metadiscourse. This sounds more like a summary of Halliday's researches since it is based on the basic ideas of M. A. K. Halliday.

So far, we may find that functional view of metadicourse very often divides metadiscourse into two parts, i. e. , textual metadiscourse and interpersonal metadiscourse. This actually overlaps some functions of the propositional part of the discourse. Obviously, the interpersonal and textual functions of metadiscourse play important parts in our linguistic actions. Interpersonal elements carry essentially social meanings and textual meanings. Without them, we would not be able to interact with our readers, form cohesive texts, and would not be able to effectively express ideational meanings in the discourse.

According to the above definitions, so far, no unanimous agreement has been reached among scholars regarding its definition and nature. It seems to us that the existence of different views and perspectives originates, very often, from different research fields in which they are interested. Despite the differences, they have tried to define it operationally so as to conduct researches conveniently.

However, many of the definitions mentioned above are to a certain degree overlapped and they all reflect the complicated nature of metadiscourse. The basic discourse function of metadiscourse is to guide the reader through the text and to comment on the use of language in the text. The focus is on the structure, discourse actions and wording of the text.

Obviously, most definitions of metadiscourse by researchers focus their attention on written text while many of them have neglected to a certain degree its ubiquitous existence in oral communication. Only by taking into account both written and oral forms can we get a relatively comprehensive understanding of human linguistic communication. To meet the needs of the present study, it is necessary to propose an operational definition of metadiscourse.

2. 3. 2   *Working definition of metadiscourse*

We intuitively value primary discourse and neglect the importance of metadiscourse to some degree when we make a distinction between "primary discourse" and "metadiscourse" as the starting point for the discussions about metadiscourse and its functions of organizing, evaluating primary discourse and guiding the audience. The word "primary" itself conveys the idea of being important, thus its status in the whole discourse. Therefore, we may figure out that people have paid more attention to primary discourse when they look at discourse.

As a matter of fact, however, metadiscourse is essential to the fulfillment of communicative ends in human verbal communication. This is because metadiscourse can not only help writers or speakers construct discourse, but also allow them to show audience how different parts of the discourse are interrelated and how they should be interpreted. Therefore, much more attention should be paid to the occurrence and the role of metadiscourse in order to understand its true nature and bring some implications to FLT and teacher training.

In existing literature, metadiscourse has long been regarded as an essentially heterogeneous category which ranges from linguistic forms even to punctuations and visual metadiscourse, such as the layout, color and typography of the discourse, etc. Judging from the literature, metadiscourse seems to be elements of the discourse that include anything regarding the organization of the proposition content. Actually, this is not always the case. We argue that this kind of taxonomy has made the concept too broad and even misleading to a certain degree. This echoes the concept of "cognition". When cognitive linguistics appears, many scholars bring too many traditional linguistic phenomena into this field. Actually, "cognition" is not all-mighty since it just interprets linguistic phenomena from one perspective. This is also true of metadiscourse. What we can do in our daily research is to narrow down the range of metadiscourse to get a relatively thorough and objective examination from our own experiences and perspective.

Therefore, it seems tous that metadiscourse can be defined either in a broad sense or in a narrow sense. Nevertheless, regarding metadiscourse as a category including visual devices perhaps has gone too far because this will add to the confusion already existed in the studies on metadiscourse.

Most studies on metadiscouse focus their attention on metadiscourse in the narrow sense. This is also true of the present study, which takes interest in the linguistic aspect of metadiscourse and attaches great importance to the ways the lecturer employs metadicourse devices to engage the audience so as to guarantee successful communication between the lecturer and the audience. To meet the specific needs of the current study, we define metadiscourse as follows:

> *Metadiscourse is the online choice of linguistic devices made by the speaker or writer in discourse to engage the audience and fulfill the communicative ends in concrete communicative situations.*

Specifically, on the one hand, this operational definition regards the application of metadiscourse in human verbal communication as linguistic choice made by the speaker. As a matter of fact, there may be several possible alternatives coming into the mind of the speaker or the writer before he/she makes a linguistic decision. And a certain form of metadiscourse chosen must be appropriate to the communicative situation, be it formal or informal.

On the other hand, it focuses on the dynamic nature of the choices of metadiscourse made by the speaker. Human verbal communication is a complicated phenomenon that involves online decision-making on the part of the speaker or writer. The dynamic nature of the process may guarantee the appropriateness of the metadiscourse chosen in the communicative situations, since the choice of certain metadiscourse devices is constrained by situational context of the ongoing communication, such as time, place, participants, etc. Therefore, the speaker or the writer is expected to adapt to all these factors and make online decisions so as to meet the requirements of the ongoing communication.

In addition, this definition pays attention to metadiscourse in both oral form and written form. As we mentioned above, metadiscourse is ubiquitous in human verbal communication, be it written or oral. And metadiscourse in verbal communication performs a variety of discourse functions without which the discourse may not go as smoothly as we expect.

It will mislead readers and scholars if we confine our definition of metadiscourse to the written form. Thus, a more comprehensive definition of metadiscourse should include these two forms of verbal communication.

What is more, the ultimate goal of the employment of metadiscourse is to fulfill the communicative purposes. And it is the communicative ends that decide what metadiscourse to choose and when to choose it in concrete communicative situations. Therefore, the specific requirement of the concrete communicative situations partly decides the choice made by the speaker or the writer.

We may employ metadiscourse to make our intention explicit; we may use metadiscourse to express our attitude towards the propositional content; we may also apply metadiscourse to organize the discourse to make it coherent. All these communicative goals will influence the speaker or writer's choice of metadiscourse in constructing discourse.

Before we elaborate on this, however, it is necessary to present how scholars have classified metadiscourse in order to grasp its nature and characteristics. And it is these taxonomies that help to enhance our understanding of metadiscourse and pave the way for further researches.

2. 4   Diversified taxonomies of metadiscourse

So far, many classification systems of metadiscourse have been proposed. In this section, we will review in turn seven major taxonomies of metadiscourse proposed by Meyer, Lautamatti, Williams, Vande Kopple, Crismore, et al., Hyland, and Rahman respectively. These seven taxonomies are classical and basic, which may help readers to get a rough idea of metadiscourse.

2. 4. 1   *Meyer's classification*

In Meyer (1975), signaling is considered to be metadiscourse, and is defined as a non-content aspect of prose which gives emphasis to certain aspects of the semantic content, or denotes aspects of the structure of the content. The scholar holds a non-propositional view on the nature of signaling, which is used to emphasize the information already contained in the content. And its main function is to show the author's perspective on the content covered in the primary discourse.

According to Meyer (ibid.), specifically, signaling falls into five categories: (1) specifying the structure of relations in the content structure; (2) prospectively revealing information that is abstracted from content but that occurs

30

later in the text; (3) summarizing statements; (4) pointer words.

Meyer's classification takes a worm's view of metadiscourse and is therefore very specific compared with many other classifications we will review later. Besides, he holds a non-propositional view of metadiscourse, which echoes the view of most metadiscourse researchers.

2. 4. 2   *Lautamatti's classification*

Like Meyer, Lautamatti (1978) also regards metadiscourse as non-topical linguistic devices in discourse. To her, written discourse can be divided into two levels of materials: one is basic, topical material, which is the material that is related to the topic of discourse, and the other is subsidiary, non-topical material (metadiscourse), which is discrete. And non-topical linguistic materials are essential to the discourse as a whole although they seem to play a secondary role in the discourse.

At the same time, non-topical linguistic materials, according to Lautamatti (ibid.), constitute a framework for the topical material, allow readers to relate the subject matter of the discourse to a larger framework of knowledge and help them understand the internal organization of the discourse as a whole.

Specifically, non-topical materials fall into five categories with functions as the criteria they play in discourse, which go as follows:

(1) metatextual markers or discourse connectives: materials used to comment on the discourse itself which may refer to the language of the text or the properties of the organization of the text itself;

(2) illocutionary markers: materials used to comment on and make explicit the illocutionary force of the statement concerned;

(3) commentary markers: materials used to comment directly to readers in order to help them know what and how to read;

(4) modality markers: materials used to comment on, indicate, or suggest the truth-value of the ideas discussed; and

(5) attitude markers: materials used to make explicit the author's own

attitude towards what he or she is discussing.

2. 4. 3　Williams' classification

Williams (1999: 47) regards metadiscourse as a stylistic variable that constrains the production of the discourse to a large extent. The definition of metadiscourse he presents is as follows:

"... writing that guides the reader (distinguished from), writing that informs the reader about primary topics... discourse about discourse"

"Metadiscourse: writing about writing, whatever does not refer to the subject matter being addressed ".

And metadiscourse, according to him, can be divided into four categories:

(1) all connecting devices (*therefore*, *however*, *for example*, *in the first place*);

(2) allcomments about the author's attitude (*I believe*, *in my opinion*, *let me also point out*);

(3) all comments about the writer's confidence in his following assertion;

(4) references to the audience (*as you can see*, *you will find that*, *consider now the problem of...*)

(ibid. : 111)

In addition, Williams (1981: 196) points out that metadiscourse is ubiquitous in argumentative writing due to the persuading nature of this kind of writing. And two categories of metadiscourse can be identified in this genre:

(1) hedges and emphatics, which express the certainty with which an author presents material;

(2) sequencers and topicalizers, which are used to guide the readers

through the organization of a text;

　　(3) attributors and narrators, which tell a reader where facts or opinions come from.

We see that William's taxonomy is very general which divides metadiscourse into two categories. However, being general means being broad in many cases. As a matter of fact, metadiscourse as a complicated concept really requires delicate examination of its nature in many respects.

2. 4. 4　*Vande Kopple's classification*

As a pioneer in metadiscourse studies, Vande Kopple (1980) also makes a distinction between propositional content and non-propositional content and the former is regarded as primary discourse. His researches have paved the way for later metadiscourse studies, since many scholars regard his taxonomy as the classical one. In Vande Kopple's (1985) system, metediscourse is divided into two categories: the textual and the interpersonal. Specifically, these two categories include seven kinds of metadiscourse: text connectives, code glosses, illocution markers, validity markers and commentary.

　　Textual metadiscourse
　　· *Text connectives* help readers recognize how texts are organized, and how different parts of the text are connected to each other functionally or semantically (e. g. , *first*, *next*, *however*, *but*)
　　· *Code glosses* help readers grasp and interpret the meanings of words and phrases (e. g. , *X means Y*)
　　· *Illocution markers* make explicit what speech act is being performed at certain points in texts (e. g. , *to sum up*, *to give an example*)
　　· *Narrators* let readers know who said or wrote something (e. g. , *according to X*)
　　Interpersonal metadiscourse
　　· *Validity markers* assess the truth-value of the propositional content

and show the author's degree of commitment to that assessment, i. e. , hedges (e. g. , *might*, *perhaps*) , emphatics (e. g. , *clearly*, *obviously*) , attributers (e. g. , *according to X*) , which are used to guide the readers to judge or respect the truth-value of the propositional content as the author wishes.

   · *Attitude markers* are used to reveal the writer's attitude towards the propositional content (e. g. , *surprisingly*, *it is fortunate that*)

   · *Commentaries* draw readers into an implicit dialogue with the author (e. g. , *you may not agree that*, *dear reader*, *you might wish to read the last section first*)

(Vande Kopple, 1985)

It is obvious that Vande Kopple's classification is based on M. A. K. Halliday's three metafunctions of language, i. e. , ideational, textual, and interpersonal functions. According to standard views, metadiscourse are only related to the non-propositional aspects of interpretation of text. Since the first function is mainly concerned with the propositional content of writing, this classification system focuses its attention on the latter two metafunctions of language, hence the system. It seems to us that Vande Kopple's model remains the classical and generally accepted one.

2. 4. 5   Crismore et al. 's classification

SinceVande Kopple's classification came into existence, many scholars have proposed revisions of the model. For example, Crismore et al. (1993) provides a reorganized classification system that runs as follows:

    I. TEXTUAL METADISCOURSE (used for logical and ethical appeals)

     1. *Textual Markers*
      · Logical connectives
      · Sequencers

- Reminders
- Topicalizers

2. *Interpretive Markers*
- Code Glosses
- Illocution Markers
- Announcements

II.   INTERPERSONAL METADISCOURSE (used for emotional and ethical appeals)

3. *Hedges (epistemic certainty markers)*
4. *Certainty Markers (epistemic emphatics)*
5. *Attributers*
6. *Attitude Markers*
7. *Commentary*

  (Crismore, Markkanen, and Steffensen, 1993: 47 – 54)

Crimore et al. 's classification of metadiscourse as textual and interpersonal types is cogent in that it focuses on the two functions served by metadiscourse and imposes an order on the chaotic items and therefore is much easier to grasp.

2. 4. 6   *Hyland's taxonomy*

On the one hand, Hyland (1998a) defines textual metadiscourse as devices which reveal the writer's intention by explicitly establishing preferred interpretations of propositional meanings, which includes (1) Logical connectives: it expresses semantic relation between main clauses; (2) Sequencers: it denotes sequence of text material; (3) Frame markers: it explicitly refers to discourse acts or text stages; (4) Endophoric markers: it refer to information in other parts of the text; (5) Code glosses: it helps readers grasp meanings of ideational material. On the other hand, interpersonal metadiscourse " reveals the author's attitude towards both the propositional information and the reader, thus contributing to the development of a writer-reader relationship " (Hyland, 1998a: 229).

According to him, interpersonal metadiscourse includes (1) Hedges: it withholds writer's full commitment to statements; (2) Emphatics: it emphasizes force or writer's certainty in message; (3) Attributors: it indicates the source of quoted information; (4) Attitude markers: it expresses writer's attitude to proposition content; (5) Relational markers: it explicitly refers to or build relationship with reader.

A much more recent model is the one proposed in Hyland, K. and Polly T (2004:169) and Hyland (2005:50 – 54), which make a distinction between interactive metadiscourse and interactional metadiscourse. The term *interactive* refers to the writer's management of the information flow to guide readers through the text, and *interactional* refers to his or her explicit interventions to comment on and evaluate material. The model runs as the following:

Category	Function	Example
Interactive resources	help to guide reader through the text	
Transitions	express semantic relation between main clauses	in addition/but/thus/and
Frame markers	refer to discourse acts, sequences, or text stages	finally/ to conclude/my purpose here is to
Endophoric markers	refer to information in other parts of the text	noted above/see Fig/ in section 2
Evidentials	refer to source of information from other texts	according to X/(Y,1990)/Z states
Code glosses	help readers grasp functions of ideational material	namely/e. g. /such as/in other words
Interactional resources	involve the reader in the argument	
Hedges	withhold writer's full commitment to proposition	might/perhaps/possible/about
Boosters	emphasize force or writer's certainty in proposition	in fact/definitely/it is clear that
Attitude markers	express writer's attitude to proposition	unfortunately/I agree/surprisingly
Engagement markers	explicitly refer to or build relationship with reader	consider/note that /you can see that
Self-mentions	explicit reference to author(s)	I/we/my/our

2. 4. 7   Rahman's classification

However, it seems to us that an even more recent study on metadiscourse by Rahman (2004) possibly provides a relatively comprehensive classification-system, which makes a distinction between metatext and metadiscourse. It should be noted that Rahman uses the umbrella term "metalanguage", which takes on a rather new meaning. The following is the details:

METALANGUAGE

METATEXT (text-about-text management)

Textual Reference to:

- Discourse entities (*In this paper, In the following section*)
- Discourse acts (*As noted earlier/above, will be discussed*)
- Discourse labels (*This argument, This question*)

METADISCOURSE (text-about-discourse management)

Performing/executing:

- Illocutionary acts (*We argue that, We agree, My question is*)
- Topic shifting (*In regard to, Now the question arises*)
- Code glossing (*namely, for example, for instance*)
- Interactive acts (*Note that, It should be noted*)

Indicating relations:

- Text connectives (*but, therefore, in addition, first, second*)

(Rahman, 2004)

As we show above, this model sounds much more systematic and easier to grasp. It adopts the term "metalanguage" to cover both metatext and metadiscourse. In a general sense, the word metalanguage is used o refer to the language, whether natural or formalized, which is used to speak of a language. More precisely, the word refers to a language whose sole function is to describe a language. Thus the language itself must constitute the sole sphere of application for the entire vocabulary of the language.

Holistically, it divides metalanguage we use into two general categories: metatext and metadiscourse. The former is concerned with text-about-text management, and the latter text-about-discourse management. Actually, these two concepts are overlapped to a certain degree since it is not easy to make a distinction between them in many cases.

Therefore, we will adopt this system with some revisions as the basis for the analysis of the occurrence of metadiscourse in academic lectures. But before we dwell on this issue, it is necessary to review some different theoretical perspectives on metadiscourse to offer a general theoretical basis for the readers.

2.5 Theoretical studies on metadiscourse

Metadiscourse is considered by many researchers and theorists to be a persuasive tool to help readers organize, understand, interpret, evaluate and react to written information the way the author intended (Crismore, Markkanen & Steffensen, 1993; Vande Kopple, 1985). As we mentioned above, an increasing number of studies of metadiscourse have been conducted due to its complicated nature, be it theoretical or practical. These theoretical studies have offered a bird-eye's view of metadiscourse in human communication.

Theoretical studies on Metadiscourse have been carried out from many perspectives, i. e. , functional, sociolinguistic, rhetorical, pedagogical, cognitive, etc. For example, some rhetoric theorists regard metadiscourse as a rhetorical device that conveys a writer's feelings toward a subject and clarifies text for the reader (e. g. Conley, 1983). And some functional linguists study metadiscourse in terms of the two metafunctions of language system, i. e. , ideational, interpersonal, and textual. We will take a look at some viewpoints held by some of these approaches in the following sections. To be honest, due to our limited capability and resources, our summary of these approaches is not inclusive to some extent. What we have done is to try our best to search for as many as possible relevant materials on metadiscourse and sort out their relation.

2. 5. 1   *Communicative perspective*

Studies on metadiscourse from communicative perspective focuses on the functions it fulfills in human communication. Generally speaking, metadiscourse is regarded as metacommunication by theorists of communication. As we can see, "metacommunication" is a term coined in the light of "communication", hence the close relationship between metacommunication and communication.

As a speech communication theorist, Rossiter (1974), believes that all messages about communication in the discourse, verbal or non-verbal, are metacommunication. In the process of interpreting a given message, metadiscourse has its role to play. As an added commentary about communicative interactions, metacommunication functions to inform others of how utterances are to be decoded by saying explicitly the writer's intentions in the ongoing discourse. Without metadiscourse, the readers sometimes would become puzzled about some points in the messages expressed by the speaker.

According to him, metadiscourse in communication possesses the following two characteristics: (1) metadiscourse is the communication about ongoing communication; (2) there are two kinds of metadiscourse — metadiscourse about one's own discourse and metadiscourse about someone else's discourse. Therefore, we can safely judge from his statements that metadiscourse is also a kind of communication which plays different roles in the discourse compared to the main body of communication itself. And metadiscourse can function to talk about both one's own discourse and other's discourse.

Similarly, another theorist of communication Wunderlich (1979) holds that it is inadequate to take communication only as being composed of propositional content, for communication is also consisted of propositional attitudes. Therefore, communication is composed of both propositional content and the writer's attitudes towards the proposition, and the latter is also essential to the successful communication between the writer and the readers.

In addition, he focuses his attention on the logical properties of human communication. According to him, human communication not only conveys information, but also shows the speaker's or writer's attitude towards the possibilities or necessity of the information. Only by taking into account of these two aspects of communication can we obtain a full picture of metadiscourse in human communication. Therefore, metadiscourse

Furthermore, Wunderlich also distinguishes between five categories of verb operators called propositional functors which can be applied to both spoken and written propositional attitudes. And the propositional functors he refers to in his study is what we called metadiscourse, without which communication would not go as smoothly as we have expected. But he uses a different term "functor", which reflects the intention of the scholar. According to him, functors in the discourse help the speaker or writer deliver the propositional content.

The five categories go as follows: (1) epistemic ones (e. g. , *know*, *think*, *suspect*); (2) doxastic ones (e. g. , *believe*); (3) ability/capability (e. g. , *can*, *may*, *be able to*); (4) motivational ones (e. g. , *wish*, *want*, *prefer*); (5) normative ones (e. g. , *ought to*, *should*). The identification of these five categories focuses its attention on the some kind of verbs that will influence the interpretation of propositional attitudes. As a matter of fact, we could obtain more accurate interpretation of an utterance in spoken or written communication through the metadiscourse devices (or *funcors* in his term) employed by the speaker or the writer.

2. 5. 2   *Sociolinguistic perspective*

Some sociolinguists consider metadiscourse used in human communication as "frame", which offers interpretive and framing information for the whole sets of other messages (Bateson, 1972; Goffman, 1974; et al.). The very term "frame" itself adopted by them reflects the functions metadiscourse fulfills in the ongoing discourse. Therefore, according to many sociolinguists, metadiscourse provides framing information for the hearer or reader to interpret the utterance or discourse in human verbal communication.

In addition, according to them, metadiscourse is constrained by the norms of a particular setting and genre, and even the experiences of speech community. Complicated as they are, the employment and interpretation of metadiscourse require delicate mental efforts on the part of both interlocutors in the communicative activities basing themselves on the interactive conventions and other factors in a given speech community.

Others (Hopper, 1980; Schiffrin, 1980; Ragan & Hopper, 1981; etc.) see metadiscourse as "alignment talk", which provides information about what others might have been taken for granted by making explicit, recasting, and transforming other messages in human communicative activities. It is the existence of such alignment talk that guides the hearer or reader to catch the intended meaning of the writer or the speaker.

For example, Schiffrin (1981) regards metadiscourse as talk about talk in human verbal interaction. She terms it "metatalk" which is used by speakers to organize and evaluate the conversation by explicitly conveying the speaker's attitude towards a certain talk. According to her, "metatalk allows a speaker to exercise control over the principal discourse at specific junctures during the production by projecting an animator who will bracket the expressive implications of what is being said" (Schiffrin, 1980: 131). This quotation tells us that, to her, metatalk serves as a tool used by the speaker to constrain the interpretation of his/her discourse on the part of the hearer.

In addition, according to the scholar, metatalk falls into two broad categories: organizational brackets and evaluative brackets. And the former functions on a referential and informational plane, and the latter the expressive, symbolic plane (ibid.). These two planes constitute the main part metatalk can play in the discourse. Actually, the classification of these two brackets is based on the functions metadiscourse plays in the discourse.

Echoing Schiffrin (1981), another sociolinguist Ragan & Hopper (1981) also terms the explicit forms of metadiscourse in human verbal communication as "metatalk". The function of metatalk, according to him, is to act as the verbal properties of another message and does aligning work in conversation to guarantee a precise interpretation of the utterance through questioning inexplicable utterances and initiating conversational repair. This is related the organizational function of metadiscourse in social interaction.

As a matter of fact, human being interacts with each other in social context since we cannot live outside the society. Our verbal communication, in most cases, is social interaction. And we communicate with metadiscourse in the society. No one can deny it. Therefore, metadiscourse from sociolinguistic perspective have enhanced our understanding of it by focusing on social variables and other factors influencing its production and interpretation in human verbal communication.

2. 5. 3 *Psycholinguistic perspective*

Apart from communication theorists and sociolinguistics, psycholinguists also take interests in metadiscourse in human conversation. As a matter of fact, they pay attention to the strategies employed in conversation by speakers to organize their ideas and to set their conversational moves. This approach to metadiscourse probes into the mental activities and strategies of the speaker or the writer and thus has provided us with a much more delicate understanding of its nature in human verbal communication.

Keller (1979), as a representative in this approach, focuses his attention on metadiscourse in conversation and refers to metadiscourse as "gambits". According to him, gambits are a set of signals that is used to introduce level shifts within the conversation or to prepare the hearers for the next turn in the logical argument. Therefore, gambits are signals or messages used by speakers or as part of their conversational strategies in order to fulfill a certain communicative task. Only by taking into account of the presence or absence of gambits can we interpret the conversation with great ease due to the essential functions gambits play in conversation.

As for its functions, according to him, gambits can fulfill the following four tasks in conversation:

(1) to structure their presentation of the topic;

(2) to structure their turn of talking in the conversation;

(3) to indicate their state of consciousness with respect to some infor-

mation, opinion, knowledge, emotion, or planned action; and

(4) to check whether communication is being passed on to the listener.

With these fours aspects of functions, gambits will add to the explicitness of
the conversation and thus facilitate the understanding of the conversation on the
part of the hearer. In addition, gambits are also a semantic introducer in conversation. They function to tell the hearer the general frame of and the speaker's attitude towards the topic in the conversation. In this respect, gambits can function to indicate the participants' communicative intention in the concrete communicative situations, and thus contributing to the success of the communication.

Therefore, generally speaking, the gambits employed in conversation by the
speakers constitute conversation strategies adopted by them to fulfill the intended
communicative goals. And the choice of certain gambits requires delicate mental
efforts on the part of the speakers and it is these strategies that help to facilitate
conversation on the parts of both the speakers and the hearers. Human communication in this respect sounds much delicate and requires the joint efforts of the
speakers and hearers. In this process, gambits act as the tool or strategy for the
participants in concrete communication.

2.5.4 *Functional perspective*

In china, many well-known linguists take interest in functional linguistics
and have gained great achievements in this area, such as Hu Zhangling of Peking University, Huang Guowen of Zhongshan University, and many other young
scholars. Many of them have introduced functional linguistics to china and
spread it to every corner of Chinese linguistic circle. No one can deny their contribution to the introduction and spreading of this discipline in China. The popularity of functional linguistics in China could possibly be traces back to the education background of M. A. K. Halliday in Peking University. And many Chinese scholars at that time went to study functional linguistics at The University of
Sidney. It should be admitted that the amount of functional studies of metadis-

course is not huge in China in spite of the popularity of functional linguistics.

Studies from the point of view of systemic and functional linguistics shed new light on the understanding of metadiscourse. As a representative systemic-functional linguist, Halliday regards language as a semiotic system and claims that the investigation of language is relevant to the understanding of both social structure and language itself. His theory offers a theoretical framework for the studies on metadiscourse and many later researches have been carried out on the basis of Halliday's idea about language use. Basing themselves on Halliday's theory, many functional linguists have conducted a huge amount of studies of metadiscourse from functional perspective. Before we elaborate on these studies, it is necessary to present a brief introduction of Halliday's basic ideas.

Halliday (1973) divides the meaning system of language into two meta-functions: the ideational, the interpersonal and the textual. To be specific, the ideational system of meaning regarding the content of language conveys a message which has specific reference to the process, persons, objects, abstracts, qualities, states, and relations of the real world; and the interpersonal function is the use of language to establish and maintain human relationships and is concerned with social meaning (ibid. : 58). And the textual function of language is concerned with the organizational role language plays in the discourse. These two metafunctions of language constitute the whole body of the meaning system of language and serve as the main vehicles for participants to fulfill communicative purposes.

What is more, the interpersonal aspect of language allows writers or speakers to make their own presence explicit in a text or other communicative situations; it also permits them to express their comments, attitudes, and evaluations of propositions and to express the relationship between writers and readers. Options in the interpersonal system enable the language users to establish human interpersonal relationships and, therefore, are concerned with social meaning. Therefore, language many function at two different levels and the ultimate goal is the successful communication between participants or interlocutors.

To describe language use from his perspective, Halliday coined the term "meaning potential" to refer to the linguistic realization of behavior potential.

44

This constitutes the choice a speaker can make from a huge amount of potential forms in the language, which are the options in human language. With these options at hand, the speakers or writers could vary their linguistic forms to realize the intended communicative goals. As a matter of fact, meaning potential is a pot of potential meanings of linguistic forms which provides the speakers or writers with the possible choices in concrete verbal communication.

Halliday's concept of the three metafunctions of language is key to later researches because it lays the theoretical foundation for metadiscourse studies. It seems that propositional meaning fulfills the ideational function of language and that metadiscourse can fulfill either interpersonal or textual functions of language (Vande Kopple, 1985). This is a typical understanding of metadiscourse from a functional perspective.

Another functional linguist Sangster (1987) holds that the categories of metadiscourse are complex, non-discrete, and fuzzy. According to him, the least overt type of metadiscourse is poetry, since poets very often violate normal rules to make choices about words, clauses or even explicit metadiscourse in order to create poetic effects on the readers. And another extreme of metadiscourse use in human verbal communication is covert metadiscourse and grammatical metadiscourse which remain the most covert form in discourse.

Sangster (ibid.) also believes that a theory of metadiscourse must take into account the phenomenon of exercising the first person pronoun as texts become less oral, such as technical reports and textbooks. To him, metadiscourse takes on different degrees of the author's presence in different communicative contexts and a functional analysis of metadiscourse should be made from the spoken discourse to written discourse because of their varying degrees of formality or style.

Similarly, Eoyang (1987) states that the taxonomy of metadiscourse might begin with oral texts that have a great deal of metadiscourse and end with written texts that have all the metadiscourse left out. Therefore, his study has depicted the whole range of the objectives for metadiscourse studies by providing two extremes of metadiscourse. Actually, metadiscourse is everywhere in human daily communication and it has its role to play in this process. These two extremes of metadiscourse use serve to prove the existence of metadisocurse and its significance.

Dillon (1981), a functional linguist, states that using metadiscourse in constructing a discourse will lead to calling attention to the act of discoursing itself. And these two acts are closely related to each other in the process of producing a discourse. According to him, typically, there are two planes or levels in concrete writing-reading situation. The first plane pays attention to a writer supplying readers with information about the subject matter of the text and expanding the referential content, and the second level in the situation is related to a writer's writing and a reader's reading the writing. Therefore, obviously, we can judge from his illustration that the second plane is concerned with metadiscourse in a discourse, which function to help to facilitate both the construction and the interpretation of the ongoing discourse.

Besides, Luukka (1992) also takes a functional perspective on metadiscourse. What he believes is that metadiscourse can fulfill a variety of functions though it is concerned with the non-propositional content of an utterance. This sounds very traditional since most traditional theories argue that metadiscourse constitutes the non-propositional content of the discourse and it only functions to help the writer or speaker organize and evaluate the propositional content of the discourse. We can quote some statements made by her as follows:

> Metadiscourse elements are not supposed to add meanings to the propositional information of texts. Thus, they could even be omitted from a text without changing its actual meaning... The actual meaning of a text is not to be regarded as propositions. ... Therefore, I do not define metadiscourse as "non-propositional elements of texts", but instead, take a more functional approach.
>
> (Luukka, 1992: 78)

Therefore, functional approach to metadiscourse focuses on the functions metadiscourse plays in the discourse and many studies are largely based on Halliday's theory of metafunctions of language in human verbal communication. As a representative approach in linguistics, functional linguistics has its role to play in metadiscourse studies and other related areas.

2. 5. 5   *Cognitive perspective*

However, many scholars take a different perspective and focus on the cognitive mechanism of the occurrence of metadiscourse in discourse rather than its formal feature. As a cognitive activity, human verbal communication involves meticulous calculation of which linguistic form to choose in order to realize the intended meaning. This is also true of metadiscourse use in our communication. And cognitive approach may bring some new light to metadiscourse studies to some extent.

For example, some scholars (Chafe, 1986; Lakoff, 1972; Palmer, 1985; etc.) refer to metadisourse as "evidentials" and have conducted many researches on the role of metadiscourse in verbal interaction. To present a much clearer picture of such studies, we can quote some thoughts of Chafe as follows:

Everything dealt with under this broad interpretation of evidentiality involves attitudes towards knowledge.

(Chafe, 1986: 161)

According to Chafe (ibid.), in addition, evidentials function to qualify knowledge in two ways: evaluating the degree of reliability of knowledge, specifying the mode of knowledge, and marking the contrast between knowledge and expectation. These two ways suggest that evidentials in the discourse may involve human cognitive activities. Apart from this, evidentials show the sources of information which can be realized in a variety of forms.

Interestingly, cognitive approach to metadiscourse claims that the main function of evidentials is to express the writer's attitude towards knowledge due to its non-propositional nature. As we can see, different from many other approaches to metadiscourse studies, cognitive approach adopts the term "knowledge" instead of "proposition". Therefore, metadiscourse studies from the cognitive perspective also pay attention to the functions it fulfills in the discourse.

2. 5. 6   *Rhetorical perspective*

Rhetorical approach to metadiscourse focuses on the rhetorical function of metadiscourse in verbal communication. Conley (1983) , for example , regards metadiscourse as rhetorical strategies used for effective communication rather than mere ornamentation in discourse. These rhetorical strategies , in most cases , refer to figures of speech applied in human verbal interaction.

The figures of speech relevant to metadiscourse , according to him , fall into three categories: the first category includes the figures of presence (e. g. , repetition) ; the second category includes the figures of focus (e. g. , similes , metaphors , and definitions) ; and the third category includes the figures of communication (e. g. , allusion , and rhetorical questions). These two categories of figures of speech and propositional content constitute a whole picture of the discourse in concrete communicative situations. And successful communication , in part , depends on the appropriate employment of the figures of speech.

Similarly , Flower (1987) considers metadiscourse as an instrument for rhetorical moves and strategies. At least three variables or features of thought have been identified in her study. Among them , the first variable is a narrative structure; the second variable is using a cautious and qualified position (hedges) , an emphatic and certain position (emphatics) , or evaluative position (evaluatives) ; and the third variable is a personal quality. These three variables of thought serve as the rhetorical tool for our communication.

Apart from these , Crismore (1989) proposes a relatively comprehensive rhetorical model for metadiscourse.

1. Metadiscourse exists , whether it is called metatalk , gambits , non-topical material , commentary , peritext , or epi-text.

2. Metadiscourse is part of the communication triangle/semiotic structure as isregular discourse , and it deserves its own model , a model which should be considered in relation to a discourse illustrates the two levels or

48

planes of discourse: (a) the primary discourse level, consisting of propositions and referential meaning and (b) the metadiscourse level, consisting
of propositional attitudes, textual meanings.

3. A metadiscourse model recognizes that most people consider
metadiscourse as a discourse—a text written by the author of the primary
discourse or by some other person.

4. Metadiscourse, like primary discourse, is part of or embedded in a
rhetorical, situatonal context that determines appropriateness of type, form,
amount, style, aim, and function. Metadiscourse is pragmatic and rhetorical—it is concerned with acts and effects of the audience/readers.

(Crismore, 1989: 89 – 90)

Therefore, according to Crismore, any discourse, oral or written, is communica-
tively rhetorical and involves three components: the author, the audience, and
the subject. The author communicates with the audience on a certain subject.
These three elements constitute the main part of the discourse in human verbal
interaction. Bearing the rhetorical aims in mind, the writer or speaker can vary
his/her employment of metadiscourse accordingly. All these will contribute to
the construction of discourse as a whole. Crismore's model examines metadiscourse from the perspective of rhetoric and focuses on the general nature or rhetorical function of metadiscourse, since the four aspects in his model about
metadiscourse confines it to the small range of rhetoric.

2.6 Summary

Theories and studies concerning metadiscourse vary in many respects due to
different stands or attitudes. To sum up, seven different classification systems
and six theoretical perspectives of metadiscourse have been reviewed in this
chapter. These studies have shed light on the occurrence and nature of metadiscourse in written or oral discourse and pave the way for the present study although they have different research focuses.

The identification of metadiscourse and its functions must depend on the particular context of the particular text. Brown & Yule (1983 : 1) holds that "The analysis of discourse is, essentially, the analysis of language in use". Therefore, we are expected to take into account the context whole studying the role of metadiscourse. This echoes the famous saying, "no context, no meaning". It is the context that gives meaning to the metadiscourse in the discourse. Sometimes, contextual meaning of a discourse may differ from its literal meaning to a large extent because metadiscourse in concrete context may trigger mental association which is related to the inferential process of meaning. In verbal exchange, the inference of meaning for a metadiscourse is systematic, since it is decodable by different interpreters in the same way. What we are expected to do is to find out the underlying systematic mechanism for the occurrence of metadiscourse in human verbal exchange.

It seems to us that most studies, however, have failed to dig into the underlying mechanism regarding the occurrence and the role of metadiscourse and a study from pragmatic perspective is likely to further our understanding of the nature of metadiscourse in verbal communication. As we know, pragmatics is the study of language in use (Leech, 1983) . As a pragmatic phenomenon, metadiscourse reflects the ways the speaker effects his/her speech by employing a variety of metadiscourse devices in the process of constructing a discourse. We believe that the choice of appropriate metadiscourse in academic lectures is dynamic, which requires the speaker or writer to vary his/her choices in different communicative situations and for different intentions or communicative purposes. A more systematic and integrated look at metadiscourse in human verbal exchange would be highly desirable.

However, it is not easy to grasp the occurrence of metadiscourse in human verbal communication. In this respect, studies of metadiscourse are expected to be put in a theoretical framework in order to gain a reasonable interpretation. Therefore, it is necessary to establish a relatively sound theoretical model to account for the phenomenon so as to achieve a better understanding of metadiscourse. The present study attempts to construct an enriched Adaptation-Relevance Model of metadiscourse use in academic lectures and explore some possible implications for teacher training and course design. With this framework, we have interpreted the occurrence of metadiscourse in academic lectures and figured out the possible underlying mechanism. Before we elaborate on this, it is necessary to have a look at the methodology and data in the present study.

Chapter Three   Research Methodology
and Data Collection

3. 1   Introduction

Good research begins with appropriate methodology and fairly large data for analysis. Research methodology is essential to scientific research, since method determines the validity and value of a research. No one can deny the value of methodology for scientific research. In addition, a description of the methodology in a research will help to build up a much better understanding of the research undertaken on the part of the readers.

Bearing this in mind, we will in this chapter elaborate on the methodology we adopt in the current study and its procedure of data collection, along with a general description of the data applied in the present study. The purpose of this chapter is to offer our readers the basic knowledge of the methods and data in the book.

3. 2   Research methodology of the present study

The goal of this study is to advance the researches regarding metadiscourse in academic lectures in the light of the Adaptation Theory and Relevance Theory. Thus, this study explores the mechanism underlying the occurrence and the role of metadiscourse in academic lectures and possible pedagogical implications for classroom teaching and curriculum design.

As a matter of fact, the methods used in this study are primarily qualitative and theory-driven. The qualitative method will be used in order not only to construct a theoretical model to account for the use of metadiscourse in academic lectures, but also to revisit the role of metadiscourse in academic lectures and elicit some possible pedagogical implications.

In choosing tocarry out a theory-driven study of somewhat sizeable corpora, we embrace the empirical principle that the more material the analysis is based on, the more reliable the conclusions drawn will be, and the more generable the results will be. As a result, we tried our best to search for and tape as many academic lectures as possible.

In this descriptive and explanatory study, a qualitative contextual analysis of the occurrence of metadiscourse in academic lectures will be made and an enriched Adaptation-Relevance Model based on Adaptation Theory and Relevance Theory will be adopted as the theoretical framework for the evaluation of both the occurrence and the role of metadiscourse features.

The present study, being qualitative by nature, offers a description and explanation of metadiscourse in academic lectures. A series of examples are selected from many authentic academic lectures to illustrate the occurrence of metadiscourse in academic lectures. After that, a detailed interpretation of the metadisocourse in three full academic lectures is presented so as to demonstrate the significance of metadiscourse in this communicative genre.

At the same time, we rely heavily on the ideas of the Adaptation Theory and Relevance Theory. Basing our analysis on these two theories, we try to revise and enrich the Relevance-Adaptation Model proposed by Yang Ping and the Adaptation-Relevance Model by Ran Yongping.

Therefore, the present study is qualitative and theoretical by nature. What is more, it has both theoretical significance and pedagogical implications. We will illustrate them in later chapters.

3. 3   Data collection of the current study

The data utilized for this study are collected from various sources and of different kinds. The first kind of data is video-taped academic lectures, including the ten lectures of George Lakoff made at Beijing University of Aeronautics and

Astronautics in 2004, and some lectures at Lecture Forum of CCTV.

The second type of data comes from some lectures we tape-recorded personally. In order to obtain a relatively rich data for the study, we have googled and yahooed on the Internet some scripts of academic lectures made by some scholars. Although they are not as authentic as the first two types of data we collected, academic scripts will contribute to the richness of the data, thus possessing reference value.

In choosing data to meet the requirements of the present study, we try to adhere to the following two principles: being exhaustive and being manageable. By exhaustive, we mean that it is necessary to collect sufficient data for the present research in order to offer a relatively complete picture. Accordingly, we have tried our best to choose some ready-made video tapes of academic lectures and video-taped some academic lectures in classrooms personally. And by manageable, we mean we must make sure that the data can be collected with limited time and personal capacity. We never do things beyond our capacities and resources. What we bear in mind in this process is that the data should be authentic to assure that the materials may reflect the true nature of metadiscourse in academic lectures.

As a matter of fact, this research is conducted within our capacities and resources. Frankly speaking, many data could be used for the analysis of the occurrence and the role of metadiscourse in academic lectures. And the diversified data will possibly present us a much more comprehensive picture of metadiscourse and add to the validity of the research. However, for the sake of convenience, we focus our attention on the ten lectures of George Lakoff and some lectures at Lecture Forum of CCTV due to their availability and easy access.

3. 4   Description of the data

The data collected in this study areacademic lectures in many fields, such as cognitive linguistics, education, etc. Among them, two major sources are the video tapes of George Lakoff's lectures on cognitive linguistics, and some lectures at Lecture Forum of CCTV. In addition, some lectures we tape recorded will add to the authenticity and vividness of the data used in the current study.

All the possible data are chosen because they constitute a relatively comprehensive data bank so as to meet the needs of the study. A content analysis is adopted based on our enriched theoretical framework.

More specifically, each academic lecture in the data is relatively long: each lasts for over 2 hours. Though limited, the data can represent the genre of academic lectures to a certain degree. And the data are used to illustrate our point of view within the framework of the Adaptation-Relevance Model.

The audience of the lectures is diversified, ranging from experienced scholars to graduates and non-professionals. This is due to the fact that an academic lecture may be used to not only exchange information among scholars, but also instruct students through imparting academic information.

Sometimes, these two functions can be combined to form an integrated whole. For example, students in academic lectures can benefit a lot from learning academic information and communicating with the lecturer and adding new information to the lectures. And our focus is on the first part of function since we value more the pedagogical implications of metadiscourse in academic lectures.

3.5　Summary

In this chapter, we have presented a general description of the methodology and data in the present study. In so doing, we hope that the reader will get a rough idea of the how the data in this book will be collected and their functions.

Besides, a theoretical framework is extremely necessary for the study in order to provide the research with a relatively sound foundation. As a matter of fact, theoretical framework may offer a direction for the study and make it manageable to some extent. The theories we have chosen is the Relevance Theory and the Adaptation Theory, which are the classical ones in pragmatics. However, we hold that these two theories have their own strength and weaknesses since they interpret linguistic facts from their different perspectives and contexts. What we are expected to do is to combine them and construct a relatively comprehensive framework for our current study. In spite of the difficulties, we have read through many monographs and articles on these two theories and elicited the core ideas in them, which are the basis for our current study. Actually, this is not an easy job at times due to limited energy and capacities. Accordingly, we have constructed an enriched Adaptation-Relevance Model from the lecturer's perspective to illustrate the occurrence and the role of metadiscourse in academic lectures. And the examples taken from our data will be examined within this framework. This is what I will deal with in the following chapter.

Chapter Four   Conceptual Framework:
An Adaptation-Relevance Model

4. 1   Introduction

Basing ourselves on a review of various taxonomies of metadiscourse and different theoretical perspectives adopted in metadiscourse studies, we have pointed out some remaining issues of the existing research and the objective of the present study. To set this study in a larger theoretical context, this chapter will try to construct a conceptual framework, with which we could obtain a better understanding of our topic.

Therefore, this chapter will discuss the possibilities of constructing an enriched Adaptation-Relevance Model to account for the occurrence and role of metadiscourse in academic lectures. And before we do that, it is necessary to introduce briefly Adaptation Theory and Relevance Theory proposed by Jef. Verscheuren and by D. Sperber & D. Wilson respectively, since our theoretical model is heavily derived from these two theories. It is known to us that these two theories are two representative classical ones in pragmatics, which constitute the core of the discipline. As a beginner in pragmatic studies, one is expected to know the basics of these theories so as to lay a solid foundation for later researches. Otherwise, he/she will not be a qualified pragmatic researcher. We do value these two theories because they are the basis for the explanation and interpretation of many pragmatic phenomena in our linguistic studies. They are powerful explanatory tool in many aspects, offering new perspectives of looking at the same linguistic facts.

4. 2 Adaptation Theory

As we know, Adaptation Theory was summarized by Jef. Verscheuren in his classical work *Understanding Pragmatics* published in 1999. This book is the embodiment of his main thoughts about the theory. As the proponent of the continental school in linguistics, he holds a perspective instead of componential view on language use. According to him, what we do in using language is to "make negotiable linguistic choices from a variable range of possibilities in such a way as to approach points of satisfaction for communicative needs" (Verschueren, 1999: 61). This reflects the main thought of Verscheuren's Adaptation Theory.

According to Adaptation Theory, specifically, the process of using language is a constant one of making linguistic choices. And this process is very complicated involving a variety of factors, since using language is "the continuous making of linguistic choices, consciously or unconsciously, for language-internal (i. e. , structural) and/or language-external reasons" (ibid. : 55 – 56).

However, a question may be raised by many researchers: why can human beings make linguistic choices due to the complexity of language use? The possible answer, according to him, is that language itself possesses three features, namely, variability, negotiability and adaptability. These three characteristics possessed by language guarantee language users the capacity to vary their linguistic forms in concrete communicative situations.

Generally speaking, variability refers to the fact that language has a range of"possibilities from which choices can be made"; negotiability means that "choices are not made mechanically or according to strict rules or fixed form-function relationships, but rather on the basis of highly flexible principles and strategies"; adaptability is defined as "the property of language which enables human beings in communication to make negotiable linguistic choices from a variable range of possibilities in such a way as to approach points of satisfaction for communicative needs"(ibid. : 59 – 61).

According to Verscheuren, any linguistic form employed by the speaker involves simultaneous choice-making at all levels in the process of verbal communication. And the linguistic choices made by the speaker in this process possess the following seven main features:

(1) Choices are made at every possible level of structure: from phonetic/phonological to syntactic and semantic.

(2) Speakers not only choose forms but also strategies. The choice of a strategy may have influence on specific choices to be made on a wide range of structural levels.

(3) The process of making choices may show different degrees of consciousness. Some choices are made very consciously or completely automatically.

(4) Choices are made both in producing and interpreting an utterance, i. e. , in a given process of verbal communication, both sides need to make choices.

(5) A language user has no freedom of choice between choosing and not choosing. Once language is used, the user is under an obligation to make choices.

(6) The choices of forms and strategies are not equivalent, because they are constrained with social and cultural factors.

(7) Choices may lead to the changes of the related linguistic or non-linguistic factors.

(ibid. : 56 – 58)

Therefore, the speaker can make linguistic choices from a wide variety of possible choices in the language system by adapting to various contextual factors that influence this process in concrete communicative situations. Besides, the process of making choices also involves strategies-choosing on the part of the speaker.

In other words, the speaker also chooses communicative strategies when the speaker makes adaptations to choose a certain linguistic form to realize his/her communicative ends. These two aspects of choices are closely related with each other and adaptation plays an essential role in the process of choice making regarding both linguistic forms and strategies. In many cases, adaption is regarded by many scholars as the strategy adopted by the speaker in communication.

4. 2. 1   Adaptation

In Adaptation Theory, Adaptability is defined as "the property of language responsible for the fact choices are not made mechanically or according to strict rules or fixed form-function relationship, but rather on the basis of highly flexible principles and strategies" (Verschueren, 1999: 59). What we should focus on is the ways speakers adapt to different contexts to realize their communicative purposes by using language in concrete communicative situations. Adaptability is coined to account for what people do when using language and the process of make adaptation is a really complicated process. That is reason why Verscheuren proposes the correlates of adaptability to interpret what it is that language or linguistic choices are interadaptable with. And the process of making adaptations involve the interaction between the the speakers and the hearers.

Therefore, adaptability is a cognitive process and a mechanism of language use, and variability and negotiability serve as the contents of adaptation. As a matter of fact, as a dynamic process, linguistic communication involves linguistic, cultural and cognitive elements.

We can quote these contextual correlates of adaptability as follows:

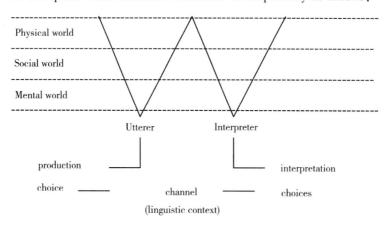

Figure 4. 2   Contextual Correlates of Adaptability

(Verschueren, 1999: 76)

As we mentioned above, linguistic communication involves making choices on the part of the speaker. These choices may take place at all possible levels of linguistic structure and pragmatic phenomenon can be related to any layer or level of structure.

But how does it work? According to Verscheuren, there are some mechanisms governing choices-making: (1) there are choices made at different levels such as languages, codes and styles. The use of language for communication requires making choices of languages, codes and styles; (2) there are choices of basic utterance-building ingredients such as sound structure (intonation, pausing, rhythm, voice quality, etc.), morphemes and words, clauses and sentences, propositions and supersentential units; (3) There are choices of utterances and utterance clusters, which can include the choices of verbal behavior and discourse types; (4) There are choices of utterance-building principles, which mainly include choices made in content organization, coherence, relevance, information structure, thematic structure, and so on. According to him, the focal points in this representation are the utterer and the interpreter. Both of them are the participants of language use without which communication is impossible. And the contextual aspects of the physical, social, and mental worlds function on the basis of the activation of the participants' cognitive processes. As a matter of fact, all the communicative activities cannot exist without human cognition which is the major body for the functioning of linguistic elements and contextual factors. Therefore, commnunicative activities are cognitive process in which human brain has its role to play.

In addition, adaptation in communication has the followingthree characteristics: (1) adaptation is a dynamic process; (2) adaptation is goal-driven; (3) adaptation has a specific object for which it is performed. In a sense, it is these features of adaptation that reflect the nature of linguistic communication and makes human verbal communication feasible and successful. The process of making adaptations is dynamic since the participants need to make different choices in different communicative situations and the communicative ends of different process may vary. Therefore, the three characteristics of adaptation in human verbal communication reflect the complicated process of making adaptation in verbal exchange.

4. 2. 2   *Context in Adaptation Theory*

Context may exert great influence upon the utterer and interpreter while they make production choices and interpretation choices respectively. Views diverge concerning the concept of "context" among metadiscourse researchers. For example, Halliday & Hasan (1976) claim that context of language use (or register) includes three elements, namely, field, tenor, and mode. The notion of register is postulated to account for what people do with their language in concrete communicative situations. When we observe language activity in the various contexts in which it takes place, we find differences in the type of language selected as appropriate to different types of situation.

They refer to field of communication as the domain and tenor refers to the relationship between the participants in concrete communication. Mode refers to the way the communication is realized, oral or written. However, many scholars agree to divide context into linguistic context and non-linguistic context. The former refers to linguistic items in the discourse, whereas the latter, which can exert great influence upon linguistic communication, is the situational factors, such as social environment, social conventions, moral standard, and cultural background.

As a means of communication, language never works independently, but is socially andculturally constrained, and it requires constant adaptation to different purposes and circumstances of language use.

Vercheuren's adaptation points out the various ingredients of context and their corresponding linguistic elements. And the most important feature of context is that it originates from the process of communicators' language use, and context is dynamic in the process of constructing discourse. Therefore, context in Adaptation Theory is closely related to the concrete use of language in communicative situations.

4. 2. 3   *Metapragmatic awareness*

Metapragmatics could be defined as the "systematic study of the metalevel, where indicators of reflexive awareness are to be found in the actual choice-making that constitutes language use" (Verscheuren, 1999/2000: 188). Among the study objects of metaprgmatics, metapragmatic awareness has its role to play.

In communicative situations, "language users know more or less what they are doing when using language" (ibid. : 187). Therefore, linguistic choice-making involves some degree of consciousness and it depends on different communicative situations. This kind of consciousness is metapragmatic awareness. The speaker or writer may employ many kinds of linguistic forms of metapragmatic awareness in communication, such as shifters, contextualization cues, etc. All these forms can help to show a certain degree of metapragmatic awareness on the part of the speaker or the writer. A wide range of indicators of metapragmatic awareness have something to do with discourse markers, pragmatic markers, discourse particles or pragmatic particles, which is related to lexical indications.

Therefore, Adaptation Theory provides us with a detailed and concrete description of human language use. It is demonstrated that Verschueren's Adaptation Theory treats language use as continuous linguistic choice making from a general cognitive, social, and cultural perspective. And it sheds new light on the understanding of diversities of human verbal interaction.

However, it is a relatively weak theoretical account of human verbal communication. For example, how can the speaker get the best linguistic choice of adaptation from the varieties of linguistic potentials? Why does the utterer sometimes make some choices consciously, and sometimes automatically? To tackle all these problems, it is necessary to search for a relatively more satisfactory explanation. And Relevance Theory provides a possible solution.

4. 3 Relevance Theory

As we all know, there are two different modes of communincation in the world: the coding-decoding mode and the inferential mode. The two modes may be applied in different communicative situations. As a matter of fact, the first mode cannot offer a full account of a given communication process since most communicative activities involve inference in human mind. It is not easy for us to show what is communicated is actually being encoded and decoded. Human verbal exchange is a complex process in which the intentions of the participants in many cases cannot be interpreted by the coding-decoding mode. It seems to most people that a combination of the coding-decoding mode and the inferential mode may be the best choice in order to provide a full description of human verbal communication. However, this is not an easy task because human verbal communication is a complex system that requires delicate examination of its nature and occurrence in concrete communicative situations. Many generations of linguists have tried their best to figure out the underlying mechanism of language. For example, Grice's 1957 article is among most representative studies. According to him, the goal of communicators in the communicative process is to have their informative intention recognized so as to convey their communicative intention. He argues,

> Our talk exchanges. . . are characteristically, to some degree at least, cooperative efforts; and each participant recognizes in them, to some extent, a common purpose or set of purposes, or at least a mutually accepted direction. . . at each stage, some possible conversational moves would be excluded as conversationally unsuitable. We might then formulate a rough general principle which participants will be expected to observe, namely: Make your conversational contribution such as is required, at the stage at which it occurs, by the accepted purpose or direction of the talk exchange in which you are engaged.

> (Grice 1975:45)

Grice's co-operative principle includes nine maxims in four categories:

Maxim of quantity

1. Make your contribution as informative as is required (for the current purposes of the exchange).

2. Do not make your contribution more informative than is required.

Maxim of quality

Supermaxim: Try to make your contribution one that is true.

1. Do not say what you believe to be false.

2. Do not say that for which you lack adequate evidence.

Maxim of relation

Be relevant.

Maxim of manner

Supermaxim: Be perspicuous.

1. Avoid obscurity of expression.

2. Avoid ambiguity.

3. Be brief (avoid unnecessary prolixity).

4. Be orderly.

Grice's Co-operative Principle (abbreviated as CP) has laid a solid foundation for later theoretical frameworks in pragmatics, such as the Adaptation Theory and the Relevance Theory. The four maxims in CP tell us many underlying
mechanisms of language use. In other words, many later pragmatic theories are
evolved from Grice's Co-operative Principle. And many later theories simplified
their interpretation of language use.

Compared with the Adaptation Theory, Relevance Theory proposed by
Sperber & Wilson takes a different view. It regards communication as cognitive
activities and is mainly hearer-oriented. Basing themselves on the Code Model
and the Inferential Model of communication, Sperber & Wilson propose Ostensive-Inferential Model of communication to explain language use:

The communicator produces a stimulus which makes it mutually manifest to communicator and audience that the communicator intends, by
means of this stimulus, to make manifest or more manifest to the audience a
set of assumptions I.

(Sperber & Wilson, 1995/2001: 155)

According to Sperber & Wilson (1986), human verbal communication involves both coding and inferential processes, and the speaker is expected to offer
an ostensive stimulus to the hearer so as to facilitate the inferential process. This

will relieve the processing burden on the part of the audience, which is related to human cognition. In order to ease the interpretation, the hearer should make manifest to an audience his intention.

What is more, the basic assumption of Relevance Theory is that every aspect of communication and cognition is governed by searching for relevance. And any conceptually represented information available to the addressee can be used as a premise in the inference process of human verbal communication. Therefore, the speaker is expected to make it manifest to the hearer that the ostensive stimulus is relevant enough, hence the presumption of optimal relevance. We can look at some relevant concepts:

Two principles of relevance:

(1) Human cognition tends to be geared to the maximization of relevance.

(2) Every act of ostensive communication communicates a presumption of its own optimal relevance.

(Sperber & Wilson, 1995/2001: 260)

Relevance

Extent condition 1: an assumption is relevant in a context to the extent that its contextual effects in this context are large.

Extent condition 2: an assumption is relevant in a context to the extent that the effort required to process it in this context is small.

(ibid. : 125)

Relevance to an individual (comparative)

Extent condition 1: an assumption is relevant to an individual to the extent that the contextual effects achieved when it is optimally processed are large.

Extent condition 2: an assumption is relevant to an individual to the extent that the effort required to process is optimally small.

(ibid. : 145)

The uniqueness of the ostensive-inferential model lies in the idea that human cognition is relevance-oriented. And the process of searching for relevance depends on whether the speaker's intention can be recognized by the audience or not. Or, put it in another way, it depends on the degree their cognitive environments overlap. Thus, it requires the speaker to make it manifest in order to ensure mutual manifestation of their cognitive environments. According to them, the assessment of relevance, like the assessment of productivity, is a matter of balancing output against input: contextual effects against processing effort. Relevance in the theory is defined as "other things being equal, an assumption with greater contextual effects is more relevant; and, other things being equal, an assumption requiring a smaller processing effort is more relevant" (ibid. :125). Sperber and Wilson have offered their explanation of their theories and concepts with many artificial examples in their famous book. To tell the truth, their theory of language use sounds quite simple but delicate in many respects. For example, they coined some terms to illustrate their ideas, such as explicature, implicature, etc. we will illustrate some of them in the following section.

4.3.1   Two pairs of concepts in Relevance Theory

Explicature and implicature are two important concepts in Relevance Theory. The former refers to an explicitly communicated assumption, and the latter an implicitly communicated assumption. Communicated assumptions are either explicatures or implicatures. Generally speaking, the difference between explicature and implicature is supposed to be that "the explicit content is decoded, while the implicatures are inferred" (Sperber & Wilson, 1995/2001 :56).

Hence, to communicate is to imply that the utterance is worth the audience's attention. Any utterance (or other act of overt communication) addressed to someone automatically conveys a presumption of its own relevance. Relevance is defined in terms of cognitive effect and processing effort.

It is clear that the presumption is not one of maximal relevance. Communicators are not always expected to give the most relevant possible information, or to present it in the least effort-demanding way, as a presumption of maximally relevance would suggest. It is impossible for the hearer to compare all the possible interpretations of an utterance before deciding on the intended one. Therefore, we need to set a lower limit on the expected degree of relevance, to spell out why such an utterance would generally not be produced.

In addition, the concepts of ostension and inference are also essential to the theory. How does the hearer understand what the speaker means? According to Relevance Theory, the hearer infers through ostension and inference by searching for relevance. Ostension and inference are two sides of the same coin of communication process. Inferential communication and ostension, therefore, are one and the same process, but seen from two different points of view: ostension is seen from the speaker's viewpoint and inference from the hearer's (ibid. : 54).

Communication involves two kinds of intention: the informative intention and the communicative intention. Ostension refers to making manifest one's intention of communication. To make his intention understood by the audience, the speaker always tries to express his information in the most ostensive way; to understand the speaker's intention, the hearer, on the other hand, must process the information in an ostensive-inferential way, speculate and make inferences.

A fact is manifest to an individual at a given time if and only if he is capable at that time of representing it mentally and accepting its representation as true or probably true. To be manifest is to be perceptible and inferable. When a cognitive environment is mutual, we have evidence about what is mutually manifest to all of us.

In so doing, the communicator needs to be aware that there are both explicit information and implicit information in communication. Explicit information is ostensible information, the explicatures, which the communicator intends to convey to his audience while implicit information is the unexpressed information, the implicatures. And implicatures are open-ended and vary along a continuum of relative strength. The stronger the implicatures, the more necessary it is conceived to be. And successful communication conveys all and only those explicatures and implicatures the utterance was intended to convey.

4. 3. 2   *Context in Relevance Theory*

Relevance Theory defines relevance as "the relation between an assumption and context", so relevance is context-dependent. As a psychological construct, context includes co-text, physical context, and individual knowledge, such as given information, assumptions, etc.

> A context is a psychological construct, a subset of the hearer's assumptions about the world. ... A context... is not limited to information about the immediate physical environment or the immediately preceding utterance: expectations about the future, scientific hypotheses or religious beliefs, anecdotal memories, general cultural assumptions, beliefs about the mental state of the speaker, may all play a role in interpretation.
>
> (Sperber & Wilson, 1995/2001: 15 – 16)

As we can see from the above quotation, context is a psychological construct, a subset of the hearer's assumptions about the world. Hence in relevance theory context does not refer to some part of the external environment of the communication partners, be it the text preceding or following an utterance, situational circumstances, cultural factors, etc. ; it rather refers to part of their "assumptions about the world" or cognitive environment.

As for its range, any set of facts that are manifest to an individual in communication belongs to context. Sperber & Wilson call this set of facts "cognitive environment" of an individual. And an individual's total cognitive environment is the set of all facts that he can perceive or infer: all the facts that are manifest to him. It is a function of his physical environment and his cognitive abilities. Cognitive environment consists not only of the facts that he is aware of, but also all others that he is capable of becoming aware of at that time in that place.

In other words, "A cognitive environment is merely a set of assumptions which the individual is capable of mentally representing and accepting as true" (ibid. : 41). As a matter of fact, the concept of "cognitive environment" could shed new light to later linguistic studies.

Human beings have the desire to optimize their resources. They want to keep the effort spent on processing a text to a minimum in order to obtain large benefits (i. e. , contextual effects) from the communication. In this regard, if a text is found to be costly to process, that means it cannot be processed with the contextual assumptions which are most easily accessible to the audience, he may spend more efforts to gain an audience an adequate return in terms of contextual effects.

As a matter of fact, therefore, the concept of "context" in Relevance Theory is different from that in many other theories, such as the Adaptation Theory. Context in Relevance Theory is a cognitive phenomenon which focuses on the mental activities of the participant in verbal interaction. Before an utterance is made, the speaker or the writer is expected to consider all the contextual correlates in concrete communicative situations to guarantee maximal contextual effect and minimal processing effort. This is a cognitive process in which the mental efforts of the speaker or the writer are required.

4. 4　Relevance-Adaptation Model proposed by Yang Ping

Different linguistic theories have different understandings of language use due to their focuses or perspectives. For example, Relevance Theory focuses its attention on the interpretation aspect while neglecting the production aspect. Adaptation Theory offers us a detailed and thorough description of the process of choice-making in communication, but it does not provide a general principle regarding the operation of choice-making. As a matter of fact, both theoretical description of choice-making process and guidelines for detailed operation are essential to the interpretation of human verbal communication. In actual linguistic research, we are expected to pay attention to these two aspects in order to render a full understanding of verbal interaction as a whole.

To integrate the two theories and establish a more rigid framework, some scholars have done some researches and put forward their own model of verbal communication. For example, Yang Ping (2001) proposes her Relevance-Adaptation Model from the speaker's perspective, the main ideas of which go as follows:

(1) The purpose of verbal communication is to achieve optimal relevance;

(2) The speaker's presumption of relevance decides his/her choices of styles;

(3) The presumption of relevance results from the speaker's adapting to the context suited to Relevance Principle;

(4) Relevance-adaptation is a dynamic process of interadaptation of contextual elements (physical world, social world and mental world) and linguistic structures (phoneme, stress, intonation; length of sentences; propositional structure and content; discourse structure and content); and

(5) Relevance-adaptation is a process of choosing strategies.

(Yang Ping, 2001)

All these five aspects are related and interact with each other in the process of verbal communication. According to this model, the process of language use is one of both making adaptations and searching for relevance on the part the speaker. These two aspects interact with each other in the process of verbal communication. The following figure can serve to illustrate her point of view regarding her Relevance-Adaptation Model:

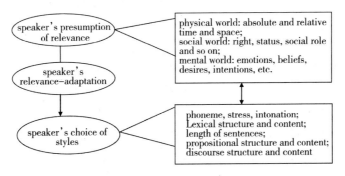

Figure 4. 4   The Relevance-Adaptation Model

(ibid. : 25)

Specifically, the speaker makes presumption about the hearer's cognitive state in order to achieve presumption of relevance, and the result of the assumption regarding physical world, social world, and mental world decides the speaker's a certain linguistic form. In addition, the process of relevance-adaptation involves choice of styles, such as intonation, lexical structure, propositional structure, discourse structure, etc.

In the process of human verbal interaction, according to Yang Ping's model, contextual adaptation and relevance seeking share the same purpose. In order to achieve maximal contextual effect, the speaker's should choose linguistic choice by adhering to the principle that a certain form chosen must be relevant enough to be worth hearer's processing effort.

4.5 Adaptation-Relevance Model proposed by Ran Yongping

Basing himself on the Adaptation Theory and Relevance Theory, another scholar Ran Yongping (2004) proposes an Adaptation-Relevance Model to explain human verbal communication by integrating the merits of these two models. According to his new model, the process of language use involves both production and interpretation, and this process is one of making contextual adaptations and relevant choice. Guangdong University of Foreign Studies is famous for its studies in linguistics, especially the Relevance Theory. Many conferences on the Relevance Theory have been held in the past decades and an increasing number of scholars are interested in this area. This has exerted great influence upon many other scholars in other part of China and more and more young scholars have joined the team, thus an academic rush in the Relevance Theory in China. As a famous pragmatician at Guangdong University of Foreign Studies, Prof. Ran Yongping is well-known for his researches on Relevance Theory. The details of his Adaptation-Relevance Model run as follows:

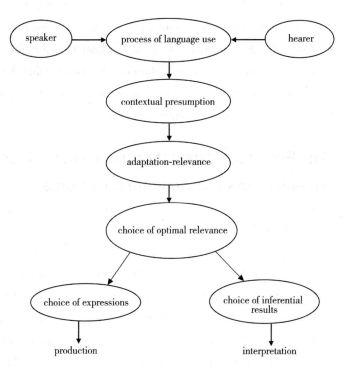

Figure 4. 5   The Adaptation-Relevance Model

(Ran Yongping, 2004)

Obviously, Ran Yongping's model takes into account both parties in human verbal communication, namely, the speaker and the hearer. According to the above figure, language production and interpretation are two distinctive but related aspects of human verbal communication, which have equal status in this process. In this process, contextual adaptation and relevance choice serve to fulfill the same ultimate communicative ends. In concrete human verbal exchange, the two aspects interact with each other to ensure the success of verbal communication.

Similar to Yang Ping's model, this model also involves the speaker's contextual presumption about the hearer's cognitive state and the process of adaptation-relevance. A certain linguistic form chosen by the speaker could be regarded as the result of his/her presumption or estimation of the hearer's contextual resources through continuously adapting to the contextual correlates. Both Yang Ping's model and Ran Yongping's model combines the core ideas of the Adaptation Theory and the Relevance Theory and gives a detailed interpretation of the process of verbal exchange. Therefore, they are applicable in the interpretation of many human communicative activities. However, we believe that their model must be modified to interpret the occurrence of metadiscourse in academic lectures due to a relatively new communicative situation.

4. 6 An Enriched Adaptation-Relevance Model of metadiscourse in Academic Lectures

4. 6. 1 Description of the model

As a matter of fact, the models proposed by Yang Ping and Ran Yongping shed a new light on linguistic studies due to the combination of Relevance Theory and Adaptation Theory. More importantly, on the one hand, Yang Ping's model illustrates the detailed features and elements involved in the process of making utterances. This will help us get a much clearer picture of the working mechanism of human language. However, this model only focuses on the speaker or the production side while neglecting the hearer or the interpretation side.

On the other hand, Ran Yongping's model, different from Yang Ping's, concerns both production and interpretation of verbal communication. This model is much more comprehensive, since it finds a connection between the speaker's relevance assumptions and the hearer's concrete contextual correlates and it makes the relevance assumption detailed as well. This model takes into account the physical, social and cultural factors involved in human communication, hence it is much more comprehensive.

However, their models deal with language use in general while neglecting the detailed use of certain category of words in human communication. For example, how does metadiscourse work in academic lectures? This is a specific area that focuses on the use of metadiscourse in a specific genre. To account for this, more revisions and enrichments are needed so as to meet the specific needs of the present study.

By combining Adaptation Theory and Relevance Theory, Yang Ping and

Ran Yongping adopt different terms for their theories, namely, "Relevance-Adaptation Model" and "Adaptation-Relevance Model" respectively. As we can see, they have put the terms "relevance" and "adaptation" in different order, which indicates their different focuses or preferences. However, we prefer the latter instead of the former, since we believe a lecturer is expected to adapt to communicative factors to achieve optimal relevance and the former term reflects the primary role "adaptation" plays in concrete communicative activity from speaker's perspective although both "adaptation" and "searching for relevance" are essential to the success of human verbal communication.

As a matter of fact, this aspect of language use constitutes an essential side of the vivid picture of human verbal communication. In order to add explanatory power to the existing models, it seems wise to revise the model to meet the requirements of the present study, instead of adhering to a model that does not sufficiently match the linguistic phenomena it sets out to describe.

In an effort to improve the existing two models, we take into account the topic in question, i. e. , the use of metadiscourse in academic lectures. We believe that the process of producing utterances itself involves both adaptation making and relevance searching on the part of the lecturer.

What is more, it strikes me that "adaptation" plays a much more important role than "relevance searching", the latter being the basis for the former. What the speaker is expected to do is to adapt to different contextual correlates through relevance searching. The differences between the original model and this enriched model lies in the fact that the latter focuses its attention on the speaker and concerns the way in which a speaker effects his/her speech by making adaptations and searching for relevance at the same time. The current study explores the ways a lecturer presents academic information in terms of metadiscourse devices.

To illustrate the details of the occurrence and the role of metadiscourse in academic lectures, we propose a tentative enriched model based on Yang Ping's model and Ran Yongping's framework. We believe that our enriched Adaptation-Relevance Model from the lecturer's perspective has its power in explaining the occurrence and the role of metadiscourse in academic lectures, since our focus will be on the ways the lecturer effects his/her lecture through metadiscourse.

This enriched Adaptation-Relevance Model is a lecturer-centered theoretical framework, within which academic lecture is regarded as an ostensive-inferential process of searching for relevance as well as making adaptations on the part of the lecturer.

Though lecturer-oriented in nature, this theoretical framework also takes into account the audience in academic lectures. In other words, the lecturer is involved in two processes at the same time, i. e. , searching for relevance and making adaptations, when he is engaged in an academic lecture. Our model run as follows:

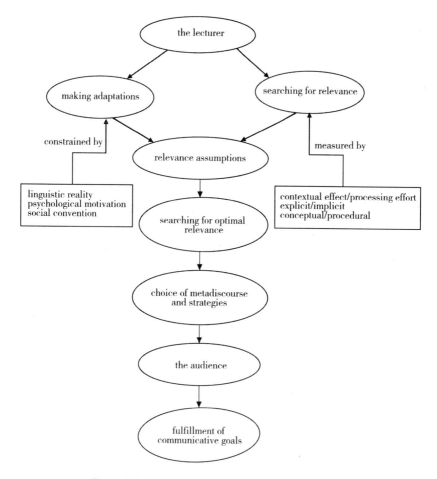

Figure 4. 6   An Enriched Adaptation-Relevance Model

In order to make adaptations to choose appropriate metadiscourse devices, the lecturer searches for relevance by considering contextual correlates and making relevance assumptions about lexical information, logical information, encyclopedic information, the audience's cognitive states, etc. Only by taking into account all the factors can the lecturer get a full understanding of the communicative situation so as to make adaptation and search for relevance in the process.

Meanwhile, the expected contextual effects will also be measured in the mind of the speaker before he/she makes adaptations based on the variability, negotiability, and adaptability of language.

In the framework of the enriched Adaptation-Relevance Model, the lecturer should firstly make assumptions and assessments of the addressee's cognitive environment and inferential ability by adapting to the audience's contextual correlates in order to choose a proper linguistic form or strategy so that the utterance can be relevant enough to be worth the audience's processing effort and also be in accordance with the addressee's cognitive ability and preference, so as to achieve optimal cognitive effect.

And the lecturer chooses a certain metadiscourse device by assuming and adapting to the audience's cognitive environment and other contextual correlates in order to achieve optimal relevance on the part of the audience, hence fulfilling the teaching objectives.

In the process of giving academic lectures, relevance assumption is the product of making adaptation and the choice of a certain metadiscourse is the result of adapting to the contextual correlates on the part of the audience. Adaptation-relevance is a feature of the choice of metadiscourse devices. Relevance here refers to that of cognitive presumption of context formed in choosing a certain metadiscourse device and that of information to be processed. Adaptation refers to choosing or creating appropriate contextual conditions to confirm, adjust or adapt to the existing presumption of cognitive context leading to lecturer's appropriate choice of metadiscourse and strategies in academic lectures. This will possibly lead to the effective interpretation of the academic information on the part of the audience.

Therefore, the process involves the subjectivity of the lecturer. And the lecturer is not certain before a certain metadiscourse is selected to fulfill the intend-ed informative and communicative goals. The process of communication is dy-namic, in which the lecturer searches for relevance and makes adaptations to choose appropriate metadiscourse and strategies.

In this process, the lecturer is expected to takes into account a variety of factors, such as social background, cultural context, the audience's psychologi-cal motivations, cognitive capacities, etc. Only when he/she obtains optimal relevance in concrete communicative situations can he/she makes adaptations to choose appropriate metadiscourse device to realize the intended ends. As a rath-er complicated communicative situation, academic lecture may be a difficult task for the lecturer.

4.6.2 Features of the Model

As a new model, our enriched framework takes a new look in pragmatics whose aim is to interpret the role of metadiscourse in academic lectures. Our new model also combines the core ideas in the Adaptation Theory and the Rele-vance Theory, since they are the theoretical ground for it. Besides that, we set our model in a new communicative situation in which the main purpose of com-munication is to impart academic information and education. In such a situa-tion, the communicative context and intended ends might be a little different. Thus, we have constructed an enriched framework to interpret the communica-tive situation in academic lectures. The main claims of our enriched Adaptation-Relevance Model can be described as follows:

First, academic lecture is relevance-oriented communication and the process of searching for relevance interacts with that of making adaptations. One essential feature of academic lectures lie in the fact that the lecturer tries to search for optimal relevance by making assumptions about the audience's cogni-tive state and make adaptations accordingly to choose appropriate metadiscourse forms in academic setting. If optimal relevance is achieved after a period of time of searching for it, part of the communicative goals is fulfilled to some extent. This echoes the communicative goals of most other forms of communicative activities.

Second, the lecturer's presumption of relevance decides his/her choices of a particular metadiscourse. The process of verbal communication indeed is a process of sharing and enlarging contextual assumptions. Only by doing so could the lecturer realize the maximal relevance and optimal relevance between lecturer's academic information and audience's cognition. This also shows the flexibility and dynamic feature and the relevance orientation of linguistic choices in the process of metadiscourse use and interpretation in academic lectures.

When the lecturer makes adaptations to contextual correlates, he/she also makes assumptions about the audience's cognitive state, encyclopedia knowledge, processing abilities, etc. And the choice of a certain metadiscourse depends on the outcome of presumption of relevance. If lecturer and audience share almost the same cognitive surrounding or contextual assumptions for one communication goal, they can make contextual adaptations and relevant choices easily. Namely, they share more contextual adaptation-relevance choices.

Third, the process of adaptation-relevance in choosing metadiscourse in academic lectures also involves choosing strategies on the part of the lecturer. In the process of choosing appropriate metadiscourse devices, the lecturer also chooses communicative strategies in order to achieve a particular communicative end. Strategies-choosing is closely related to metadiscourse-choosing and a certain metadiscourse chosen can be regarded as part of the result of strategies-choosing. Therefore, in a sense, strategies-choosing always accompanies metadiscourse-choosing in the process of giving academic lectures. As a complicated cognitive process, academic lectures may be interpreted from this perspective.

As we can see from the above, the first and second claims are the theoretical ground for the third one. As a matter of fact, the third claim of the enriched Adaptation-Relevance Model suggests the underlying mechanism of the metadiscourse in academic lectures. We will illustrate this in the following chapter.

4. 6. 3   Significance of the model

The establishment of the enriched Adaptation-Relevance Model from the

79

lecturer's perspective guarantees adequate explanation of the occurrence and the role of metadiscourse in academic lectures, since our focus in the present study is on how a lecturer monitors his/her speech in concrete communicative situations by searching for relevance and varying the choices of metadiscourse devices in order to make the lecture progress smoothly and efficiently. As we mentioned above, the study in the book is qualitative and explanatory. What we are trying to do in this book is to do our part to get us closer to the mechanism of meadiscourse in academic lectures.

The significance of our enriched model lies in the fact that it tailors to the requirements of the specific research, i. e., the occurrence and the role of metadiscourse in academic lectures. Metadiscourse use may be different in different genres, and academic lecture is a genre in which scholars can both spread academic information to the students and communicate with other scholars. Due to limited space and resources, this book mainly focuses on the first aspect.

But similarity is that both of these two situations involve the exchange of academic information, namely, the processes of imparting and interpreting academic information. As a matter of fact, the efficiency and success of the process depend on a variety of factors, such as the lecturer's and the audience's encyclopedia knowledge, the nature of the subject, etc. And metadiscourse can play an essential role in this process, hence the significance of theoretical explorations on it.

4. 7 Summary

In this chapter, we have proposed an enriched Adaptation-Relevance Model from the lecturer's perspective by reviewing some relevant theories and models. Some features and specific elements of our model are also presented and discussed in order to present a much clear picture of the theoretical framework. It is our hope that the model we proposed here could offer theoretical support for our later analysis.

The significance of the enriched model lies in the fact that it paves the way for the detailed illustration of the occurrence and the role of metadiscourse in academic lectures. This will enhance our understanding of metadiscourse in terms of its theoretical significance. But how can we account for the phenomenon from such a pragmatic perspective? This is the task we will turn to in the next chapter.

Chapter Five Metadiscourse in Academic Lectures: An Adaptation-Relevance Account

5. 1 Introduction

Within the framework of the enriched Adaptation-Relevance Model, this chapter probes into the occurrence of metadiscourse in academic lectures and analyzes the mechanism underlying its occurrence in this particular genre. The purpose of this chapter is to apply our enriched Adaptation-Relevance Model to the interpretation of metadiscourse in academic lectures so as to justify the significance of our theoretical model and find out the underlying mechanism.

The analysis is based on the examples selected from the data we collected on various topics, which identifies various functional categories of metadiscourse found in academic lectures and explores an Adaptation-Relevance account of metadiscourse in academic lectures. All the examples are selected at random and analyzed within the framework of the enriched Adaptation-Relevance Model.

As a matter of fact, metadiscourse plays an essential role in fulfilling the communication between the lecturer and the audience. It is our belief that a study of metadiscourse in academic lectures within the framework of the enriched Adaptation-Relevance Model will obtain some theoretical support and shed some new light on our understanding of metadiscourse in the particular genre. Before we probe into the mechanism of metadiscourse, it is necessary to take a look at its occurrence in academic lectures.

5. 2   Occurence of metadiscourse in academic lectures

Many studies have investigated metadiscourse in various areas, such as written genres in business (Hyland, 1998b), in science (Crismore & Farnsworth, 1990; Harris, 1991), and in persuasive writing (Crismore, et al. , 1993). Scholars in this field have conducted many researches on metadiscourse according to their own interests or focuses.

Functionally, metadiscourse aims not only to help writers with discourse production, but more importantly, it aims to help readers with discourse interpretation. Therefore, the issue regarding metadiscourse is rather complicated.

Rather than building up new propositions for the completion of a thought, metadiscourse plays the role of facilitating primary discourse, enabling readers to interact with writers and to encounter as little difficulty as possible in capturing writer's intention while reading and orienting writers to the dimension along which a text production goes.

As we mentioned in Chapter Two, the fact that so many classification systems of metadiscourse have been proposed reveals a typology problem: we lack consensus on its classification and interpretation. And the identification of metadiscourse and its function must depend on the particular context of the particular text.

Therefore, the present study is only a tentative one on the nature of metadiscourse in academic lectures, which can add to our understanding of it. We will firstly investigate whether or not metadiscourse is pervasive in academic lectures in terms of a classification system. After that, a theoretical account of the occurrence of metadiscourse in academic lectures will be offered.

Among the taxonomies of metadiscourse proposed by different scholars, the classification system by Rahman (2004) sounds much more systematic and plausible. It adopts the term "metalanguage" and divides the metalanguage we use in writing into two general categories: metatext and metadiscourse. The former is concerned with text-about-text management, and the latter text-about-discourse management. This also reflects the multifunctional nature of metalanguage. A detailed analysis of the occurrence of metadiscourse in academic lectures may offer the readers a relatively clear idea of its working mechanism in academic lectures. We can take a look at the detailed corresponding categories of metadiscourse occurring in academic lectures in the following parts of this chapter.

5. 2. 1   Metatext (text-about-text management) in academic lectures

Metatext is defined by Rahman as "text-about-text management" that applies explicit references to the text managing acts. It can help the readers better understand the whole writing process. This is also true of academic lectures. In the process of giving academic lectures, the lecturer may employ such strategies to engage the audience.

a. Reference to discourse entities

In this respect, the lecturer may also refer to the entire lecture, individual sections, or tables and figures used in the lectures. This technique will contribute to a better understanding of the lecture as a whole. For example:

[1] *In the previous lectures* I have gone through the basic mechanisms for mind, that is, image schemas, prototypes, metaphors, blends and so on.

[2] What I am going to do *in the next few lectures* is go over a lot of work that I've done, I can not believe it over the last 41 years.

b. Reference to discourse acts

By mentioning what has been talked about, the lecturer can draw the audience's attention to the academic information, hence facilitating the progression of the lecture. For example:

[3] At the very beginning, I've *mentioned* in previous talks and in *metaphor we live by*, metaphor goes with love is a journey in which lovers are understood as travelers and relationships as vehicles and difficulties in the relationships as impediments things that get in the way of traveling to its

destination.

[4] We've *discovered* that there are over twenty ones, that every different verb of force, motion if you use a different logic of causation like bringing, carrying, growing and so on, they all can be used in causal sentences but with different logics.

c. Reference to discourse labels

In the process of giving academic lectures, the lecturer may also refer to a discourse act by using discourse labels. For example:

[5] So if you try to understand language acquisition in terms of an abstract mathematical system, you will never reach *this conclusion*.

[6] And *that logic* was the logic not of the human mind necessarily. It could be the human mind but was the logic of the world, and if you are smart you could grasp the logic of the world with your mind. That was the assumption. And *that assumption* carried through up until 1963.

5. 2. 2   Metadiscourse (text-about-discourse management) in academic lectures

a. Executing illocutionary acts

The illocutionary acts in lectures show the audience that the lecturer has made or will make a statement concerning the topic. Thus, the reader could easily catch the main point of the lecture. For example:

[7] What *we claim* is that the end state that you put on the top is actually infinity in all the cases. And then there are special cases.

[8] What *I argued* in the first lecture was that that metaphor did not work. That was false.

b. Topic shifting

In the process of giving an academic lecture, the lecturer often gives a clue to the audience when he/she wants to change the topic. For example:

[9] And *as for* the people coming on the planes, they just came off the planes and she asked them at the moment they came off the planes the same question.

[10] Now *there is another* really, really important prototypes, and that is, what we call radial categories-central cases and non-central cases.

c. Code glossing

Code glossing, such as *for example*, *for instance*, helps the audience interpret the meaning of some statements or arguments. For example:

[11] Now, can a metaphor be true? And the answer is yes. *For example*, it is possible for someone to waste an hour of your time...

[12] In terms of selection, verb selects the meaning of the head, it selects the head that will go compatible with it. *For example*, if you have a verb like believe. Believe requires a human being.

d. Interactive acts

Interactive acts inacademic lectures reveal that the lecturer keeps the audience in mind. For example:

[13] Now *notice* a simple thing: we came crying hither, we came hither. "Came" literally is moving, but there is a general metaphor that existence is location here, birth is coming into existence, that birth is arrival, death is departure.

[14] *Notice* that here this is an underlying structure, you'll never guess who John invited; but so is this, you can't imagine what kind of a party John invited someone to, that is also an underlying semantic structure or deep structure;...

e. Text connectives

By employing text connectives, the writer can make his/her writing coherent. Words like *first*, *second*, *next* help to organize the text in a logical way. As for the lecturer, he/she is also expected to present what he/she wants to say in a coherent way to avoid confusing the audience. For example :

[15] Now, why is this important? *First*, in terms of philosophy and semantics, it is vitally important. . . . *Next*, it is important because of what is called distinction between literal meaning and non-literal meaning.

[16] *First*, there are many concepts that are graded that have degrees like "tall". . . . But, *in addition*, there were discovered in the 1970s by a woman named Eleanor Rosch, a very famous professor, one of my colleagues at berkeley, phenomenon called prototypes.

5. 3   Contextual adaptation of metadiscourse in academic lectures

The production of academic lecture discourse is a communicative process of dynamic adaptations on the part of the lecturer. In this online process, the lecturer makes choices of appropriate metadiscourse to convey his/her informative intention and communicative intention. Constrained by a variety of factors, these choices in academic lectures are also characterized by variability, negotiability and adaptability.

As a result, the lecturer very often adapts to many contextual factors, such as linguistic reality, psychological motivations, social conventions. By so doing, the lecturer can make sure that the metadiscours chosen is appropriate to the concrete communicative situations and can fulfill the intended communicative purposes.

To present readers with a much more comprehensive picture, we will illustrate these two main types of adaptations in turn with both English and Chinese data as examples in the following part of the book. The reason for our selection of examples from two languages is that we believe contextual adaptation of metadiscourse is a universal phenomenon in academic lectures in different languages in spite of possible slight differences among different languages or language communities. Due to limited time and space, it is a pity that we will not touch this aspect in the present study.

5. 3. 1 *Adaptation to linguistic reality*

Linguistic reality is the linguistic elements and linguistic structures of language, which reflect the real nature of certain rules of that language, i. e. , the grammatical rules of that language when people use it. It is concerned with the way the elements of language are organized together in a certain language. Therefore, linguistic reality constrains what to choose and how the words or expressions chosen should be organized in the discourse in order to produce coherent discourse.

And linguistic reality in the present study is considered to be the linguistic elements in the broad sense, viz. , we are concerned with the relationship between the use of metadiscourse and its linguistic context in academic lectures. In other words, we do not confine the concept of linguistic reality to grammatical rules of a certain language, but linguistic usage in a language. Linguistic context in discourse, a factor influencing the choice of metadiscourse in academic lectures, mainly refers to the concrete environment in which linguistic communication takes place, i. e. , co-text. And adaptation to the linguistic reality here refers to the occurrence of metadiscourse in academic lectures for linguistic reasons or language usage, such as coherence of discourse.

As a matter of fact, the lecturer very often adapts to the contents in the whole discourse so as to choose appropriate metadiscourse based on the psychological state of the audience, social context, and linguistic context. Although the degree of metapragmatic awareness varies from one lecturer to another, a lecturer is likely to adjust his/her communicative strategies (consciously or unconsciously) to make the metadiscourse he/she chooses appropriate. The reason is that the process of communicating through language is, in a sense, that of the interaction between utterance and its linguistic context.

As a result, the choice of appropriate metadiscourse through making adaptations to linguistic reality on the part of the lecturer will lead to the successful communication between the lecturer and the audience. To illustrate our point of view in detail, we can cite some examples from Lecture Forum of CCTV and George Lakoff's lecture series.

[17] *And that logic* was the logic not of the human mind necessarily. It could be the human mind but was the logic of the world, and if you are smart you could grasp the logic of the world with your mind. That was the assumption. *And that assumption* carried through up until 1963. It was assumed that the study of all rational structures in the universe, and mathematical logic was supposed to be the mathematics of that structure and that rational thought limit the structure of the universe. That was an assumption, just taken for granted about the nature of reasoning and logic.

[18] 所以我们现在可以概括起来，什么叫科学思想？第一，懂得承认和尊重规律；第二，懂得违背规律是要受到惩罚的；第三，懂得干什么事情都必须弄清它的根本原理，都必须抓住最基本的东西。所以这是一个现代国民的素质问题，我们把这些呢，又叫做理性的观念。

Coherence of discourse can be realized in a number of ways. In example 17, the whole discourse of George Lakoff centers around the logic about the human mind and the world, which is the assumption made by the lecturer. The use of discourse labels *and that logic* and *and that assumption* meets the requirements of the discourse, without which the whole discourse will sound incoherent.

Similarly, in example 18, text connectives "第一", "第二" and "第三" help the lecturer to illustrate his scientific thoughts in a logical way. The employment of these two metadiscourse devices also contributes to the coherence of the discourse. In fact, the organization of the information in this way sounds so natural that we even do not notice that. If a lecturer says "第二" or "第三" without "第一", however, the whole discourse will sound illogical and leave the audience the impression that the lecturer lacks linguistic competence to present his/her point of view in a proper way.

5. 3. 2   *Adaptation to psychological motivations*

Only by taking into account of both the writer or the speaker and the audience can we get a full picture of verbal communication. As the counterpart of
the writer or the speaker in human verbal interaction, audience interprets information and exerts influence upon the way the writer or the speaker presents information.

In the domain of writing, Grabe and Kaplan (1996: 207 – 211) list five
main parameters of audience that influence writing:

1. The number of readers — whether a text is written for oneself, a
single person, a small group or a large heterogeneous group will have an
impact on linguistic and rhetorical choices.

2. Whether readers are known or unknown – the degree of closeness to
the readers is likely to influence the extent of interactional and involvement
features in the text.

3. The relative status of participants — metadiscourse choices will also
vary depending on whether the writer has an equal or lower status than the
reader. In spoken contexts it seems that equal status creates more interactional negotiation.

4. The extent of shared background knowledge — writers are likely to
be more explicit in their use of metadiscourse where they assume the
reader's lack of cultural, institutional or social familiarity with issues.

5. The extent to which specific topical knowledge is shared — how far
writers can rely on readers knowing about the topic will influence not only
the amount of detail that can be included, but also the elaboration of ideas
and assumptions through code glosses, the amount of evidential support required, the frequency of explicit transitions and so on.

As shown in the above quotation, Grabe and Kaplan focus their attention on
five main parameters concerning audience in the process of writing. The parame-

ters, which constrain the writing process, include the number of readers, familiarity, relative status of participants, mutual knowledge, and shared specific topical knowledge.

Therefore, a good writer is expected to take into consideration all these factors so as to improve writing efficiency and produce excellent writing. As a matter of fact, these parameters are not distinctive features of written communication, but also applicable to oral communication, such as academic lectures.

Widdowson (1990: 45) also holds that the meaning of discourse does not lie in the discourse itself, but in the interpretation on the part of the audience. Academic lecture is in essence a cognitive activity involving the production and recognition of the explicit meaning and contextual effects. This echoes Blakemore (1992: 18), who states that successful cognitive communicative activity depends on the choosing of appropriate contextual assumptions.

Actually, this activity is related to the psychological motivations of the audience. Motivation, which is derived from the Latin term *motives*, refers to the forces acting either on or within a person to initiate behavior. As a psychological process, motivation reveals the activating properties in doing something or saying something.

As far as academic lecture is concerned, psychological motivations in communication, as language-external factors, constrain not only the production of discourse on the part of the lecturer, but also influence the audience's interpretation of the lecturer's utterances. Therefore, the psychological motivations of the audience are essential to the successful exchange of academic information on the part of both parties in academic lectures.

However, the cognitive assumption of the lecturer in most cases does not overlap that of the audience. As a result, it is not easy to activate the cognitive structure of the audience, which will possibly lead to communicative failure.

Therefore, the lecturer should take into account the cognitive contexts, such asthe processing capacity, the knowledge structure of the audience while making adaptations and searching for optimal relevance. Metadiscourse is such a possible means as can be applied by the lecturer to realize his/her communicative aims.

The lecturer can employ metadiscourse to lessen the processing efforts on the part of the audience, thus enlarging contextual effects. This is also based on the assumptions made by the lecturer about the cognitive and psychological state of the audience.

It is believed by many scholars that human verbal communication is, in essence, a cognitive activity involving interpreting and inferring. This is also true of academic lectures. In this kind of communicative activity, the lecturer needs to make assumptions about and adapt to the cognitive and psychological state of the audience in order to teach to different audiences.

To view academic lectures as a process of adapting to psychological motivations therefore means examining discourse features and making assumptions in terms of the lecturer's projection of the perceptions, interests and needs of a potential audience. Managing psychological motivations of the audience is crucial in presenting academic information through academic lectures because a lecture communicates effectively only when the lecturer has correctly assessed both the audience' resources for interpreting it and their likely response to it. This, in part, can be achieved through the employment of metadiscourse which may take a variety of linguistic forms constrained by many contextual factors.

Among them, psychological motivations of the audience have their part to play in this process. The reason is that the psychological motivations of the audience is essential to his/her processing capacity and the application of metadiscourse in academic lectures can help the audience to catch and follow the logical order of its presentation, thus relieving the processing burden. Bearing this in mind, the lecturer will achieve his/her communicative ends much more smoothly. For example:

[19] Now those properties form a frame for bachelor. But now there are tricky cases. Suppose you think of an Arab sheikh, who has only two wives but can have four. Is he an eligible bachelor? ... *Take another example* "the pope". Is the pope a bachelor? Well, he has not been married. But you know he is really eligible to be married? Oh, not really, possibly he could quit the church to get married but it is sort of odd to call the

pope a bachelor.

[20] *What we are going to do is* understand the imperfective case, potential infinity where things go on and on and on in terms of the iterative case that stops after the finite number is out. . . . *What we claim is that* the end state that you put on the top is actual infinity in all the cases. And then there are special cases.

The main function of code glossing such as *for example*, *for instance* is to help the lecturer illustrate ideas, concepts, or propositions in detail, and guide the audience in the interpretation of the academic contents. In example 19, the metadiscouse device *take another example* can be viewed as the result of the process of making adaptations and searching for relevance.

Before the lecturer chooses the metadiscourse *take another example*, he/she may search for relevance and make assumptions about the cognitive states of the audience. The lecturer may assume that the audience might have little knowledge about what "bachelor" really means and more examples are needed in order to offer the audience a clearer picture of the concept. As a result, the lecturer makes adaptations to the cognitive states of the audience and chooses code glossing *take another example* to illustrate the issue in detail.

Therefore, the use of *take another example* in example 19 can be regarded as the result of adapting to the psychological state of the audience, since many people can not easily grasp the connotation of *bachelor* and a detailed explanation is therefore a must. Therefore, the lecturer chooses the metadiscourse *take another example* to connect the example of Arab sheikh and the pope with the concept of *bachelor*. This will facilitate the understanding of the concept *bachelor* on the part of the audience.

Similarly, a general introduction or reminding the audience of the ongoing lecture is a must when the lecture is relatively long and complicated. This very often happens at the beginning of a lecture, since this act can provide the audience with a clear idea of the logical sequence and main content of the ongoing lecture. The metadiscourse *what we are going to do is* and *what we claim is that* are the results of searching for relevance and adapting to the psychological motivations of the audience.

The existence of this kind of metadiscourse can help the audience get a clear idea of the main structure of the ongoing lecture, hence helping the audience catch the real intention the lecturer wants to convey in the lecture. This is because metadiscourse of executing illocutionary acts is the act of explaining to the audience the main points under discussion in the lecture. In addition, it can be seen that the lecturer often uses the future tense and the imperative mood when choosing such metadiscourse devices to indicate the main contents of the lecture.

Example 20 shows the lecturer's high degree of sensitivity to the linguistic needs of his audience as result of making adaptations to the psychological motivation of the audience; this is evidenced not only by his explaining a word which has a specific meaning in the subject, but also by linking it with words that the students might be more familiar with and even providing an etymological, linguistic explanation.

Recipientor audience design occurs because lecturers in academic lectures invariably tailor their talk to the interactive needs of their audience. Academic lecturers display a particular care and attention to the audience's needs and the linguistic manifestations of this constitute one of the characterizing features of lectures as a genre. In fact, among these linguistic features, metadiscourse are most frequently used to cater to the audience's needs in academic lectures, since metadiscourse in many cases may direct the audience in the process of academic lectures.

5. 3. 3   *Adaptation to social conventions*

As we know, context means different things to different scholars and social conventions are part of the non-linguistic context in verbal communication. For example, as we mentioned above, Halliday & Hasan (1976) distinguish three elements of context, i. e. , field, tenor, and mode. Field of context refers to the domain in which the interaction takes place, such as scientific discussion, classroom teaching, etc. Tenor of context is the relationship between the participants involved in the communication, such as teacher-student relationship. And mode of context refers to the way verbal communication is realized, oral or written. Most linguists, however, agree to divide context into linguistic context and non-linguistic context. Social conventions belong to non-linguistic context and include many factors, such as social environment, moral principles, cultural background, etc. These factors can exert influence upon human linguistic interaction.

As social animals, we behave within certain social constrains in communicating with each other. We cannot live without society, i. e. , we are social animals. To make our communication successful, we need to abide by some rules set by the social conventions although there may exist slight difference in different social communities. These social conventions may include various laws, rules, customs, norms, etc. And these rules are commonly agreed upon by most of the members of the society, any violation of these rules will possibly cause damage to the society or the relationships between people.

In our society, language remains the major way of conducting our social behaviors and thus language use is essential to this process. Therefore, due attention should be paid to the social conventions that constrain human verbal communication in order to guarantee the successful interaction between participants.

As a kind of social communication, academic lecture is also constrained by social conventions. We believe that the application of metadiscourse is related to social and communicative environment and the use of metadiscourse makes us clearer about the interactional feature of metadiscourse in academic lectures. In a sense, language is applied to human communication in similar ways in spite of a certain degree of differences among different cultures.

Therefore, the lecturer is expected to search for relevance and adapt to social conventions and the specific social environment in which the communication takes place to choose appropriate metadiscourse devices. In so doing, the lecturer could easily engage the audience and strengthen the solidarity between the lecturer and the audience. For example:

[21] *Notice* that here this is an underlying structure, you'll never guess who John invited; but so is this, you can't imagine what kind of a

95

party John invited someone to, that is also an underlying semantic structure or deep structure;...

[22] 第一个关系，我认为是义与利的关系。就是说战争这个东西肯定不好玩，要死人的，从道德的意义上讲、从人道的意义上讲，战争是不应该有的，但是从历史发展角度讲、从实际的利益来讲，战争又是不可以没有的。

Metadiscourse of interactive acts *notice* in example 21 conforms to social conventions, since it makes the audience believe that the lecturer keeps him/her in mind, thus meeting the face needs of the audience. This reflects the contextual adaptation to social conventions on the part of the lecturer.

This is also true of hedges in academic lectures, such as *kind of*, *sort of*, *a little bit*, *loosely speaking*, etc. They can also be regarded as the result of searching for relevance and adaptation on the part of the lecturer. Hedges like "我认为" in example 22 reflect the lecturer's modest attitude towards academic research, which is considered to be the necessary virtue possessed by a scholar in academic circle.

At the same time, the use of hedge "我认为" here can be used to help the lecturer express his viewpoints in a mild way and thus maintain the face need of the other scholars in the same research field.

As an essential element in social conventions, politeness helps to build up solidarity between the lecturer and the audience. Crismore and Vande Kopple (1988) investigate the effects of hedging (e. g. , metadiscursive devices that express the writer's commitment to the truth value of the proposition being made) on reading retention. This kind of metadiscourse accounts for a large part of politeness phenomenon not only in writing, but also in oral interaction.

As we know, politeness is a universal phenomenon in human communication. Thus, interlocutors in verbal interaction are expected to be polite in order to achieve their intended goals as expected. Closely related to politeness phenomenon, the concept of "face" in human communication was first proposed by Goffman (1967). According to him, "face" is "the positive social value a person effectively claims for himself by the line others assume he has taken during a particular contact" (ibid. : 5).

Besides, Brown and Levinson (1987) develop this notion and regard "face" as "public self-image that every member of a society wants to claim for himself. " There are two aspects of "face"—"positive" and "negative". The former refers to the desire that this self-image be accepted and approved of, and the latter is the basic claim to territories, personal preserves, rights to non-distraction, i. e. , to freedom of action and freedom from imposition. An individual's positive face is reflected in his or her desire to be liked, approved of, respected, and appreciated by others (Thomas, 1995 : 169).

It is Leech who first introduces the Politeness Principle as a necessary supplement for Grice's Cooperative Principle. In order to "rescue" the CP, Leech (1983) proposes the Politeness Principle that runs as follows :

> *Minimize (all things being equal) the expression of impolite beliefs ;*
> *Maximize (all things being equal) the expression of polite beliefs.*

More specifically, the Politeness Principle has 6 maxims :
1) Tact maxim
a. Minimize cost to other
b. Maximize benefit to other
2) Generosity maxim
a. Minimize benefits to self
b. Maximize cost to self
3) Approbation maxim
a. Minimize dispraise of other
b. Maximize praise of other
4) Modesty maxim
a. Minimize praise of self
b. Maximize dispraise of self
5) Agreement maxim
a. Minimize disagreement between self and other
b. Maximize agreement between self and other

6) Sympathy maxim

a. Minimize antipathy between self and other

b. Maximize sympathy between self and other

(Leech, 1983:81)

Politeness is such a universal phenomenon that it also abounds in academic lectures as result of the lecturer's searching for relevance and making adaptations to social conventions. This is also related to the interpersonal function of language. According to Halliday, the interpersonal function of language enables users to participate in communicative acts with other people. This function concerns the interactional aspect of language, typified by vocatives, mood options, and modality.

Hedges, such as *perhaps*, *probably*, *it seems that*, etc. , are some of the typical forms to show politeness in academic lectures. Lecturers tend to use hedges widely in their academic lectures, since hedges can perform many functions in the process of giving lectures.

For example, they could tone down their points of view by mitigating the force of the verb or prediction so as to make them socially more acceptable, and negotiate meaning in face-to-face interactions, especially in academic lectures. For example:

[23] You *generally* don't make requests of the things that you know are impossible in the normal situation. Now you *might* for certain reasons want to do this, for certain rhetorical reasons you might want to request something impossible of your parents, for example.

[24]也许大家现在都知道，中国在近代有很多流动人口，比如我们上海，有好几百万外来的人口，但这些是不是我们讲的移民呢？不完全是，因为移民不等于流动人口，或者就是一般性的，迁移的人口。我们所研究的移民，一般地来说，是带有定居性质的，所以我给它定义，就是应该在迁入地，居住了相当长的时间。那么具体多少年呢，我想在不同的时期，对不同的人，标准是不完全统一的，但都有一点，他们要在迁入的地方，居住了相当长的一个阶段，各位在座的同学，我想绝大多数人，可能不是生长在上海的。

98

The topic in example 23 is making requests in some situations. In the process of presenting his point of view, the lecturer makes contextual adaptations to the norms of social conventions through employing the hedges *generally* and *might*. This is because making adaptations to social conventions and airing our viewpoints in a mild way is considered to be an appropriate in most cases. Otherwise, it will leave the audience the impression that the lecturer is a little arrogant and therefore impolite.

Similarly, in example 24, the lecturer centers on what "*immigrant*" means and tries to offer the audience a precise definition of the concept of "*immigrant*". In order to present the academic information in a proper way, the use of hedges "也许", "我想", and "可能" plays an essential role in coating his point of view. The lecturer makes assumptions about the social conventions and makes adaptations to choose such metadiscourse devices to show politeness accordingly.

It should be noted that hedges are also found in academic lectures to be used with a modal verb toning down the statement or with a modifier as a complex unit. A typical academic lecture includes many of these metadiscourse devices, which also suggest the politeness concern on the part of the lecturer. Hedging with this kind of complex structure reflects the cautions calculating in the mind of the lecturer and could be regarded as the result of making adaptations to the social conventions. For example:

[25] There is a great Shakespeare poem, sonnet 73, and it's about death. . . . Now a lot of complicate English. *I think* this *would* take days to unpack all those metaphors. But let's take a couple.

[26] 关于人生、关于世界、关于历史，也包括自己怎么活着。这些问题在各种不同的影片里，都得到过反映。那么你要去欣赏这样一些电影，并不一定要对它顶礼膜拜，只是它带给你某种很难说在一个黑屋子里看电影，跟大家一块儿哭、一块儿笑就带得给你的那种东西。而这种东西我以为是一个有文化的欣赏者所应该从电影中得到的，因为电影本身已经提供了这些。

99

In example 25, the lecturer quotes a sonnet of Shakespeare and explains to the audience the complicated nature of the poem and metaphors in particular. Through a complex unit of hedge *I think* with the modal verb *would*, the lecturer expresses his point of view, and thus makes adaptations to social conventions successfully.

Example 26 discussesthe methods of appreciating movies which may include human life, the world, history, and how we shall lead our lives. And the use of the hedge "我以为" with the modal verb "应该" helps the lecturer present his idea in an appropriate way as a result of making adaptations to social conventions.

Another way of showing politeness is to use pronouns that include the lecturer himself/herself in the criticism or opinions while presenting the lecturer's point of view so as to minimize FTA. This will lead to the solidarity of the whole group or the academic circle as a whole. For example:

[27] So what *we* have is a model for binding that assumes that you have simultaneous firing. If that is wrong, *we* could construct a different model to try to fit those other facts. *We* also have spreading activation throughout the network with, what is called, a probabilistic inference mechanism.

[28] 下面我讲第二个问题，我觉得《孙子兵法》的意义，不完全在它兵法的本身。我们现在就要说，一本两千五百年以前的兵书，为什么到今天大家还要学，还要关注，甚至有的时候还想运用？它本身就有非常值得人思考的内容。我们知道，文化或者说文明有两种形态，有一种现在我们也很重视，就是说它是当时很辉煌、很有价值的东西。比如说我们中国的甲骨文、商朝的文字，我们今天肯定有人要，当然人很少了，要去研读这些文字，但是研读这些文字，并不是说我们现在书写什么电脑输入法，比如方正输入法，它不会去发明，用不着了，因为它已经是死的了。我们用它去了解商朝的历史可以，我们去了解文字的演变史可以⋯⋯

The employment of the person pronoun *we* in example 27 is a popular way of presenting and illustrating academic information, since the inclusion of both the lecturer and the audience in the viewpoints or criticism sounds much more natural and polite. This is also true of example 28, in which "我们" plays a similar role.

Besides, the lecturer very often leaves the impression that he/she is addressing an audience personally although academic lectures may address hundreds of people at one time. This kind of politeness can be achieved through person markers, such as *you*, *we*, *I*, etc. Such act may leave the audience the impression that he/she always keep them in mind and pays attention to their concern or feelings. Such metadiscourse devices can also help to create sense of solidarity and fall into the domain of interpersonal function of language. For example:

[29] *You* are assuming that the other person is willing to undertake this. That is the least possible, and the other person is able to do it. *You* generally don't make requests of the things that *you* know are impossible to do this, for certain rhetorical reasons *you* might wan to request something impossible of your parents, for example.

[30] 也就是说，你必须要加上自己的思索，当作品提供了这种思索空间的时候，这个是个前提的。那很多电影你用不着想，它也不让你想。但是这样的电影，是很多的。尤其是现在我们有了其他载体，可以看到各种各样的电影，和一百年来，前人拍的很多电影的时候，你就更需要建立自己这样一种带思索的欣赏习惯。因为这个可以获得的东西就不仅仅是电影本身了，它可以佐证很多你在别的领域里正在思索的问题，或者你希望能够得到举一反三的思索的这种线索。

In both examples 29 and 30, the person marker *you* or"你" is frequently used by the lecturer to create solidarity between the participants in academic lectures. This can also be regarded as the result of the lecturer's making adaptation to social convention, since the lecturer is concerned about politeness when choosing a certain metadiscouse to realize his/her communicative ends.

5. 4   Relevance-searching of metadiscourse in academic lectures

As we have shown above, within the framework of the enriched Adaptation-Relevance Model, the appropriate metadiscourse chosen in academic lectures can be regarded as the result of making adaptations to contextual factors which constrain the process of delivering academic lectures. We have categorized three aspects of contextual factors that may influence the choice made by the lecturer in this process, namely, linguistic reality, psychological motivations, and social conventions. The analysis supports our viewpoints about the mechanism underlying the occurrence of metadiscourse in academic lectures.

Meanwhile, within this framework, the metadiscourse could also be considered to be the outcome of the lecturer's searching for relevance. This aspect of metadiscourse use can be illustrated with three pairs of distinctions, i. e. , contextual effect/processing effort, explicit / implicit, and conceptual/procedural.

5. 4. 1   Contextual effect / processing effort distinction and metadiscourse in academic lectures

The concept *relevance* in Relevance Theory is defined in terms of contextual effect and processing effort. The relevance of an utterance depends not only on the positive effects achieved but also on the amount of mental efforts required to achieve them. Other things being equal, the smaller the processing effort required, the greater the relevance of the utterance will be.

It should be noted that within the enriched Adaptation-Relevance Model, relevance is also a matter of degree, depending on the size of effect achieved and the amount of effort required for deriving the effect. Humans have the natural tendency to maximize relevance because our perceptual mechanisms tend automatically to pick out potentially relevant stimuli and our memory retrieval mechanisms tend automatically to activate potentially relevant assumptions.

Contextual effect, also named cognitive effect in later studies, is achieved

102

when newly presented information interacts with a context of existing assumptions in one of the following three ways:

(1) It may strengthen an existing assumption;

(2) It may contradict and eliminate an existing assumption;

(3) It may be combined with an existing assumption to yield a contextual implication, i. e. , a logical implication derivable from the contextual assumptions and the new information combined.

(Sperber & Wilson, 1986: 109)

Sperber & Wilson believe that "the addressee is entitled to expect a level of relevance high enough to warrant his attending to the stimulus, and which is, moreover, the highest level of relevance that the communicator was capable of achieving given her means and goals" (Sperber & Wilson, 1995:270 – 271).

Besides, the processing of an utterance in a context of available assumptions achieves relevance when it yields a positive cognitive effect, making a worthwhile difference to the individual's representation of the world.

And the processing effort needed to derive the cognitive effects of an utterance is determined by a variety of factors, such as a) the linguistic complexity of the utterance; b) the accessibility of the context; c) the logical complexity of the utterance; d) the size of the context; e) recency of use; f) frequency of use; and g) the inferential effort needed to compute the cognitive effects of the utterance in the chosen context (Ifantidou, 2001:63).

Within the framework of the enriched Adaptation-Relevance Model, the process of giving academic lectures is in a sense that of the interaction between utterance and contextual factors, in which the lecturer searches for relevance and making adaptations based on different psychological states, social environments and linguistic contexts, etc.

The lecturer needs to make assumptions about the audience's processing abilities, contextual resources, and intertextual experiences. And the appropriate metadiscourse chosen could be the result of focusing on both participants of the interaction by searching for relevance and making adaptations.

The processing of an utterance in a context of available assumptions a-chieves relevance when it yields a positive cognitive effect, making a worthwhile difference to the individual's representation of the world. Other things being e-qual, the greater the contextual effects achieved, the greater the relevance. The relevance of an utterance depends not only on the contextual effects achieved but also on the processing efforts required to achieve them.

A lecturer aiming at optimal relevance should try to formulate his/her utter-ance in such a way as to spare the audience gratuitous processing effort, so that the first acceptable interpretation to occur to the audience is the one the lecturer intends to convey.

Therefore, relevance is measured in light of contextual effects and process-ing efforts. In terms of processing effort/contextual effects distinction, it is likely that the audience will also benefit from the ostensive effort of the lecturer in achieving optimal relevance. For example:

[31] Now, *that doesn't mean* we have made a full model of the brain or anything like that. *What we intended to do is to* make higher-level mod-els of clusters of neurons and we will talk about those. These are called lo-calist models, and in them the units are not individual neurons but whole clusters, *we will talk about clusters momentarily.*

[32]他说的一句话是怎么说呢?就是"不以法为守",你不要死守教条,"而以法为用",你要把它灵活来运用;"常能缘法而生法"根据法来生法。原则上生出新的原则来,新的战法来,与时俱进,生出新的高明的道道来;"与夫离法而合法",表面上你做的事情是跟原则好像有距离,实际上你的精神核心是合法的,表面上是离开的,但是实际上是吻合的。这才是用《孙子兵法》、理解《孙子兵法》、运用《孙子兵法》的最上层的境界。也就是说,要把《孙子兵法》当作古代的哲学原理来看,不要把它当作一种教条,或者说标签来用。

In example 31, the lecturer talks about models of clusters of neurons which is a difficult topic for many people. Bearing this in mind, the lecturer employs many metadiscourse devices to relieve the processing burden on the part of the audience and achieve maximal contextual effects. These devices include *that doesn't mean*, *what we intended to do is*, *we will talk about clusters momentarily*, etc.

The metadiscourse in example 32 also serves to relieve the processing burden and spare the audience's gratuitous processing efforts, such as "他说的一句话是怎么说呢", "就是", "这才是", "也就是", "或者说", etc. As a result, the audience benefits a lot from the ostensive efforts made by the lecturer in achieving optimal relevance with minimal processing efforts in the process of interpretation.

Consciously or unconsciously, therefore, the lecturer will try to choose the appropriate metadiscourse by making adjustments of communicative strategies on the basis of the results of searching for relevance and making adaptations.

It is this act that makes possible the successful communication between the lecturer and the audience. The lecturer in academic lectures goes to great length to tailor the discourse to the needs of their students, selecting his/her metadiscourse to make it as accessible as possible for his/her audience.

As far as searching for relevance is concerned, the lecturer will keep a balance between contextual effect and processing effort in the process of choosing the appropriate metadiscourse devices to fulfill his/her communicative goals. To realize such a balance, the lecturer should take into account various contextual correlates and search for optimal relevance.

And the ideal way of doing so is to achieve maximal contextual effects through minimal processing efforts, which is very often a big challenge for the lecturer. And metadiscourse could be a solution to the challenge so as to improve the efficiency of academic lectures.

5. 4. 2   Explicit / implicit distinction and metadiscourse in academic lectures

Coming to the distinction between explicit and implicit, we have the concept of explicature within the framework of the enriched Adaptation-Relevance Model, parallel to Grice's notion of implicature. The propositions recovered from developing a linguistically encoded logical form are the explicature of an utterance, which reflects another aspect of meaning for the utterance. Meanwhile, the concept of explicature can bring some light on the understanding of the occurrence of metadiscourse in academic lectures.

Specifically, Sperber and Wilson also make a distinction between the proposition expressed and the higher-level explicatures. The explicitly communicated content of an utterance is either the basic proposition expressed by the utterance or any higher-level explicatures obtained by embedding the proposition expressed under a speech-act verb or a propositional-attitude description.

The definition of explicitness offered in Sperber and Wilson (1986/1995: 182) runs as follows: an assumption communicated by an utterance U is explicit if and only if it is a development of a logical form encoded by U.

According to them, an explicitly communicated assumption is explicature and any assumption implicitly communicated is implicature. And explicature is a result of a combination of decoding and inference. The explicitly communicated content of an utterance is either the basic proposition expressed by the utterance or any higher-level explicatures obtained by embedding the proposition under a speech-act verb or a propositional-attitude description.

However, we look at the distinction between explicit and implicit in the broad sense. For us, any explicit use of language to state the structure or the speaker's attitude towards the proposition is the explicit aspect of communication. As a mater of fact, many metadiscourse devices encode information about the explicatures of the utterance.

The lecturer's decision to convey academic information implicitly or explicitly by metadiscourse depends on the searching for relevance based on his/her assessment of the audience's contextual resources. The lecturer who does expect his/her utterance to be interpreted in a particular way must assume that the contextual assumptions required for the recovery of this interpretation are immediately accessible. In some cases, the lecturer will access the required assumptions of his/her own accord.

When giving academic lectures, an excellent lecturer will do well to make his intentions explicit by taking into account the cognitive environment of the audience to achieve better contextual effects.

Generally speaking, the lecturer will try to express the lecture information

106

explicitly and clearly by choosing appropriate metadiscourse to make sure that the audience can interpret the information with minimal efforts. For example:

[33] That is a list of properties and that everything is either in a category or out of acategory. And that the defining features are what are called the essence of this category. This is a classical theory. It has been around for over 2500 years and it doesn't work. *Unfortunately*, it would be nice if it works, but it is not true.

[34]但是这样一个巨大的尸体死而不僵的巨大的尸体，从死亡到收尸入殓，居然用了 1600 年的时间，这要一直到罗马帝国，把它埃及变成罗马帝国的一个行省，居然用了 1600 年的时间，实际上埃及早就已经不存在了，那么<u>我觉得非常有讽刺意义的非常有象征意义的是</u>，埃及文化的典型象征就是金字塔和木乃伊。而埃及文明的命运恰恰就是金字塔和木乃伊，它成为一个文明的金字塔，一个文明的木乃伊，或者用汤因比的话来说，它成为文明的化石所以它消失了。

The process of making explicit the lecturer's intention through metadiscourse is constrained by various contextual factors, which includes: minimizing the processing efforts on the part of the audience and maximizing the contextual effects of metadisocourse. The adverbial *unfortunately* in example 33 indicates explicitly the lecturer's attitude towards classical categorization theory, thus saving the audience gratuitous processing efforts.

Similarly, metadisourse"我觉得非常有讽刺意义的非常有象征意义的是" in example 34 is also an explicit way of expressing the lecturer's attitude towards pyramids and mummy in Egypt. Otherwise, it will take the audience much more processing efforts to figure out the communicative intention of the lecturer, or it may even lead to communicative failure.

From the perspective of the enriched Adaptation-Relevance Model, the use of metadiscourse communicates to the audience an assumption which is readily accessible to them, and the relevant aspect of the implicature is made explicit, which enables the audience to process it with minimum effort. Hence, the audience will be able to achieve the contextual effects intended by the lecturer.

Therefore, the lecturer makes decisions not only about whether what they want to communicate is to be explicated or implicated by a certain metadiscourse, but also about the extent to which they will constrain the audience's recovery of implicatures. Clearly, this decision to choose a certain metadiscourse device will be affected by the speaker's estimation of the hearer's contextual and processing resources.

5. 4. 3   *Conceptual / procedural distinction and metadiscourse in academic lectures*

The distinction between conceptual and procedural meaning was proposed by Blackmore (1987), which is the result of a move away from the assumptions underlying the speech act theoretical distinction between describing and indicating.

Within the framework of the enriched Adaptation-Relevance Model, metadiscourse in academic lectures could also be analyzed in terms of whether they encode concepts (conceptual meaning) or indicate to the audience what type of inference process he is in (procedural meaning). For example, different kinds of metadiscourse in academic lectures also have different contextual effects in the discourse.

It is generally believed that two distinct processes are involved in utterance interpretation, i. e. , decoding and inference. And linguistic form could encode not only the constituents of the conceptual representations that enter into inferential computations but also information which constrains the computations in which these computations are involved in human verbal communication.

Some metadiscourse encode information constraining the inferential process of constructing higher-level explicatures, i. e. , information about computations rather than representations. It directs us to process utterances with such metadiscourse.

The meaning of a metadiscourse in academic lectures is procedural if it constrains the inferential phase of comprehension by indicating the type of inference process that the audience is expected to go through in order to satisfy his/her expectation of relevance and make adaptations. The relevance in discourse is not a property of discourse, but rather of an interpretation which is mentally represented and derived through cognitive processes.

The role of linguistic meaning in utterance interpretation is not exhausted by encoding concepts. It can also guide pragmatic inferencing by encoding information about the type of pragmatic procedures.

Metadiscourse can be analyzed in terms of whether they encode concepts or indicate to the audience what type of inference process he is in. For example, *but*, *however* make a contrastive procedure, *in addition*, *for example* are strengthening procedure.

And metadiscourse in academic lectures indicates the ways of searching for relevance for the audience to achieve contextual effects. As a matter of fact, the process of searching for relevance and making adaptations is not an easy task in concrete communicative situations. It involves constant comparing and inferring with the aid of contextual assumptions before a certain metadiscourse is fixed.

On the one hand, the lecturer tries to provide the audience with relevant metadiscourse in accordance with the cognitive environment of the audience. For the lecturer, the appropriate metadiscourse chosen makes explicit his/her informative intention and conveys his/her expected contextual effects.

On the other hand, the audience is likely to pay attention to the metadiscourse relevant to his/her cognitive environment in order to interpret the communicative intention of the lecturer.

To illustrate our viewpoint in detail, we could consider the following examples:

[35] And a modifier can modify the object or what's measured, no problem, either one depending on the semantics. *So* in the construction grammar, this is no problem, but in X-bar grammar it's impossible.

[36] 这个事情，东方人对此还颇有微词，因为东方人觉得诱拐妇女当然不是一件好事，不是一件荣誉的事情，但是如果妇女们不同意，她大凡是不会被诱拐的。因此，为了这件事情而大动干戈，这似乎大可不必。

Metadiscourse so and "因此" in example 35 and example 36 respectively constrains the inferential phase of interpretation on the part of the audience, hence encoding procedural meaning. In other words, metadiscourse like these can be regarded as the expression that does not encode concepts, or contribute to the truth conditions of utterances, but as indicating to the audience what type of inference process he/she is in.

During the process of giving academic lectures, the lecturers search for relevance by integrating all the contextual information at hand, and then make adaptations to choose the appropriate metadiscourse to guide the audience to achieve the expected contextual effects of the lecturers in the process of interpreting lecture information.

Besides, the metadiscourse chosen by the lecturers will also constrain the searching for relevance and inferring the lecturers' communicative intention on the part of the audience. To achieve maximal contextual effects, the audience will infer the relevance between the metadiscourse employed and the contextual assumptions so as to perceive optimal relevance and recognize the lecturers' real communicative intention.

Metadiscourse in academic lectures is not a homogeneous class of expressions, but expressions with diversified characteristics. It should be noted that different metadiscourse in academic lectures may perform different functions in the utterance.

But the similarity among them is that the choice of a certain metadiscourse can be regarded as the result of searching for relevance in order to meet the need of the ongoing discourse. In other words, the ultimate goal of choosing a certain metadiscourse device is to achieve optimal relevance to meet the requirements of the discourse.

5.5 Metadiscourse in academic lectures as choice of both making adaptations and searching for relevance

As we know, academic lecture is a very economic and convenient way of delivering academic information and communicative intention to the audience through language. A lecture usually lasts about two hours with the exception of serial lectures. And the crucial thing for an academic lecture is the realization of the successful interaction between the lecturer and the audience.

As we mentioned above, however, only a few studies on metadiscourse in the past have explored the theoretical support for the occurrence and the role of metadiscourse. These studies have paved the way for later theoretical explorations in metadiscourse researches. Ifantidou, whose dissertation focuses on metadiscourse, is a distinguished scholar who has conducted some studies on the theoretical aspect of metadiscourse use in human verbal interaction.

For example, Ifantidou (2005) has probed into the semantics and pragmatics of metadiscourse in the framework of Relevance Theory. The paper holds that (a) at the semantic level, metadiscourse may contribute to the propositional content of utterance and (b) at the pragmatic level, metadiscourse is indispensable to the effective interpretation of academic discourse. It is also pointed out in the paper that sentence adverbials may affect the truth-conditions of an utterance. In the example *"Not surprisingly, most men responded well."* The adverbial *not surprisingly* will mark the ground-floor assertion and add to the strength of the claim.

Meanwhile, the descriptive/interpretive distinction of language use is also applied inthe study. As a theoretical research, this paper touches upon the mechanism underlying the occurrence of metadiscourse within the framework of Relevance Theory. Although Ifantidou's study is carried out from the perspective of Relevance Theory, it is not systematic and comprehensive, and pays little attention to spoken metadiscourse.

Our present study aims to explore the theoretical mechanism underlying the occurrence of metadiscourse in academic lectures. Within our framework, the lecturer is believed to be involved in the process of both making adaptations and searching for relevance in a dynamic way so as to realize his/her communicative aims through metadiscourse devices. These two aspects of the process interact with each other and form an integrated whole.

To be specific, they are constrained by each other despite the differences between the two aspects. It seems to us that the process of making adaptations and searching for relevance is characterized by two elements, i. e. , adaptation-relevance and dynamism. The former is related to the content of the whole process, and the latter nature of the process. And these two elements are essential to the appropriate choice of a certain metadiscourse in concrete academic lectures.

5. 5. 1 *Adaptation-relevance as a feature of metadiscourse choice*

As we mentioned in the previous sections, metadiscourse can be regarded as the result of contextual adaptations. We have illustrated this point from two aspects, namely, adaptations to linguistic reality, social conventions, and psychological motivation. Besides, metadiscourse in academic lectures also involves relevance-searching without which the process of seeking for appropriate metadiscourse is not complete. Our analysis through two distinctions suggests that metadiscourse in academic lectures

Basing himself on a variety of factors involved, such as linguistic environment, social conventions, and psychological motivations of the audience, the lecturer makes adaptations and seeking optimal relevance with a certain degree of awareness. And the main purpose is to choose a certain appropriate metadiscourse device to fulfill the intended communicative purposes.

What is more, the lecturer should firstly make assumptions and assessments of the addressee's cognitive environment and inferential ability by adapting to the audience's contextual correlates in order to choose a proper linguistic form or strategy so that the utterance can be relevant enough to be worth the audience's processing effort and also be in accordance with the addressee's cognitive ability and preference, so as to achieve optimal cognitive effect.

And the lecturer chooses a certain metadiscourse device by assuming and adapting to the audience's cognitive environment and other contextual correlates in order to achieve optimal relevance on the part of the audience, hence fulfilling the instructive objectives.

In the process of giving lectures, relevance assumption is the product of adaptation and it is the choice of metadiscourse that adapts to the contextual correlates on the part of the audience. Adaptation-relevance is a feature of the choice of metadiscourse devices. Relevance here refers to the cognitive presumption of context formed in choosing a certain metadiscourse device and that of information to be processed. Adaptation refers to choosing or creating appropriate contextual conditions to confirm, adjust or adapt to the existing presumption of cognitive context leading to the lecturer's appropriate choice of metadiscourse and strategies in academic lectures. This will possibly lead to the effective interpretation of the academic contents on the part of the audience.

And the enriched Adaptation-Relevance Model is alecturer-oriented theoretical framework, within which metadiscourse in academic lectures can be regarded as the result of the process of the ostensive-inferential process of searching for relevance and the dynamic process of making adaptations. In other words, the lecturer searches for relevance in cognitive environment and makes online adaptations accordingly in order to find out appropriate metadiscourse device.

As a result, the lecturermakes adaptations to choose proper metadiscourse so as to achieve enough contextual effects by conveying his/ her informative intention and communicative intention.

For example:

[37] This is a very useful metaphor to use, but still there's no force there, and there's still you, not just geometry. *So, what I'm suggesting is that* all sciences, especially physics, is metaphorical, and that it's necessarily metaphorically.

[38] 比如有人说它是和绘画相通的，因为"书画同源"。有人说它和建筑相通，因为都要强调那个平衡和稳定。也有人说它和舞蹈相通，因为一个一个字就像舞蹈家的舞姿那么优美。还有人说它具有诗美，因为它像诗歌一样很能够启发人的联想和想像。也有人说它具有音乐美，因为和音乐一样，具有内在的节奏和旋律，韵律。更加有意思的一种说法说书法它具有人体结构和人体的仪态之美，说我们人看书法写得好坏，根据自己的人体结构和我们的表情、姿势来看这个书法。这些说法都有一定的启示作用，但是还没有抓到书法艺术最根本的特征。

Within the framework of the enriched Adaptation-Relevance Model, the employment of metadiscourse in both example 37 and example 38 could be regarded as the consequence of making adaptations and searching for relevance on the part of the lecturer.

In these two examples, the lecturer tries to search for relevance and chooses metadiscourse by taking into account various cognitive resources of the audience. This process is also carried out on the basis of variability, negotiability, and adaptability. The use of *what I'm suggesting is that* is the result of both making adaptations to social conventions and an explicit way of conveying the lecturer's communicative intention to ensure maximal contextual effects with minimal processing efforts on the part of the audience.

To be specific, on the one hand, this metadiscourse reflects the lecturer's concern about the polite way of presenting academic information. This is because hedge could mitigate the claim held by the lecturer to a certain degree. On the other hand, the employment of the metadiscourse device relieves the audience's processing burden, since it makes explicit what the lecturer claims on metaphor.

Interestingly, therefore, the metadiscourse employed fulfills these two functions at the same time. This is also true of metadiscourse in example 38, in which the code glossing "比如" and "更加有意思的一种说法说" can be regarded as the result of the lecturer's adaptations to the audience's cognitive state and searching for relevance through making assumptions about the audience's processing capacity in this respect. Because the audience perhaps is not very clear about the art of writing and more details, illustration is a must for the audience in the process of giving academic lectures.

5.5.2 *On-line adaptations-making and relevance-searching in metadiscourse choice*

It should be pointed out that the lecturer is not certain about which metadiscourse is appropriate until he/she achieves optimal relevance and makes adaptations to contextual correlates in order to choose a certain metadiscourse. This is because academic lecture is such a complicated form of verbal communication that it involves a variety of factors influencing its occurrence.

These factors may include encyclopedia knowledge, logical information, psychological motivation, social and cultural factors, etc. It should be pointed out that this process is dynamic, during which the lecturer makes on-line adaptations on the basis of searching for relevance. And it is this feature that guarantees the successful carrying out of searching for relevance and making adaptations on the part of the lecturer when facing the influencing factors.

This dynamism, which guarantees to a certain degree the successful progression of communication, can be regarded as one of the defining features of the occurrence of metadiscourse in academic lectures. Without the dynamic choice through making adaptations and relevance-searching, the communication would not possibly does smoothly and even come to a failure.

Therefore, the process of choosing metadiscourse in academic lectures is dynamic and inferential, and the lecturer makes on-line adaptations to choose appropriate metadiscourse through searching for relevance. The dynamic nature of this process lies in the fact the lecturer has to adjust to the communicative situations and make adaptations, etc. And its inferential feature refers to the fact that the lecturer should make assumptions about the audience and search for optimal relevance.

For example:

[39] *Now think about* what this means for theory of grammar. *It means that* this exclamation which means something else, a negative statements, *that is*, if you have the sentence "because" and the meaning of that is a negative statement, you can express it with this. In the theory of grammar, *could* you tell exactly where "who could stop Yao" can occur without looking at what it meant?

[40] 但是现在大家知道，从录像带诞生以后，有了 VCD，现在特别是 DVD 的普及，我前几天看到一个报道，像美国，美国是世界上最发达的电影国家，它今年到现在还不到年底，它今年的电影院的票房已经突破了一百亿美元，美国市场是和加拿大合在一起的，它们

北美市场是统一的。本土市场到了一百亿美元这是一个非常大的数字，但是就在这个统计出来之前，那个 DVD 行业已经宣布，它们今年的 DVD 出售的销售额，已经突破了 102 亿美元了。那么再加上它的有线电视、无线电视和其他的一些后电影的开发，比如说游戏，比如说相关产品、品牌效应等等，那么美国的现在的一部电影的收入，20% 来自影院，80% 来自与其他那三个渠道，是这样一个局面。

As a dynamic process, the choice of a certain metadiscourse is constrained by a range of factors, such as the audience's encyclopedia knowledge, communicative need of concrete situations, etc. in example 39, the metadiscourse *now think about*, *it means that*, *that is* could be regarded as a dynamic adaptations and relevance-searching of the audience's cognitive state in order to ensure the successful interpretation of the academic information about theory of grammar. And metadiscourse *could* in the question is applied to check whether or not the audience can follow the lecturer in the process of lecture.

Similarly, metadiscourse "但是现在大家知道" and "但是就" in example 40 are used to mention some facts that the lecturer considers to be appropriate in the communicative situation. They are also a dynamic adaptations and relevance-searching to the current cognitive state of the audience. This is also true of the repeated use of metadiscourse "比如说" in later discourse.

Therefore, the adaptation-relevance process of metadiscourse choice in academic lectures is dynamic, which involves the complicated subjective efforts on the part of the lecturer while delivering lectures.

5.5.3 *Adaptations-making and relevance-searching as strategy in metadiscourse choice*

As we mentioned above, within the framework of the enriched Adaptation-Relevance Model, choosing an appropriate metadiscourse in academic lectures is a dynamic process that involves adaptation-making and relevance-searching on the part of the lecturer. As a matter of fact, the process is complicated and requires delicate mental efforts of the lecturer.

116

It should be noted that, at the same time, the relevance-searching and adaptations-making of the lecturer is also a dynamic process of choosing strategies. And the process of strategies-choosing accompanies that of relevance-searching and adaptations-making.

As we know, strategy is the delicate way of choosing what to do and the ways of doing in the process of doing something. Strategy in this sense is critical to the success of the process of delivering an academic lecture, since a good strategy will possibly change the total situation due to its positive role in it.

To be a good academic lecturer, he/she is expected to adopt the best strategy so as to choose appropriate metadiscourse to fulfill his/her communicative ends. Facing a variety of possible metadiscourse choices, the lecturer has to decide on which one is the most appropriate form in concrete communicative situations. This reflects the strategy choosing process on the part of the lecturer.

Therefore, within the framework of the enriched Adaptation-Relevance Model, the process of making adaptations and searching for relevance is that of adopting strategies. And the lecturer is expected to choose the best strategy so as to employ the most appropriate metadiscourse device to meet the need of the on-going discourse in the process of delivering academic lectures.

For example:

[41] *Why it is that you study linguistics?* My first linguistics teacher was a great linguist Roman Jakobson. My other second linguistics teacher was another linguist Noam Chomsky. They had two opposite views. Roman Jakobson viewed language as central to human activities. *What he said is this that* when you study language you study everything, that to study language is to study thought,...

[42]这个非常真实，就是在我们的电影院里也会出现这样的情况，就是人们用惟一的集体观赏的方式看电影的时代，但是这个不仅仅是在说观赏本身，又说了一个为什么这个小镇上的人民，因为这部影片是一部埃及电影，我们中国也演过，那个时候，记得看《流浪者》，比如说印度的《流浪者》，那真是有一点万人空巷的意思。他更多的人是从那个电影里除了听那个歌，看那些我们没有见过的异国

风情，更主要是对故事本身所说的那个人物的命运所吸引、所感动，<u>那么这就说到我现在要说的下面一个问题。</u>

In example 41, the employment of metadiscourse *why it is that you study linguistics*? suggests that the lecturer adopts the strategy of questions to introduce the audience to the addressed topic. This could possibly improve the efficiency of delivering academic lectures. And metadiscourse *what he said is this that* reflects the strategy of explaining directly the intended academic information on the part of the lecturer. This strategy has relieved the processing burden of the audience.

Similarly, in example 42, metadiscourse "这个非常真实，就是在我们的电影院里也会出现这样的情况" is the comment and complementary element added by the lecturer to enrich his statement about the very topic movie. It is a strategy adopted by the lecturer to guarantee the audience a full picture of the main points in the lecture. And the use of metadiscourse "那么这就说到我现在要说的下面一个问题" in this example is also a strategy employed by the lecturer to lead smoothly the audience to the next topic he will address in the following part of the academic lecture. The audience will get a general framework of the following part of the lecture through such metadiscourse devices. On surface, such words seem to be a waste of time in some cases. However, such psychological preparation on the part of the audience is half success for the lecture due to its function in the process.

5.6 Summary

Up to now, we have tried to account for the occurrence of metadiscourse within the framework of the enriched Adaptation-Relevance Model. The discussions above suggest that lecturers tend to search for relevance and make adaptations to choose the appropriate metadiscourse device at the same time in the process of giving academic lectures. And the process of searching for relevance and making adaptations of the lecturer goes on dynamically.

As a dynamic process, contextual adaptations of metadiscourse may be constrained by a variety of factors, such as linguistic reality, social conventions, audience's psychological motivation, etc. These two aspects have been elaborated on in this chapter.

Meanwhile, the process of searching for relevance of metadiscourse could be measured in terms ofthree pairs of distinctions, namely, contextual effect/ processing effort, explicit/implicit, conceptual/procedural. We have discussed the process from these six aspects respectively in order to offer a relatively detailed interpretation of the occurrence of metadiscourse in academic lectures.

Our analysis within the framework of the enriched Adaptation-Relevance Model suggests that these three aspects could be combined and a certain metadiscourse chosen is the result of searching for relevance and making adaptations on the part of the lecturer.

It seems to us that the occurrence of metadiscourse is closely related to the role it plays in academic lectures and they share some common grounds. What role, then, does metadicourse play in academic lectures? Can we address this hot issue from the perspective of our enriched Adaptation-Relevance Model? This is the issue that we will turn to in the next chapter.

Chapter Six Role of Metadiscourse in Academic Lectures Revisited

6. 1 Introduction

We have so far selected some data to illustrate the occurrence and role of metadiscourse in academic lectures within the enriched Adaptation-Relevance Model. The findings of the previous chapter suggest that we could enhance our understanding of metadiscourse in academic lectures from this perspective.

To further our understanding of this interesting issue, this chapter will reinvestigate another relevant aspect of metadiscourse, i. e. , the role of metadiscourse in academic lectures within the same theoretical framework. This will possibly also shape the views held by many scholars in the research field and bring some new light to metadiscourse studies.

Before we embark on this issue, however, it is necessary to review briefly some representative views on the role of metadiscourse so as to set a research background for our detailed discussions. As a matter a fact, we have elaborated on some viewpoints in this respect in the previous chapters. And what we will do in this chapter is to briefly present some representative approaches to the role of metadiscourse and revisit the role of metadiscourse in academic lectures within our framework in order to clarify some relevant concepts and interpretations.

6. 2 Role of metadiscourse in past studies

As we mentioned in the previous chapters, literature on metadiscourse is pervasive and views diverge regarding the occurrence and the role of metadiscourse, which reflects the complicated nature of metadiscourse. As far as its role is concerned, opinions diverge and overlap to some extent at the same time.

In other words, on the one hand, there are some common grounds among many past studies on metadiscourse due to similar focuses or concerns. On the other hand, they are also with slight differences among them because of different perspectives or experiences. For example, a common characteristic of most metadiscourse studies is that they are conducted from the writer's perspective.

Generally speaking, a brief look at the literature tells us that most metadiscourse studies in the past have focused their attention on the role of metadiscourse in written communication and less emphasis has been put on metadiscourse in oral interaction. Specifically, they focus on how the writer uses metadiscourse to organize the discourse which contributes to its interpretation and evaluation on the part of the readers, and neglect to a certain degree its use in oral communication. ‾

Some researches focus on the "facilitator" role of metadiscourse in the ongoing discourse. Here, "facilitator" refers to the elements that help to organize the primary discourse and facilitate the interpretation of the discourse as a whole. Obviously, they focus on the functions that metadiscourse performs in the discourse and metadisourse is regarded as a tool or device used by the writer to organize the discourse. In other words, the role a metadiscourse plays in the discourse is not essential, but supplementary. The metdiscourse just helps the discourse constructor organize and evaluate the primary discourse.

Crismore (1989) claims that metadiscourse functions to structure discourse, guide readers through a text, and help them to organize the content in an appropriate way. According to her, metadiscourse is also an important persuasive resource used to influence readers' reactions to texts due to existing values and conventions of a given discourse community.

Vande Kopple (1989) argues that metadiscourse can also supplement the primary text in accomplishing persuasive goals, thus its persuasive function. It is obvious that he focuses his attention on the way the writer employ metadiscourse in order to persuade readers.

Hyland (1998a) believes that metadiscourse reveals how writers attempt to influence readers' understanding of both the text and their attitudes towards the content and the audience. And the role of metadiscourse is "to signal the writer's communicative intention in presenting propositional matter".

Many scholars believe that metadiscourse plays a text-organizing role. This corresponds to Halliday's textual metafunction. Crisomore (1989), Crismore and Farnsworth (1990), and Hyland (1998a) take a comprehensive view which includes not only text-organizing elements, but also interactive elements such as the expressions of the author's attitudes and certainty, usually associated with Halliday's interpersonal metafunction.

Besides, they very often describe metadiscourse in a certain form of written communication, such as essays, ads, etc with little theoretical support, thus being descriptive in nature. As a matter of fact, many of them explain facts in terms of facts. This suggests that many studies on metadiscourse lack rigid theoretical support.

However, some scholars have noticed this point. For example, Christina Haas and Linda Flower (1988) describe the functions of metadiscourse in explaining how readers used these devices to construct representations of the author and context.

In fact, the term "metadiscourse" itself suggests that it is subjected to the primary discourse, which serves as the "facilitator" of the procession of the whole discourse. As we have discussed in Chapter Two, metadiscourse is very often defined as "discourse about discourse" or "talk about talk", which highlights its role guiding the audience in understanding the primary discourse or talk.

Of course, this distinction confines metadiscourse to secondary discourse, which is text about the evolving text, or the writer's explicit commentary on his/her own ongoing discourse. As secondary discourse, according to many scholars, metadiscourse does not constitute the content of the discourse, but facilitates the production and interpretation of the primary discourse.

And many scholars make a distinction between "primary discourse" and "secondary discourse", or "propositional content" and "non-propositional content". As a result, many green researchers take the distinctions made in some traditional studies for granted without questioning its validity. This represents the stands of most metadiscourse researchers.

Therefore, opinions on metadiscourse diverge and the role of metadiscourse remains a controversial issue. To obtain a better understanding of it, more rigid theoretical studies are called for.

6. 3   Role of metadiscourse in academic lectures: a revisit

6. 3. 1   Significance of a revisit of the role of metadiscourse

As we know, academic lecture is perhaps the most typical form of academic information transfer in our academic circle. The typicality of academic lecture lies in the fact that it abounds in the teaching activities in education institutions and academic information presentation and discussions in symposiums for scholars from different regions.

Due to its efficiency and economy, academic lecture is suitable for both discussions among scholars and academic information imparting between the lecturer and the students. And the main focus of the present study is the latter, i. e. , how the lecturer conveys academic information effectively to the students through appropriate metadiscourse chosen in concrete communicative situations.

And metadiscourse plays a central role in both the lecturer's delivering academic lectures and the audience's learning experiences and interpretation of lecture information. Without metadiscourse, the lecturer may not convey his/her intention smoothly and the audience could not possibly contextualize the lecture information in many cases.

Increasing evidences suggest the significance of metadiscourse in academic lectures. Surprisingly, however, little is known about the role of metadiscourse in academic lectures, compared to the wealth of recorded evidences about academic writings and speech in the past two or three decades. Investigation into the role of metadiscourse will, in reverse, help to enhance our understanding of the mechanism underlying the occurrence of metadiscourse in the discourse.

What is more, few pragmatic studies have been conducted with regard to the role metadiscourse plays in academic lectures and the way the lecturer monitors his/her speech through metadiscourse to fulfill the intended communicative goals. That is the reason why the present study probes into the occurrence and the role of metadiscourse in academic lectures from a pragmatic perspective.

As a matter of fact, the role of metadiscourse in academic lectures remains a complicated issue, thus requiring further explorations and discussions. And this chapter aims to demonstrate how metadiscourse in academic lectures is used as a manifestation of linguistic choices made by the lecturer as a result of adapting to specific contexts and searching for relevance in the process of academic communication.

6. 3. 2   Role of metadiscourse in academic lectures within the enriched Adaptation-Relevance Model

We do not agree to some traditional views on the role of metadiscourse held by many scholars, which are incomplete and lack theoretical support to some extent. Besides, some distinctions made by them will even mislead many researchers in the field. This, in a sense, reflects a kind of bias on metadiscourse held by many scholars in metadiscourse studies.

Specifically, on the one hand, many traditional studies regard the role of metadiscourse as secondary elements in the discourse compared to primary discourse. Actually, this will fix metadiscourse in a minor position and confine it to elements that only organize primary discourse.

It seems to us, however, that the role of metadiscourse is not "secondary", but "special" to some extent, since the term "secondary" can be associated with "minor" and thus implies that metadiscourse plays a less important role in the discourse. And term "special" adopted by us suggests a new perspective of looking at metadiscourse and the rest of the discourse.

On the other hand, it will mislead many young scholars or readers in this field when a distinction between propositional content and non-propositional content is made in traditional metadiscourse studies. It is because this distinction

124

will exclude metadiscourse from propositional content of the discourse. As a matter of fact, views vary regarding whether metadiscourse is related to propositional content, hence a controversial issue. What we are expected to do is to leave the discussion open and welcome different interpretations of the role of metadiscourse in the discourse. This will possibly bring some new light to the study.

Therefore, the distinction between "primary discourse" and "secondary discourse", or "propositional" and "non-propositional", is a kind of "metadiscourse discrimination" to a certain degree although it only serves as the starting point of the researches on metadiscourse for some scholars. It is possibly the reason why so many studies on metadiscourse in the past decades were confined to the discussions on the functions metadiscourse can perform in order to facilitate the construction and interpretation of "primary discourse".

What we believe, however, is that metadiscourse and the other part of discourse have different focuses and functions in a discourse, oral or written. From the perspective of the enriched Adaptation-Relevance Model, the role of metadiscourse in academic lectures is related to the process of searching for relevance and making adaptations on the part of the lecturer.

As a matter of fact, metadiscourse functions to influence both the lecturer and the audience in academic lectures. And the appropriate use of metadiscourse will lead to the successful communication between the lecturer and the audience. For the lecturer, metadiscourse helps him/her construct coherent and effective academic discourse based on searching for relevance and making adaptations.

Therefore, the role of the appropriate metadiscourse chosen is the result of searching for relevance and making adaptations on the part of the lecturer. These two aspects in the process of seeking an appropriate metadiscourse interact with each other and form an integrated whole.

Within the framework of the enriched Adaptation-Relevance Model, metadiscourse in academic lectures could add to the explicitness and relevance of the utterance the lecturers produce. In addition, metadiscourse indicates the lecturer's assessment of the cognitive demands the lecture may possibly poses on the audience by searching for relevance and making adaptations to contextual correlates.

What is more, the significance of metadiscourse in academic lectures also lies in its role in explicating a context for interpretation, and suggesting one way in which acts of communication define and maintain academic lecture as a genre. In this particular genre, the lecturer employs metadiscourse dynamically to construct academic discourse basing on the process of searching for relevance and making adaptations.

Therefore, the role of metadiscourse in academic lectures is the discourse constructor that constructs discourse through searching for relevance and making adaptations to contextual correlates by the lecturer. And the role of metadiscourse in academic lectures is not a passive "discourse facilitator", but an active "discourse constructor" in essence due to its active part in constructing academic discourse.

Specifically, on the one hand, we consider the role of metadiscourse in academic lectures as the result of searching for relevance and making adaptations on the part of the lecturer. These two aspects take part in the process constructing the discourse and have been illustrated in detail in the discussions above.

On the other hand, we use the term "discourse constructor" instead of "discourse facilitator". This could possibly highlight the active role of metadiscourse in the process of constructing the academic discourse. The activeness feature of metadiscourse lies in the fact that it contributes to the on-line production and dynamic interpretation of the discourse.

For example:

[1] *So, in addition*, here is multimodal integration. The premotor cortext as a whole. *Let me stop for a minute and tell you about the premotor cortex.* If I perform an action, like lifting up this bottle and grasping it, two different parts of the brain are active at least. One is the motor cortex up here, where neurons that fire control individual movements, for example, this and this, opening and closing he elbow, opening and closing the hand, turning individual movements;...

126

[2]当然，我们也要说，科学观念是现代观念的重要组成部分，但不是一切，科学使人明白过去做不出来的东西我们可以做出来了，但是做出来的东西也可能造福于人类，也可能不。你比方原子弹，生物武器，对人类造成伤害。所以我们还要有人文思想，而人文思想呢，它始终关心一个问题：就是人。尊重人，关心人，爱护人，就是把创造出来的东西，始终造福于人类，而把它对人类的危害降低到最低程度。所以下面呢，我们就介绍一下什么叫人文观念。

The topic in example one is premotor cortex, which sounds difficult for many people. As a result, the lecturer has employed many metadiscourse devices to construct coherent and appropriate academic discourse by searching for relevance and making adaptations to contextual correlates.

For example, metadiscourse *so* is used to construct a discourse that may suggest what can be concluded by previous discussions. This is procedural information employed to guide the audience to interpret the utterance and achieve maximal contextual effects by minimal processing efforts. Meanwhile, it also indicates the lecturer's adaptations to the contextual correlates because the audience may lack profound knowledge about the topic to a certain degree.

Example 2 discusses humanistic conception compared to scientific conception. Similarly, metadiscourse devices in this example also serve to produce the discourse based on searching for relevance and making adaptations. And the role of metadiscourse in the lecture is to construct the academic discourse through searching for relevance and making adaptations.

For example, firstly, the use of metadiscourse "所以下面呢,我们就介绍一下什么叫人文观念" frames the main structure of the whole discourse by indicating what is to follow in the discourse. Secondly, it reflects the lecturer's explicit way of organizing the discourse so as to relieve the processing efforts on the part of the audience. Thirdly, it also indicates the lecturer's making adaptations through making assumptions about the audience's cognitive state.

Therefore, the role of metadiscourse in academic lectures could be regarded as the active discourse constructor through searching for relevance and making adaptations to contextual correlates. And realizing the essential role of metadiscourse in academic lectures will possibly result in an awareness of metadiscourse both in the production and the interpretation process of academic discourse.

6. 4 " Metadiscourse awareness " in academic lectures

It is generally acknowledged that the use of metadiscourse can engage the audience's attention and sustain their interest during the lecture, and this qualifies a good lecturer to some extent. Metadiscourse in academic lectures can help to present academic information in a clear, convincing and interesting way so as to promote acceptance and understanding, as well as lecturer-audience solidarity.

The employment of metadiscourse in academic lectures displays an awareness of the ongoing discourse on the part of the lecturers, which we term "metadiscourse awareness". When lecturers give lectures, consciously or unconsciously, they may apply metadiscourse devices to achieve certain communicative aims through searching for relevance and making adaptations.

Based on a brief review of traditional opinions on the role of metadiscourse, we have revisited the role of metadiscourse in academic lectures within the framework of the enriched Adaptation-Relevance Model. As a result, the role of metadiscourse in academic lectures could be regarded as the discourse constructor through searching for relevance and making adaptations on the part of the lecturer. And the role of metadiscourse in academic lectures is not a passive "discourse facilitator", but an active "discourse constructor".

As a matter of fact, metadiscourse awareness in academic lectures is also the manifestation of politeness. Politeness is a universal phenomenon in human verbal communication. The Cooperative Principle is essential to successful communication, so does the Politeness Principle. Thus, participants are expected to follow the PP in order to achieve their intended goals. Before we illustrate the Politeness Principle, a brief introduction of the concept of "face" seems necessary since they are closely related. The notion of "face" in human communication was first proposed by Goffman (1967). For him, "face" is "the positive social value a person effectively claims for himself by the line others assume he has taken during a particular contact. " (1967 : 5). Goffman further points out that "Following Chinese usage, one can say that ' to give face ' is to arrange for another to take a better line than he might otherwise have been able to take, the other thereby gets face given him, this being one way in which he can gain face. " (ibid. : 9).

Later, Brown and Levinson (1987) develop this notion and regard "face" as " public self-image that every member of a society wants to claim for himself. " There are two aspects of "face"—"positive" and "negative". The former refers to the desire that this self-image be accepted and approved of, and the latter is the basic claim to territories, personal preserves, rights to non-distraction, i. e. , to freedom of action and freedom from imposition. An individual's positive face is reflected in his or her desire to be liked, approved of, respected, and appreciated by others (Thomas, 1995 : 169).

In many cases, face is likely to be threatened by the speaker or the addressee. These run contrary to the face wants of the addressee and/or the speaker' (and hence threaten face). All these acts are called face-threatening acts (FTAs). Thus, the maintenance or enhancement of face is crucial to successful communicative interaction. This is also true of academic lectures. In academic lectures, the lecturers need to take into consideration the face of the audience to avoid face-threatening acts. In the process of academic lectures, what the lectures say and the way the lecturers deliver academic information may possibly threaten the face of the audience to some degree. If the lecturers ignore the face of the audience, academic lectures may come to a failure in many situations.

In pragmatics, the CP is considered to be an important principle that governs human conversations. However, people do not always observe the Gricean maxims in conversations. It is G. Leech who first introduces the Politeness Principle as a necessary supplement for H. P. Grice's Cooperative Principle. In order to "rescue" the CP, Leech (1983) proposes the Politeness Principle that runs as follows:

129

Minimize (all things being equal) the expression of impolite beliefs;

Maximize (all things being equal) the expression of polite beliefs.

More specifically, the Politeness Principle has 6 maxims:

1) Tact maxim

a. Minimize cost to other

b. Maximize benefit to other

2) Generosity maxim

a. Minimize benefits to self

b. Maximize cost to self

3) Approbation maxim

a. Minimize dispraise of other

b. Maximize praise of other

4) Modesty maxim

a. Minimize praise of self

b. Maximize dispraise of self

5) Agreement maxim

a. Minimize disagreement between self and other

b. Maximize agreement between self and other

6) Sympathy maxim

a. Minimize antipathy between self and other

b. Maximize sympathy between self and other

(Leech, 1983:81)

Each maxim has two sides of problem. The former is other-oriented while the latter is self-oriented. Tact maxim is applicable to other's request while generosity maxim is about how to help others. Metadiscourse in academic lectures, in a sense, demonstrate the lecturer's consideration of politeness in the process of the lectures. Such metadsicourse awareness helps to facilitate the communication between the lecturers and the audience. Actually, the lecturers are expected to keep in mind the audience and consider their needs so as to improve the solidarity between them. To some degree, the success of the lectures lies in the degree of their solidarity in the process of the lectures. Therefore, more importance should be attached to the solidarity between the lecturers and the audience.

It should be noted that "metadiscourse awareness" displayed by the lecturers in the process of giving academic lectures is a matter of degree. It may vary from one lecturer to another, depending on their personalities and other contextual factors. We cannot force the lecturers to possess metadiscourse awareness in the process of academic lectures. What we can do is to raise their metadiscourse awareness so as to facilitate the delivering process and achieve their intended communicative goals in academic lectures.

As a result, the degree of metadiscourse awareness has something to do with the success of the academic lectures. Ignorance of metadiscourse may lead to the failure of the academic lectures in many cases. To evaluate a lecturer, it seems to us that metadiscourse awareness could be one of the criteria due to its functions in improving communicative efficiency. An experienced lecturer is likely to display a certain degree of metadiscourse awareness and monitor his speech through metadiscourse to fulfill his/her communicative goals.

Therefore, one the one hand, metadiscourse devices in academic lectures may be applied to achieve certain communicative aims through searching for relevance and making adaptations. On the other hand, metadiscourse awareness on the part of the academic lectures is the manifestation of politeness so as to improve the solidarity between the lecturers and the audience.

6. 5 Summary

Basing ourselves on a brief review of traditional opinions on the role of metadiscourse, we have revisited the occurrence and role of metadiscourse in academic lectures within the framework of the enriched Adaptation-Relevance Model. Besides, we have proposed the concept of "metadiscourse awareness" to highlight its role in discourse.

As a result, the role of metadiscourse in academic lectures could be regarded as the discourse constructor through searching for relevance and making adaptations on the part of the lecturer. And the role of metadiscourse in academic lectures is not a passive "discourse facilitator", but an active "discourse constructor". As these two words suggest, the lecturers in academic lectures try their best to construct discourse through metadiscourse, since metadiscourse plays an active role in this process. Thus, the active role metadiscourse plays is not facilitator due to its essential functions. What we are expected to do is to pay more attention to the role of metadiscourse in academic lectures.

And a certain degree of metadiscourse awareness a lecturer displays will contribute to the quality and efficiency of academic lectures. This is also true of foreign language teaching activities. In FLT contexts, it has been posited that metadiscourse awareness is particularly useful in helping teachers impart foreign language knowledge to the students. The significance of this study lies in the fact that it may shed light on foreign language teaching. The pedagogical implications of metadiscourse will be illustrated in detail in the next chapter.

Chapter Seven   A Detailed Analysis of the Role of Metadiscourse in Three Full Texts of Academic Lecture

7. 1   Introduction

In the former chapters, we have applied our enriched Adaptation-Relevance Model to illustrate the occurrence and role of metadiscourse in academic lectures. Our study suggests that the lecturers search for relevance by integrating all the contextual information at hand, and then make adaptations to choose the appropriate metadiscourse to guide the audience to achieve the expected contextual effects of the lecturer in the process of interpreting lecture information. What is more, the metadiscourse chosen by the lecturers will also constrain the searching for relevance and inferring the lecturers' communicative intention on the part of the audience. To achieve maximal contextual effects, the audience will infer the relevance between the metadiscourse employed and the contextual assumptions so as to perceive optimal relevance and recognize the lecturers' real communicative intention. And the ultimate goal of choosing a certain metadiscourse device is to achieve optimal relevance to meet the requirements of the discourse.

In this chapter, we will illustrate the role of metadiscourse in two full texts of academic lectures made by George Lakoff made at Beijing University of Aeronautics and Astronautics in 2004. These three academic lectures in the appendix are about cognitive linguistics which sounds theoretical and philosophical to many readers. Actually, many students feel frustrated when they first encounter cognitive linguistics in their studies, since many theories and concepts in it are very abstract and therefore difficult to understand. That is part of the reason why we have chosen George Lokoff's academic lectures which illustrate cognitive theories and concepts in a friendly way. George Lakoff is a well-known linguist whose broad knowledge and penetrating thinking makes the subject easy to understand. However, due the oral nature of academic lectures, the three texts are with many grammatical or syntactic errors and slip of tongue which have nothing to do with the good quality of his academic lectures. It is our belief that George Lakoff's academic lectures are vivid and audience-friendly. To present out readers a full description of his academic lectures, we may look at some of the ungrammatical utterances.

For example:

[1] You have motor programs for interacting with the table or you're sitting in the chair, motor programs for turning on lamps, but no motor programs for dealing with all and only the furniture. Nothing that is to do with your body for all and only the furniture. That doesn't happen. So what she pointed out was a very special kind of category, basic level category. Notice the same is true for something like a "car".

[2] No 1 tall. So it is not the case that everything is between zero and one—something is very tall and some people are not tall. So that one problem with that is that you need to extend the theory of categories to include graded categories.

[3] This is something again embodied, it is not something you can do in formal semantics. You think about the system, you say how would you do any of this in terms of set theory. It is hopeless. This is why you need cognitive linguistics. You need something that has to do with the way you are embodied, the way your mind is embodied, the way you interact with the world.

[4] You can inflame the situation, make people more angry. And many, many others: "his sincere apology adds fuel to the fire. " Make the other person more angry.

[5] Now what is an organizational structure that persist over time? One, a society; two, a theory. Physical structure that remains erect is a

building. So what you have is a whole structure of basic metaphors that have been fixed together as pieces like building blocks to make other metaphors.

[6]And she said "I don't really understand this very well. You know maybe you can help me get, understand it. " So we said, "Look, if it's hit a dead-end street, you can't keep going the way you have been going. You may have to turn back. " And then we realized that English have a lot of expressions in which love was seen as a kind of journey.

[7] You don't have electricity, electric lights of your theory. You don't have the plumping of your theory, the floor of your theory. Look around the building, most of the things aren't there. The air-conditioning of your theory, nothing.

[8] Now why is that is so small? Why there only something is mapped and not others? It's the fact that works this way. And what the theories have to do with building? Why should theories have anything to do at all with buildings? These are the questions asked by a student of mine Joe Grady, who wrote a very interesting dissertation based on observations like this.

[9]That is, there is a neuron that fires in phases. It computes the aspect of grasping, the central part and the final part. There is other neurons which fire in the beginning parts when you are going to. That is, there are neurons that fire controlling the phases of the action, and you can find them one by one.

[10]When you do that, you are making connections to new special cases, but you already know the generalization, because they are part of the special cases. That something that's true of the neural system of the human brain. It's not something that abstractly true of a mathematical system — nit's certainly not true in a mathematical system.

In example one, the sentence "Nothing that is to do with your body for all and only the furniture" is ungrammatical. In example two, "No. 1 tall" is fragment and sound a little colloquial. In example two, the sentence "You think about the system, you say how would you do any of this in terms of set theory" is ungrammatical. In example four, the sentence "Make the other person more angry" is ungrammatical since we very often say "angrier". In example five, the sentence "Now what is an organizational structure that persist over time? One, a society; two, a theory" is ungrammatical. In example six, the sentence "You know maybe you can help me get, understand it" is ungrammatical. In example seven, the sentence "The air-conditioning of your theory, nothing" is ungrammatical. In example eight, the sentence "Now why is that is so small? Why there only something is mapped and not others? It's the fact that works this way. And what the theories have to do with building" is ungrammatical. In example nine, the sentence "There is other neurons which fire in the beginning parts when you are going to" is ungrammatical. Last but not the least, in example ten, the sentence "That something that's true of the neural system of the human brain" is ungrammatical.

As a matter of fact, we can find out a lot of such ungrammatical sentences in his academic lectures. All the examples suggest that there are many grammatical errors in his academic lectures. Some of the errors are slip of tongue due to the oral nature of academic lectures. Different from written communication, oral academic lectures require less time for preparation and thinking. Sometimes, academic lectures can reflect the speaking styles of the lectures. In most cases, there are many fragments in academic lecturers since oral communication tent to be simple and short. This tends to be a feature of excellent academic lectures because fragments help to deliver lecturers' communicative intention directly. The audience may also catch the main information in a short time, thus the improvement of teaching efficiency. At the same time, body language is applied in the video which is not the subject of current study. Future researches may focus on body language in academic lectures in order to present a full picture of academic lectures. This belongs to the domain of cross-cultural communication studies. We hope that more and more researchers will take interest in this area and do their part.

Despite the grammatical errors or slip of tongue, the three academic lectures act as a good example of excellent academic lectures. We will focus on the metadiscourse applied in them and illustrate its role as the result of making adaptations and searching for relevance within our enriched Adaptation-Relevance Model.

7. 2   Types of metadiscourse in the three academic lectures

In previous chapters, we have adopted the taxonomies of metadiscourse proposed by Rahman (2004). It adopts the term "metalanguage" and divides the metalanguage we use in writing into two general categories: metatext and metadiscourse. As a matter of fact, our concept of "metadiscourse" includes both metatext and metadiscourse. We can take a look at the detailed corresponding categories of metadiscourse occurring in the three academic lectures. The detailed analysis of the specific categories may present a relatively full picture of the occurrence and role of metadiscourse in academic lectures.

7. 2. 1   Metatext (text-about-text management) in the three academic lectures

As we mentioned above, metatext is defined by Rahman as "text-about-text management" that applies explicit references to the text managing acts. It includes many specific categories, such as reference to discourse entities, reference to discourse acts, and reference to discourse labels.

a. Reference to discourse entities

In this respect, the lecturer may also refer to the entire lecture, individual sections, or tables and figures used in the lectures. This technique will contribute to a better understanding of the lecture as a whole. For example:

[11] *We have come very far from the idea that* meaning is in the relationship between symbols and sets in the world. Meaning is in your brain. Meaning has to do with things like this. Meaning components arise because your brain has a certain structure.

[12] Now then you will ask how does this work on poetry, and so on.

137

We will get to that in a while. Notice why Aristotle gave the definition he gave. He had to. Aristotle was the inventor of logic.

[13] *We are going to talk about what we call amodality.* The traditional theory implicitly claims that even action concepts like grasp did not make use of the sensory-motor system. As a concept, according to the traditional theory, *grasp* must be embodied.

b. Reference to discourse acts

By mentioning what has been talked about, the lecturer can draw the audience's attention to theacademic information, hence facilitating the progression of the lecture. In addition, what has been mentioned will pave the way for the later part of academic lectures. For example:

[14] In 1963, I *mentioned* that I was one of the people bringing the study of logic into linguistics in order to study meaning. And let me tell you what that meant exactly. It meant that if you have a formula such as f (a, b): something like John hit Bill, something of that sort, and its predicate with two arguments.

[15] He had *figured out* how the brain processes color vision, again working with Monkeys, with macaque monkeys, so you can do operations on the brain, and had figured out that in general, color vision works by your two color cones in your eye, two types of color receptors. They form circuits of very complex kinds so that there are six types of color circuits.

[16] So, what he did was then *figure out* what metaphors they were linking the physical actions to the economics. We worked tha tout like a linguist with a little help from his friends. And then he asked, could the same circuity that can move the body do the reasoning about economics correctly, using the part about falling into a recession, pulling out, stumbling and so on.

c. Reference to discourse labels

In the process of givingacademic lectures, the lecturer may also refer to a discourse act by using discourse labels. For example:

[17] So this is a famous experiment in which, let me give you an example. A duck is not quite a typical bird, right? It is atypical, sort of in the middle. The experiment went like *this*.

[18] *That*'s the classical theory of meaning completely disembodied, has nothing to do with the mind, the brain, the body, anything else, a purely mathematical theory.

[19] Now, *here* is the neuron firing. You have the monkey in this region and what you are doing *here* is showing what happens when you put something into space at various angles *here*, *here*, *here*, and so on, and you see the amount of firing varying. The maximum firing is right next to the check. And *this* is the region in which you get any firing at all. Here is how this works in another experiment.

7. 2. 2   *Metadiscourse (text-about-discourse management) in the three academic lectures*

Metadiscourse in this sense focuses on the part of discourse management, including executing illocutionary acts, topic shifting, code glossing, interactive acts, and text connectives. We will look at the specific examples in the three academic lectures.

a. Executing illocutionary acts

The illocutionary acts in lectures show the audience that the lecturer has made or will make a statement concerning the topic. For example:

[20] So what she *pointed out* was this is a very special kind of categorization, and it was a category, basic level category. Notice the same is true for something like a "car". You can get a mental image of a car, you do certain things with the car, you drive it, you shift, etc, or you press the paddles.

[21] That isn't true about the rest. So in general, what Rosch *conclu-*

ded from this was something important. Basic level categories are defined by your bodily interactions with the world. That is the ability to have gestalt perception, form a mental image and interact physically with your body.

[22] So what she *pointed out* was this is a very special kind of categorization, and it was a category, basic level category. Notice the same is true for something like a "car". You can get a mental image of a car, you do certain things with the car, you drive it, you shift, etc, or you press the paddles.

b. Topic shifting

In the process of giving an academic lecture, the lecturer often gives a clue to the audience when he/she wants to change the topic. For example:

[23] *Now what is interesting about this is the following.* Normally when you apply an adjective to a category, all the properties of the category hold plus the properties of the adjective.

[24] Now there are *other kinds of* prototypes that are very important. These are the very special case prototypes. There are cases that are called salient exemplars, a terrible technical term that only a psychologist could make up.

[25] *Now there is another really, really important case of prototypes*, and that is, what we call radial categories-central cases and non-central cases. Take the category "mother"-simple category "mother". Now a "mother" is defined by many frames.

c. Code glossing

Code glossing, such as *for example*, *for instance*, helps the audience interpret the meaning of some statements or arguments. We may find lots of such examples in academic lectures. For example:

[26] It is a theory about what the world is like, and the assumption is that the world is structured according to logic. So, *for example*, if the water

is in the room, then the water is in the room and that is seen as a fact about the world. And that logical statement is true of the world that the water is in the bottle, and is true of the world that the bottle is in the room, and is true that of the world that the water is in the room.

[27] *For example*, if you close your eyes, you can get a mental image of a chair. Now, close your eyes and try to get a mental image of a generalized piece of furniture, not a chair, not a table, no particular kind, just a general piece of furniture, and you can't do it.

[28] The subject, we claim, is simulating the same action, *that is*, the subject's brain is carrying out what he sees. I see you going to lift that and I'm carrying out automatically because my parietal cortex is getting the visual information.

d. Interactive acts

Interactive acts in academic lectures reveal that the lecturer keeps the audience in mind and the interaction between participants in communication makes academic lectures smoother. The interaction between participants also helps to catch the attention of the audience. For example:

[29] Those are impossibilities in those theories of semantics that are not cognitive theories: discourse representation theory is not a cognitive theory, it's a formal theory just like, *you know*, set of set theoretical models where you have a bunch of sets in sequences.

[30] *Notice* that love and travel are not similar in themselves. The metaphor is not based on similarity. It is not in the words. It is in the concepts. And I notice in each case you have a frame, a frame of traveling being mapped onto love.

[31] Now, *think about* it, that is kind of interesting, because it's firing for grasping any kind at all, but what is actually doing is something different with its mouth and with its arms. So, what we know from general purpose neurons; what do they achieve in theories of concepts; partially universality, their firing correlates with a goal-oriented action of a general

type, regardless of effectors, that is arm or mouth, or manner, that's how you do it.

e. Text connectives

By employing text connectives, the writer can make his/her writing coherent. Words like *first*, *second*, *next* help to organize the text in a logical way. The audience may also benefit from the logical organization of academic content. For example:

[32] And they asked them two questions. *First*, find out the range of the colors, what the range was. You know, you have a bunch of color chips, and the range here, and the range here, and the range there and so on.

[33] Now the *second* one was just as revolutionary, and seems revolutionary in the similar way. That was a lecture given by Eleanor Rosch. Eleanor Rosch was the person who first discovered the prototype theory, and we'll talk about that in a little while.

[34] Now, what the schema that controls actions. This is what the executing schema, what the Narayanan called the Controller X – schema, which controls action: *first* do this, and *then* do this, and *then* do this.

All the examples and studies suggest that the taxonomies of metadiscourse proposed by Rahman (2004) are applicable in the three academic lectures. Throughout the three lectures, we have found many corresponding examples of all the categories which help the lecturer to deliver his academic content in an efficient way. The purpose of this chapter is to investigate the occurrence of metadiscourse in the three academic lectures so as to confirm the role of metadiscourse in academic lectures. As a matter of fact, the three academic lectures are not enough to insure the validity of the study. However, we have tried our best to present a relatively valid investigation of the occurrence of metadiscourse in academic lectures so as to pave the way for later metadiscourse researches.

An increasing number of evidences show that excellent academic lectures tend to employ appropriate metadiscourse in the process of delivering academic information due to its essential functions of improving teaching efficiency. This may act as part of the criteria for evaluating the quality of academic lectures. In most cases, excellent academic lecturers are good at choosing appropriate metadiscourse to fulfill their communicative ends while ordinary academic lectures may ignore the essential role of metadiscourse to a certain degree and spend less time and efforts on metadiscourse study. What we call for is the due attention to the metadiscourse in academic lectures on the part of the academic lectures, since appropriate use of metadisocurse may facilitate teaching and learning.

7.3   Role of the metadiscourse in the three academic lectures

As we mentioned in the past chapters, within our enriched Adaptation-Relevance Model, the role of metadiscourse in academic lectures could be regarded as the discourse constructor through searching for relevance and making adaptations on the part of the lecturer. And the role of metadiscourse in academic lectures is not a passive "discourse facilitator", but an active "discourse constructor". In the process of giving academic lectures, the lecturers try their best to construct discourse through metadiscourse, since metadiscourse plays an active role in this process. This is also true of the metadiscourse in the three academic lectures, since they provide vivid examples for metadiscourse analysis. It is obvious that the academic lectures on linguistics by George Lakoff is really a hit in China because many Chinese students and scholars have benefited greatly from them and achieved a lot in this area in their later cognitive linguistic studies. In other words, George Lakoff has exerted great influence upon many Chinese students and scholars in the area of cognitive linguistics.

The purpose of the three academic lectures is to deliver knowledge of cognitive linguistics to the audience so as to pave the way for cognitive linguistic studies in China. For most people in our China, cognitive linguistics is very abstract and difficult, thus requiring more efforts on the part of the audience or students.

In the process, the lecturer has employed a wide range of metadiscourse to facilitate his teaching. As a matter of fact, metadiscourse is not all-mighty and the lecturers in academic lectures are expected to employ appropriate metadiscourse in different communicative situations.

7. 4   Summary

In this chapter, we have presented a relatively detailed analysis of the occurrence of metadiscourse in three full academic lectures. By mentioning the grammatical errors in the lecutures, we mean academic lectures are colloquial communication in which the lectures have less to think and prepare. By mentioning the types of metadiscourse in the lectures, we focus on the occurrence and role of metadiscourse in them, hence the essential role of metadisocurse. However, our analysis is not enough to some extent and more related studies are called for to probe into the nature and role of metadiscourse in academic lectures.

Chapter Eight　Role of Metadiscourse and Metadiscourse Awareness: Possible Pedagogical Implications

8. 1　Introduction

The findings regarding the occurrence and the role of metadiscourse highlight the significance of metadiscourse in academic lectures. As a major form of teaching activities or academic exchange in symposiums, academic lectures remain a relatively efficient and economical way of conveying academic information in a classroom or lecture hall setting. As a result, we cannot ignore the existence of metadisocurse in human verbal communication as well as academic lectures. Generally speaking, metadisocurse is essential to not only academic lectures, but also other forms of communication in the world. Due to limited time and space, we only deal with the first aspect in our book. More and more related metadiscourse researches are called for in other forms of communication, which may render a relatively full picture of metadiscourse in human communication. We just do our part to raise people's metadiscourse awareness in order to make it attractive and meaningful to more scholars in this area.

And the concept of "metadiscourse awareness" brings metadiscourse into the spotlight of both the lecturer (teacher) and the audience (students) due to its significant part in improving teaching or information exchanging efficiency. Due to limited time and space, our discussion in the present study will focus its attention on the pedagogical aspect of metadiscourse. When we coin the term "metadiscourse awareness", we hope that our linguistic circle and other related disciplines will attach great importance to metadiscourse in our verbal communication. The word "awareness" means the internal or conscious focus on some-thing. Actually, we call for due attention to metadiscourse in classroom teaching so as to turn unconscious application of metadiscourse into conscious employ-ment. This requires time and efforts on the part of teachers and students. Maybe many people have neglected the existence of metadisocurse to a certain degree in our communication due to its non-propositional role in the discourse while focu-sing on the content of classroom teaching. As a matter of fact, the role of metadiscourse cannot be confined to non-propositional role and the intended meaning of the discourse cannot be fully conveyed without metadiscourse. We have elaborated on the issue in the past chapters. That is the reason why we put forward the term "metadiscourse awareness". It is our belief that no one can de-ny the essential role of metadiscourse in our verbal exchange and it deserves more attention and concern.

As far as foreign language learning and teaching is concerned, metadis-course from our perspective has its part to play. Our findings in previous discus-sions may shed light on this respect. Therefore, more attention should be paid to this notion in order to improve teaching efficiency in foreign language learning and teaching as a whole. It should be admitted that this cannot be achieved in a short time. A joint effort is required and more actions are expected to be taken. What we can do is to try our best to propose some possible implications of this study foreign language teaching and learning.

Following this line, we have found some possible implications for FLT, teacher training, and even curriculum design for English learning and teach-ing. These sound much more practical and constitute our main concern in this chapter. To present a relatively detailed picture, we will illustrate these two as-pects one after another. All the suggestions, to be honest, are not mature to some extent. More suggestions and criticism are welcome to push forward the re-form and innovation in foreign language teaching and learning. We do hope that teaching efficiency will be improved in the near future in China.

8. 2   Possible implications for FLT

With the ever-increasing importance of foreign languages, FLT (here especially English teaching) has become a common phenomenon in China. And lectures are perhaps the major form of imparting English knowledge and communicative skills to the students. On the one hand, teachers in FLT are expected to vary their ways to organize lectures so as to improve teaching efficiency and quality. On the other hand, students also need to learn skills to interpret the structure of lectures and detailed information in them in order to catch the teachers and improve learning efficiency.

Some English teachers, however, lack the necessary skills of structuring their lectures to present themselves efficiently. This is also true of some students and they can improve learning efficiency through metadiscourse. They need to have some knowledge about metadiscourse and how to catch the macro structure of lectures in order to understand the main points in lectures, since metadiscourse provides a possible solution to discourse construction and interpretation.

Vande Kopple (1991: 14) observes that specific instruction on metadiscourse can be useful to help L2 readers learn to distinguish factual content from the writer's commentary. Steffensen & Cheng (1996) have conducted an experiment to investigate the effect of targeted instruction on metadiscourse on the writing abilities of native speaker university students. An experimental group that had been taught the form, function and purpose of metadiscourse learned to use it effectively and produced compositions that earned significantly higher scores than those of a control group, which had received no instruction on metadiscourse.

As we mentioned above, metadiscourse plays a vital role in academic lectures and the concept of "metadiscourse awareness" brings into prominence the significance of metadiscourse. As a form of interaction between teacher and students, FLT also involves presenting academic information and interpreting it, and thereforeis similar in nature with academic lectures.

Although teachers need not spend a significant amount of their class time

147

teaching metadiscourse in FLT, there is a need to make learners aware of the metadiscourse devices and their appropriate use and pragmatic functions in concrete teaching activities. This will help to improve teaching efficiency and learning efficiency in the long run, since both teachers and students could benefit from focusing on metadiscourse in teaching activities.

Previous analysis within the framework of the enriched Adaptation-Relevance Model suggests that metadiscourse is the result of searching for relevance and making adaptations. And the role of metadiscourse in academic lectures is not a passive "discourse facilitator", but an active "discourse constructor".

The findings of the present study have offered us theoretical support and motivation for the employment of metadiscourse in FLT. As an adaptation-relevance process, FLT also involves searching for relevance and making adaptations on the part of the teacher in order to choose the appropriate metadiscourse to frame and construct his/her teaching. The choice of the appropriate metadiscourse will help to guide the students in the process of listening to the lecture.

In classroom teaching, the lectures with no or inadequate metadiscourse may pose some difficulties for the students to interpret the macro structure and content of the lecture. What is worse, this sometimes will make some students feel frustrated and even give up foreign language learning. Therefore, the teacher is expected to make assumptions about the students' cognitive states and make adaptations to choose appropriate metadiscourse so as to cater to the students' communicative needs.

Besides, within the framework of our enriched Adaptation-Relevance Model, metadiscourse could be regarded as the result of searching for relevance and making adaptations. This sounds much theoretical to some extent. However, it may provide FLT activities in classroom with some practical strategies. We prefer the combination of theory and practice because practice is the ultimate end of theoretical researches. Otherwise, there will be no sense in theoretical studies. What we should bear in mind is that theory should serve practice in one way or another, which is the true meaning and life of theoretical studies.

To improve FLT efficiency, some teaching strategies with regard to metadiscourse could be offered.

1. Raising students' metadiscourse awareness

Metadiscourse awareness is an important concept we proposed in the previous chapter. We have discussed its significance in academic lectures within the framework of the enriched Adaptation-Relevance Model. This is also true of foreign language teaching. It is necessary to raise metadiscourse awareness on the part of both the teachers and the students. With our efforts, an increasing number of teachers and students will come to realize the significant role of metadiscourse in classroom teaching and learning.

On the one hand, the teachers can employ appropriate metadiscourse in his/her lectures to organize the lecture and engage the students. The lecturing skills can be trained through teaching and metadiscourse awareness can be raised in the same way. The quality of good teachers is that they can improve themselves to meet the needs of new situations if they are willing to do so. Actually, all the teachers hope to improve their teaching efficiency and quality. More knowledge of metadiscourse is one of the choices. On the other hand, the major goal of students is to acquire knowledge through classroom teaching activities. As a matter of fact, many students do not know the best techniques of learning in classroom. And a good method is half the success for them. Our study suggests that they can employ metadiscourse to understand the main structure of the lectures, and interpret the teachers' communicative intention. Despite its theoretical investigation from the perspective of the enriched Adaptation-Relevance Model, our research has its pedagogical implications. It is beneficial to both the teachers and the students in academic lectures. What we can do is to pay attention to the two aspects of teaching and learning.

Bearing this in mind, the students are expected to raise their metadiscourse awareness in their daily foreign language learning. Such increased awareness could provide foreign language learners with an access to these metadiscourse devices in appropriate situations outside the classroom as part of their learning capacities. This could be part of the curriculum before it is carried out. We believe more and more people will come to realize the significance of metadiscourse in classroom teaching and learning so as to improve the efficiency of teaching and learning.

Therefore, metadiscourse awareness can be used as one of the criteria to judge whether or not a foreign language teacher is good at presenting information. In most cases, good teachers tend apply appropriate metadiscourse to organize academic lectures because they understand the significance of metadiscourse and possess metadiscourse awareness. What is more, this criterion can be employed to evaluate students, since metadiscourse awareness can enhance learning efficiency on the part of the students. Students with metadiscourse awareness have the advantages over those without it due to the significance of metadiscourse in classroom learning.

2. Making a list of common metadiscourse

As we mentioned in the past chapters, metadiscourse is a very complicated phenomenon, regarding its definitions and terminologies. Many students may feel puzzled when they encounter metadiscourse at the very beginning, since it is not easy to catch its core ideas and mechanism. A list of common metadiscourse in verbal communication, oral or written, should be provided in order to make sure that the students have a clear idea what metadiscourse is and its categories. This kind of list could be found in the appendix of many books about metadiscourse. With the list, the students can become familiar with common metadiscourse in human communication and easily pick out metadiscourse in written works or foreign language lectures. However, we can make a long list of metadiscourse from different perspectives. What we can do is to figure out typical ones and classical theories and perspectives. As a matter of fact, the list should be concise and vivid instead of being too long and boring, since students prefer manageable and interesting one in learning. It is our task to turn difficult terms into easier ones through researches.

3. Providing rich reading and video materials with adequate metadiscourse

It is not enough to provide the students with a list of common metadiscourse we use in verbal communication, since such a list is not vivid and lacks appropriate contexts for the use of metadiscourse. As a common saying in pragmatics goes, "no context, no meaning", which suggests the importance of context for language use. Excellent examples may offer an relatively authentic context for students to interpret the mechanism underlying the occurrence of metadiscourse in learning materials.

Therefore, it is necessary to offer the students rich vivid learning materials with adequate metadiscourse, written or visual. Such learning materials serve as examples for the students to make appropriate use of metdiscourse in different contexts. And the students could understand the mechanism underlying the occurrence of metadiscourse so as to employ metadiscourse in a proper way in later learning or teaching activities. Similarly, the learning materials are expected to be excellent and classical. Otherwise, they will exert bad influence upon them and lead to a failure on the part of the students.

4. Evaluating with students the metadiscourse in teaching materials and their functions

While teaching, the teachers may appreciating with the students the metadiscourse used in teaching materials, pointing out their functions to help the students to become aware of the way good teachers use metadiscourse and master the appropriate use of metadisocourse in human verbal communication which will contribute to knowledge construction.

And our enriched Adaptation-relevance Model of metadiscourse could offer some guidelines for the analysis of the occurrence and the role of metadiscourse in such teaching materials. Bearing this in mind, both the teachers and the students can take a new look at metadiscourse compared with traditional understanding of metadiscourse in the teaching materials.

In addition, the teachers may leave students adequate time for pair and small-group interaction in class to analyze metadiscourse use. Classroom practices can be conducted to recognize the occurrence and the role of metadiscourse in signaling information, organizing main points, and creating situations for the interaction between the teachers and the students, etc.

Such analyses are useful for teaching purposes, in particular for FLT, where students could, for example, master the most common forms and patterns of metadiscourse, along with their associated functions. The communication between them helps to establish a bridge for better teaching and learning efficiency.

5. Conducting classroom activities through highlighting the role of metadis-

course

Our discussions in previous chapters within the framework of the enriched Adaptation-Relevance Model suggest that the role of metadiscourse is not just a "discourse facilitator", but a "discourse constructor". This will possibly change our point of view on metadiscourse teaching and guide our teaching activities.

Classroom activities regarding metadiscourse could be conducted to highlight the role metadiscourse plays in human verbal communication. These practices can take various forms, such as writing compositions or giving lectures in foreign languages, multiple choice exercises, spot dictation, filling blanks, etc.

The purpose of such activities is to raise the students' metadiscourse awareness and train the students to apply appropriate metadiscourse in their foreign language communication. Therefore, the students could possibly be trained to be good learners through activities concerning metadiscourse.

8.3 Possible implications for teacher training

It is generally acknowledged that a vital factor in determining the success of education in the long run is teacher training although the practice of teacher training is far from being satisfactory. Despite the great efforts made by governments and educators, there is a relatively large gap between what scholars have expected and the status quo concerning teacher training.

To narrow the gap between the ideal and reality, many people keep arguing about a better way of teacher training. But what can we do? The current study suggests that much emphasis should be put on how to teach, in particular, how to employ appropriate metadiscourse to improve teaching efficiency. This is concerned with teaching approach or methodology.

The present study regards academic lecture as a process of searching for relevance and making adaptations to choose appropriate metadiscourse on the part of the lecturer. To do so, the lecturer should make assumptions about the audience. It is true that traditional foreign language education pays attention to cultivating students in many respects, but the focus perhaps is what the students need to learn, not how to help the students follow the lectures and other leaning activities.

Therefore, teachers also need to raise metadiscourse awareness and try to apply appropriate metadiscourse to facilitate his/her teaching. The teaching of metadiscourse and the raising of metadiscourse awareness can be a need for teachers. These can be an essential part of teacher training. Through this teaching methodology, perhaps we could improve teaching efficiency and produce more qualified foreign language teachers to meet the need of the society.

Specifically, we could teach future teachers about the rhetorical processes appropriate to a community and appropriate use of metadiscourse. And we could possibly tell them that the choice of appropriate metadiscourse is constrained by a range of factors, such as the cognitive state of the students, communicative situation, etc.

In addition, the specific function of metadiscourse could be introduced. For example, hedges and attributors could be employed to strengthen an argument. Due to limited time and space, we will not go much further on this issue.

8. 4   Possible implications for curriculum design

As the guide of a course, curriculum design, or "curriculum development" by some scholars, is the premise for the teaching of any subject. It specifies the teaching objective, structure, content and evaluation procedure, etc. of a course. Therefore, the quality of curriculum design will exert great influence upon the teaching result of a course, hence the importance of curriculum design.

With people's increasing awareness of FLT, more courses are designed for foreign learners in many universities in China. However, there still exists such doubt as whether students' needs are well satisfied and if they could benefit more from such courses. This is a challenge for foreign languages curriculum designers.

So far, few researches have been carried out on the inclusion of metadiscourse learning in curriculum design. To optimize the objectives of foreign language teaching, more researches are called for to improve course design and thus improve teaching efficiency and quality in the long run.

As a matter of fact, many foreign language learners in China will possibly become teachers after some years of learning. It is not enough to learn foreign language knowledge and communicative skills, since teaching is a rather different situation compared with learning.

To shoulder the responsibility of foreign language teachers, they should master some efficient teaching skills. Among these skills, the capacity of employing metadiscourse is one important aspect without which teaching could not possibly be perfect.

In traditional FLT, the teaching of teaching methodology pays too much attention to the introduction of teaching approaches in applied linguistics and less attention has been paid to the specific teaching skills in classroom teaching, such as the use of metadiscourse devices. And the teaching and practicing of such teaching skills can engage the students and equip them with some useful techniques for a qualified foreign language teacher.

The findings of the present study suggest that metadiscourse is the result of the searching for relevance and making adaptations on the part of the lecturer. In a sense, FLT is also such a process that requires appropriate use of metadiscourse on the part of the teacher. The reason is that the employment of metadiscourse devices could contribute to the success of teaching.

And the use of metadiscourse here includes two aspects, i. e. , the choice of appropriate metadicourse and the appropriate amount of metadiscourse, since different metadicourse has different functions in FLT and too much metadiscourse is also a disaster for teaching.

Therefore, the teaching of appropriate metadiscourse should be included as an essential content in the curriculum design for foreign language learners. This can serve to bring to the spotlight how metadicourse can be employed and why.

8. 5 Summary

This chapter has demonstrated the need of including metadiscourse teaching in pedagogical activities in order to improve teaching efficiency and result due to the significant role metadiscourse plays in the field. Specifically, we have illustrated our points of view from two aspects, namely, FLT, teacher training, and curriculum design.

So far, we have dealt with both theoretical and practical aspect of metadiscourse within our enriched Adaptation-Relevance Model. It is time to harvest the major findings and discuss the limitations of the current study. This is what we will turn to in the next chapter.

Chapter Nine   Conclusion

9. 1   Introduction

As we arrive at the end of this book, it is necessary to take stock of what we have fulfilled in the preceding chapters. In doing so, we could find out the limitations of the present study and pave the way for future researches.

In Chapter One, we have presented a brief introduction of the research orientation, rationale, objective, methodology, and outline of the current study and the introduction of the main parts of this book along with remaining problems of the existing studies. Basing themselves on our discussion, the readers may get a rough idea of how things are going in the present study.

In Chapter Two, we have reviewed various definitions and taxonomies of metadiscourse. It is on the existing definitions of metadiscourse and our discussions about them that we have decided on a working definition of metadiscourse to meet the need of the present study. Altogether, we have presented seven taxonomies of metadiscourse in order to lay a rigid theoretical background for the current study.

Chapter Three is a brief introduction of the methodology employed in the current study. Some details about our procedure of carrying out the present research have been presented in this chapter.

Chapter Four tries to create an enriched Adaptation-Relevance Model based on the Adaptation Theory, Relevance Theory, and two Adaptation-Relevance Models proposed by two scholars respectively. And we have presented a detailed description of our conceptual framework in this chapter.

The task of Chapter Five is to apply our enriched Adaptation-Relevance

Model to account for the occurrence of metadiscourse in academic lectures in order to bring some light to our understanding of the role of metadiscourse and
FLT. In this chapter, our viewpoints have been illustrated through examples
from our data.

And the reinvestigation into the role of metadiscourse in academic lectures
and some possible pedagogical implications are the topics of Chapter Six and
Seven respectively. We have discussed the role of metadiscourse within the enriched Adaptation-Relevance Model.

The goal of the present study was to present a qualitative analysis of how
metadiscourse is employed by the lecturer as a linguistic choice to adapt to specific context and academic audience and searching for optimal relevance. It in-
vestigates the occurrence and the role of metadiscourse in academic lectures
within the framework of the Adaptation-Relevance Model.

The result offers a support to the positive role metadiscourse plays in its
contribution to both the speaker and the audience in academic lectures. Along
with theoretical aspect, the present study also explores the pedagogical implications of the current investigation.

9. 2   Summary of the major findings

First, we have constructed an enriched Adaptation-Relevance Model to account for the occurrence and the role of metadisoccourse in academic lectures. A
relatively detailed description of the model was presented in order to illustrate
the applicability of the framework. When we construct our enriched theoretical
model, we heavily depend on Relevance Theory, Adaptation Theory, and the
integrated studies of Yang Ping and Ran Yongping. As a matter of fact, these
theories we based on have illustrated language use from their own perspectives
and focuses. We can not simply judge them in terms of the criteria of right or
wrong.

In fact, the enriched Adaptation-Relevance Model we have constructed is
lecturer-oriented and designed to meet the requirements of the current investigation into the occurrence and the role of metadiscourse in academic lectures.

Therefore, some details about academic lectures is added the framework to make it more applicable to our current discussions.

Second, we have probed into the ways the lecturer employs metadiscourse devices to convey communicative intentions and fulfill his/her intended goals within the framework of our enriched Adaptation-Relevance Model. A demonstration analysis was presented. On the one hand, we found that the lecturer in academic lectures may make adaptations to linguistic reality, social conventions, and psychological motivations in order to choose appropriate metadiscourse. On the other hand, we have discussed the process of giving academic lectures regarding the choice of metadiscourse.

Our discussion suggests that the lecturer searches for relevance by integrating all the contextual information at hand, and then makes adaptations to choose appropriate metadiscourse to guide the audience to achieve the expected contextual effects of the lecturer in the process of interpreting lecture information. This process of choosing appropriate metadiscourse is dynamic.

Besides, the metadiscourse chosen by the lecturer will also constrain the searching for relevance and inferring the lecturer's communicative intention on the part of the audience. Previous analysis within the framework of the enriched Adaptation-Relevance Model suggests that metadiscourse is the result of searching for relevance and making adaptations.

Third, we have found that the choice of metadiscourse is very often accompanied by the choice of strategies. For example, the lecturer very often chooses reference to discourse at the beginning of the lecture to present a holistic picture to the audience, and summary in the end of the lecture to impress the audience. And this dynamic process progresses with the ever-increasing overlapping of the cognitive state of the lecturer and that of the audience.

Fourth, we have revisited the role of metadiscourse in academic lectures. As a complicated issue, the views concerning the role of metadiscourse vary in the field of metadiscourse studies. It seems to us that these different views are based on different perspectives or theoretical frameworks on the part of the scholars. In our present study, we have constructed an enriched Adaptation-Relevance Model to account for the occurrence and the role of metadiscourse in aca-

demic lectures. And the role of metadiscourse within the framework of the enriched Adaptation-Relevance Model is the result of searching for relevance and
making adaptations on the part of the lecturer. And the role of metadiscourse in
academic lectures is not a passive "discourse facilitator", but an active "discourse constructor".

Fifth, we have proposed the concept of "metadiscourse awareness" based
on our analysis of the occurrence and the role of metadiscourse in academic lectures. This concept brings into prominence the essence part metadiscourse plays
in academic lectures. In addition, we have found that metadiscourse awareness
accompanies the process of searching for relevance and making adaptations to
choose appropriate metadiscourse. But due to limited time and space, we have
not threaded our way into this issue.

Finally, we have probed into some pedagogical implications of metadiscourse. These pedagogical implications within the enriched Adaptation-Relevance Model may raise our metadiscourse awareness in foreign language learning
and teaching. The implications may serve as a reference for foreign language
teachers and other scholars concerned. Therefore, we are expected to pay attention to the part metadiscourse plays in our pedagogical activities.

9. 3   Limitations of the present study

It would be misleading to suggest that we have drawn a complete and final
picture of metadiscourse in academic lectures from the perspective of the enriched Adaptation-Relevance Model. As a hot topic in pragmatics and discourse
analysis in recent years, the study of metadiscourse will continue to trigger attention and heated discussions from linguists and scholars from other research
fields.

The near future is likely to witness some of what we have illustrated in this
book modified, or even replaced, by more adequate explorations, since the research on the same topic from different perspectives and new experiences could
bring new light to a research topic. In addition, with diversified research methodologies, scholars in the near future may possibly achieve more new results on

metadiscourse studies.

What is more, a research bears its own limitations due to limited resources, personal experiences and understandings, methodologies, etc. As for the current study, it is far from being perfect and therefore inevitably possesses some limitations in terms of width and depth. Future studies on metadiscourse may serve as a significant complement to the present study.

First, the present study is carried out from the lecturer's perspective, focusing on how a lecturer chooses his/her metadiscourse to fulfill the intended communicative goals within the framework of the Adaptation-Relevance Model.

As we all know, human verbal communication involves at least two parties, i. e., the speaker and the hearer. However, the present study focuses only on the lecturer in academic lectures and seems incomplete and insecure to some degree, since it leaves the audience's part untouched. To present a comprehensive picture of the occurrence of metadiscourse in academic lectures, studies from the audience's perspective will possibly do its part.

Second, the data used in the present study is limited. In choosing the data for the current study, we have tried our best to follow some principles, such as being exhaustive, manageable, etc. And we have field-recorded some academic lectures in order to keep the authenticity of the data. But the data we collected are still inadequate due to limited time and energy. To make the result of the present study much more valid, more data are called for in future researches.

Apart from the quantity of data, consideration of the diversity of data is also necessary in order to compare both genre differences and disciplinary differences. In other words, researchers in the future can collect data from different academic fields, such as art, science, etc. This will bring us much closer to the true nature of metadiscourse in academic lectures and that of metadiscourse as a cluster of expressions. As a result, more convincing research results could possibly be obtained.

Third, no prosodic features accompanying the occurrence of metadiscourse in academic lectures have been touched upon in the current research, hence its incompleteness. And a full picture of actual occurrence of metadiscourse in academic lectures must include non-verbal contextual or pragmatic cues, such as facial expressions, intonation, tone, body language, etc. Contextualization cues like prosody are usually considered paralinguistic cues which add to the vividness of communication in an interaction in a particular way.

Fourth, the present study is a qualitative study with examples to illustrate our points of view and less attention is paid to the frequency of metadiscourse occurrence in academic lectures. A study of metadiscourse in academic lectures or other genres by a combination of both qualitative and quantitative method would likely bring about new understandings on the topic. The conclusions made in such research may sound much more convincing to a certain degree.

Finally, we have not probed into the cultural differences of metadiscourse in academic lectures due to limited time and space although we have selected examples from both English and Chinese data. As a matter of fact, cultural differences may always be there when we employ metadiscourse device to fulfill our communicative goals. This aspect may sound interesting to many of us.

9. 4   Suggestions for further researches

As we mentioned above, the current study bears its own limitations and docs not present a full picture of metadiscourse in academic lectures. Therefore, more researches in the future are called for to enhance our understanding of the topic.

First, as we mentioned above, most metadiscourse studies have been conducted from the speaker's perspective. And the focus of these studies is how the speakers produce certain appropriate metadiscourse devices in concrete communicative situations. Therefore, studies from the hearer's (or writer's) perspective are extremely necessary in order to enrich our limited understanding of metadiscourse from the other party's perspective (hearer or reader). Only by taking into account of both the speaker and the hearer can we obtain a full picture of metadiscourse use in human verbal interaction, thus the significance of the hearer's perspective.

Second, later studies could pay more attention to the prosodic aspect of metadiscourse in human verbal communication. Only by focusing on the prosodic aspect as well as linguistic forms can we get a full picture of metadiscourse use in human verbal communication. The reason is that the prosodic aspect constrains metadisourse use and its interpretation to certain degree.

This is also true of body language in human verbal interaction, since body language accompanying the use of metadiscourse can add to the vividness of verbal communication and also influence the interpretation on the part of the hearer, thus being worth further investigating. It is really interesting to take a look at these issues in future study, which could offer us a much more comprehensive understanding of verbal communication as a whole.

Third, a corpus-based quantitative study of the distribution of metadiscourse in academic lectures will possibly yield rich and delicate findings. This kind of research could possibly probe into the occurrence and the role of metadiscourse in academic lectures in a more objective way.

As a popular approach of linguistic studies in recent days, corpus-based research possesses many advantages compared with the traditional way of linguistic researches due to the assistance of the computer. With computer and corpus, researchers could retrieve data easily and make statistical analysis through software such as SPSS with great accuracy. This will possibly offer us a brand new understanding of metsdiacourse in academic lectures or in other genres.

Fourth, a contrastive study of metadiscourse can also be carried out in order to elicit some cultural differences of usage between different nations or communities, the findings of which can serve as the guideline for the appropriate use of metadiscourse in different language communities and the translation of metadiscourse devices.

What makes us feel relieved is that some scholars have studied metadiscourse comparatively in order to understand differences in usage across cultures (e. g. , Mauranen, 1993; etc.). However, this is far from enough as far as enhancing our cross-cultural understanding of metadiscourse is concerned. Therefore, more efforts could be put to this aspect of metadiscourse use.

Fifth, we have obtained some implications of metadiscourse studies for effective FLT. This respect is also worth further investigating because of its pedagogical value. As a hot topic in many research fields, metadiscourse not only

162

contribute to the organization of discourse, but also construct the discourse.

Crismore (1989), as a typical study in this respect, summarizes a study by P. Intaraprawat, which found that metadiscourse use "varied as a function of the students' language and skill". The findings of the research show that accomplished writers use more metadiscourse and use it more appropriately than less skilled writers.

In addition, researches on learner's acquisition of metadiscourse devices may also find out some patterns or ways the learners follow in the process of acquiring such words to provide FLT with some guidelines and references. For example, how do students realize what metadiscourse is appropriate to use for specific communicative situation? And why do they follow a certain pattern in the process? All these could be research topics for future researches.

Finally, the findings of the present study could be used for the purpose of dictionary or textbook compiling, such as learners' dictionaries and teachers' guidebook that might include common patterns and functions of metadiscourse, and the contexts when a certain metadiscourse could be chosen as the appropriate word. Obviously, such works will heavily depend on more relevant studies on metadiscourse regarding its occurrence mechanism in human verbal communication.

The birth of such dictionaries or guidebooks will not only contribute to the creation of an academic atmosphere for metadiscourse researches, but also raise metadiscourse awareness on both foreign language learners and teachers. Admittedly, there is a long way to go in this area. What we hope is that our efforts could push similar studies in the field a step forward.

Appendix

Lecture One　Cognitive Semantics: The Basic mechanism of Thought(1)

I want to start out by talking about the theory of meaning that comes out of Anglo-American philosophy and logic. And this theory of meaning defined what semantics was in early linguistics. In 1963, I mentioned that I was one of the people bringing the study of logic into linguistics in order to study meaning. And let me tell you what that meant exactly. It meant that if you have a formula such as f (a, b): something like John hit Bill, something of that sort, and its predicate with two arguments. That formula which was taken to be a formal set of symbols could only be evaluated in the world. And there was an assumption, a philosophical assumption holding since the time of Aristotle to many logicians in the present time that the word itself at any given moment is made up of entities, things like you, you, and you, each entity.

This is an entity, with properties—this is white, it is made of chalk, those are properties, and relations holding between them. This chalk is my hand-being in is a relation, being in my hand, the relation between the chalk and my hand. And the idea was that at any point in time, the entire world could be seen in terms of entities with properties and relations, and that any predicate, like *the chalk is white*, *white* is predicate, any predicational statement like *is white* could be understood in terms of what Aristotle called a category, a classical category, that is a category of things in the world defined by an essence, the idea of whiteness out there in the world, and that every predication in language could be understood as category statement about the world, so that *is white* means is in the category of white things. OK? And that *is in my hand* is relationship between my hand and anything in the world that happens to be in my hand, like that. OK.

That the assumption that the world could be understood that ways has held from within the theory of logic from the time of Aristotle until present day logicians. It is a theory about what the world is like, and the assumption is that the world is structured according to logic. So, for example, if the water is in the room, then the water is in the room and that is seen as a fact about the world. And that logical statement is true of the world that the water is in the bottle, and is true of the world that the bottle is in the room, and is true that of the world that the water is in the room. So the idea in classical logic was that logic consisted of the logical structure of the world, and that reasoning was something that human-beings could do to reflect the logical structure of the world, and that language got its meaning by fitting the logical structure of the world. That is the assumption behind classical semantics.

Now, in formal semantics, you take what is called set theoretical models. That is, you assume that there is a set of abstract entities, like letters A, B, C, D, E, or something like that, some abstract entities, and you from set. So for example, the property of white things in the world would be represented in a set of theoretical model by the set, and you'd understand that as the set of all white things. And a relation like is in for the chalk and my hand would be given by an ordered pair of sets (A, B), where this is the set, this ordered pair would be that all the things that was in something else. For example, *this chalk* and *my hand* would be in the set $IN = (A, B)$, or this order in the bottle, *order bottle* would be in the set IN. and the idea was that that way, set theory could mirror and model the structure of the world. And if you could do that, then you could understand semantics in purely mathematical terms, you have a set theoretical model, you have formulas in logic, and you could map them from the formulas in logic to the set theoretical models, with the models were taken as models of the world. Ok, that is what the classical theory of semantics is about, and this completely disembodied, it has nothing to do with human beings, all it has to do is just about abstract formulas and abstract set theoretical models. It's a purely mathematical construction.

And what makes it semantics is that if you can attribute these formulas to language, and you can attribute the model, you can say that the bottle models to the world with entities, properties and relations, then that is supposed to give it meaning. So the idea was that formulas were given meaning right by being mapped onto the world. That is the classical theory of meaning. And many people still believe it. In addition to that, this goes along with the classical theory of truth. The idea there is that truth is the relationship between symbols and the world, and that a sentence is true: like *the chalk is in my hand* is true just in case the entity representing the chalk and the entity representing the hand, and that ordered pair of entities is in the entity set of ordered pairs representing IN. Or, *the chalk is white* is true just in case this piece of chalk is in the set of white things in the world. That's the classical theory of meaning completely disembodied, has nothing to do with the mind, the brain, the body, anything else, a purely mathematical theory.

Now, in addition to that, in order to handle certain other problems, again brought up by Aristotle, like necessity and possibility, logicians made up an extension of this, in which they talked not only about the actual world, but about possible world. So, for example, it could be the case that the chalk in my hand is yellow, but it happens to be white. But you could imagine another possible world just like this one, with everything else the same except that this piece of chalk is yellow, that is in the set of yellow things in that world and not the set of white things. Ok, that's what a possible world is—just like this one, but the other one: it's yellow instead of white. That's a kind of possible world. And the study of possible world semantics came about because of sentences like: it could be possible for this chalk to be yellow. Right? It isn't yellow, but it could be yellow. It is a possibility. So, that kind of sentence was handled by possible world semantics at that time, and it still is. Current possible world semantics assumes the following thing: possible world semantics is not a cognitive theory, not a psychological theory, not a biological theory. Nothing to do with that, purely and abstract disembodied mathematical theory.

Now, when I was working in generative semantics, that was the only theory of semantics that existed. And I tried to make it work. I spent 12 years, developing different kinds of logic, different kinds of models and so on. And difficulties, let me try to give you a sense of the difficulties. In 1968, my friend James Deley McCawley, a great great linguist, one of the greatest linguists of all times, was giving a lecture—we were giving a class together at a linguistic institute. And McCawley at the time had a favorite actress Brigitte Bardot (BB) 1968, long time ago, and he made up a sentence and the sentence went like this: I dreamt that I was BB and that I kissed me. (not I kissed myself)—impossible.

Now, normally, the sentence*I kissed me* would make no sense, because there was no reflexive, not even if you kissed your arm or something, you wouldn't say you kissed me, you need a reflexive. But in this sentence it works, because you are dreaming that in the dream you are Brigitte Bardot, you are experiencing the world as Brigitte Bardot, you see this handsome guy McCawley, and you go and you kissed him. Right? I dreamt I was Brigitte Bardot and I kissed me.

Now, there are two possible worlds: the real world and the world of the dream. But they are related in an interesting way. Because if you look at the real world (R) and the world of the dream (D), here you have Brigitte Bardot, Mc-Cawley, and D: BB, McCawley. But McCawley has two parts his center of consciousness called his mind and the rest—his body and everything else about him. And here in the world of dream, you have Brigitte bardot has a body, a mind and McCawley's mind is mapped onto Brigitte Bardot's mind. When you say I dreamt I was BB, it doesn't mean that BB lokks like James McCawley. She looks like Brigitte bardot. You know she is very sexy, she is a woman, she is not James McCawley at all, all right? So, his mind is being mapped onto that.

Now, classical model theory with possible world semantics can not do this. It is a technical thing; it can not do that. And in particular, if you think about it, it's very strange how could one person's mind be another person's mind. This is not something that is true of the world, or even relations between possible worlds. This has to do with the way you understand something. It's about a dream. It's about your cognition.

Now, at the time I tried to deal with this, with what was called Counterpart Theory in model logic—this was a theory made up by logician Davis Luis, but even that didn't work. We tried and it didn't work. It was really no way to do this, but we knew that you had to be able to break a person up into mind and the rest of them, and to be able to do these projections across possible situations. So, here was a case where classical possible world theory broke down, and this is the beginning of mental space theory. At that time, Gilles Fauconnier was a beginning graduate student in linguistics and got a paper about this sentence, and his career since then has been about talking about how you need mental spaces, a cognitive theory of possible situations rather than a theory of situations out there in the world, and possible worlds are taken as being, you know, kind of real, not parts of people's minds, but out there.

So, these are very strange things, this was a very difficult case. Let me give you another case like this. Take the sentence: *If I were you, I'd hate me.* Now, you can't say I hate me, you have to reflexivize. You can say *I hate myself.* You could say *if I were you, I'd hate myself.* But *if I were you, I hate me* means one thing, and *if I were you I hate myself* means something completely different. Let me explain. In the first one, it says, imagine the situation: you are really a nasty person, you do mean things to other people, then *if I were you, I hate myself.* Now, consider a situation where I'm a mean person, I do nasty things, I've done nasty things to you, and I can say *if I were you, I hate me.* Totally different meanings. Right? And again, you have to have a situation like this: only it's not a dream, you have a situation where my center of consciousness of mind is projected on to yours, and then you say *I hate me* versus *I hate myself.* Now, these are interesting hard problems that are never discussed in model theory. Now, since the days of the 1970s, model theory has advanced. Richard Montague's student Hans Kopf, has invented what he calls Discourse Representation Theory, which does a lot more interesting model theory than before, and allows you to do things in sequence and so on. But discourse representation theory can not break something up into mind and body. They just can't do either of those. Those are impossibilities in those theories of semantics that are not cognitive theories: discourse representation theory is not a cognitive theory, it's a formal theory just like, you know, set of set theoretical models where you have a bunch of sets in sequences. Now, it was because of this, cases like this, that problems first began to arise with the theory of model theoretical semantics. I saw these cases in 1968, and I said I don't know how to do this, these are problematic, and I talked about them, I talked to Fauconnier and I talked to many other people. And then I just kept working; I kept working within that paradigm.

Now, in 1975, there was a very interesting institute at Berkeley. It was an unannounced underground institute. I got a small grant from the National Science Foundation to invite 8 people to a seminar at Berkeley, and I got some very famous logicians, computer scientists and so on. And a rumor got out that we were going to have something interesting happening in Berkeley, and 188 people showed up. So we formed communes. It was 1975, there were no communes in Berkeley yet. People, lots of people rented out houses together and so on. And we formed an institute that went for 6 weeks, and the rules were these: we had two classrooms and a sign-up sheet. Anyone could lecture on two-days notice, and sign up on the sign-up sheet, on any topic, and that went for 6 weeks with 188 linguists, all interesting people, and they all came out and did whatever they were doing. And during those lectures I went to probably about a third to a half of them. I heard a series of lectures that completely changed everything I believed.

The first one was a lecture by Paul Kay, my colleague at Berkeley. Like most of my colleagues at Nerkeley, Paul kay at that time was an anthropologist at that time and he since moved over to linguistics. He and Brent Berlin had written a famous book about color and color terms. When they were graduate students, they were taught that the languages of the world could have any number of colors and they could just break up the color spectrum anyway at all. They didn't believe this, so they decided to do an experiment. They went to a paint company, a company that sold paints and had little chips of paint. And the paint company had these chips with a hundred and forty-four chips of paint, 12 by 12, where there are colors, the whole spectrum out there of all the colors. And they got a hundred of these paint samples, and they sent them to one hundred anthropological field workers, people studying various languages and cultures around the world. They asked the people there to find out what the color terms were and pure color terms, not color terms that meant grass or blood, or something like that, but just something like blue or green that were colors but not other things. So they went out and they got people to do that. And they asked them two questions. First, find out the range of the colors, what the range was. You know, you have a bunch of color chips, and the range here, and the range here, and the range there and so on. Here is blue, here is green, and here is maybe purple, here is red, and so on. Then they asked another question. They said: ask each person what is the best example of each color. They sent these around the world to people who some of them have just two colors in their languages. There are some languages with only two color terms, one for the warm colors red, yellow and orange; another for the cool colors blue, green, black, and so on. Others have two colors, four colors, six colors, eight colors, and so on. English has eleven, Russian twelve. And so they sent these out and they got them back and they discovered that everybody had the same central colors, the same best examples, but the ranges were different, but they had the same best examples. So if you had a language with no word distinguishing blue and green. That's one language for both blue and green. They said the best example would be central blue or central green, not something in the middle. Now, a very striking example. That was their famous research.

In his lecture, Paul kay put that research together with a study by Russell Diveley, a famous neural scientist who recently died about two months ago, who was then at Berkeley. He had worked out the neural physiology of color vision. He had figured out how the brain processes color vision, again working with Monkeys, with macaque monkeys, so you can do operations on the brain, and had figured out that in general, color vision works by your two color cones in your eye, two types of color receptors. They form circuits of very complex kinds so that there are six types of color circuits. The circuits form pairs like red green, blue yellow, white black, and then they have responses curves so that when you see light reflected off something, like the blue chairs that you are sitting on, you see light reflected off that, that will activate a certain set of wave lengths, and that will activate the color cones in your eye, that will in turn activate the neural circuitry, and there will be certain responses. So, for pure blue,

170

you get a high response curve for central blue, and for something like purple, it might be between red and blue. Partially, here is a response curve for red, a response curve for blue where it meets in the middle is purple; response curve of yellow, response curve for red, where it meets in the middle is orange. The best example is when you have the highest response with nothing else, no other color. It turns out that everybody with a few certain perhaps other difficulties which we discovered later but most people have pretty much the same range of colors, the same best examples because of their physiology, because of their color cones in their brains. Now there are people who are color blind, and then there are interesting variations discovered later that men and women differ slightly. Apparently, the color cones, the chemicals there have to do with the genetic material with chromozones, white chromozones. It turns out that there are two types of men in terms of color, but they are very close. The central greenness is like two nanometers apart, but there are sixteen types of women, in terms of color. It is not that women are most sensitive; it is that there are more differences among women, many more differences. Now but that means that the color you see is different from someone else, if you are one type versus another type.

Now, I don't know if this happens in China, but in America, it is very common for men and women to disagree about color. For a husband to say that's brown, the wife says it is not brown, that's orange. What's interesting is that they can both be right because they can have slightly different color cones. Now what is the point of this for Paul Kay was that they showed that there was a physiology, a physiological reason for the universals of color, for color, there have been certain central colors, not only a certain limited range of possible color terms, and so on. There are not, you know, five thousand pure color terms, there are, up to twelve and so on. His idea there was that you could explain something about language, language of universal in terms of neural physiology, but for me, this meant really something much more interesting. I remembered the classical theory of semantics. Remember, it says *the chalk is white* just in case it is in the set of white things in the world. The chalk is yellow if it is in the set of yellow things in the world. The chair is blue if it is in the set of blue things in world. There is no set of blue things in the world. Blue and all other colors have to do with the interaction between you and the world. The idea is color is not in the world. Color is not just a matter of wavelengths that are reflected. Colors have to do with many wavelengths. In fact, in color television, they put together different wave lengths to get a million different colors. The idea here is that color is not wavelengths. Color has to do with the way that wavelengths hit your color cones and the neural circuitry in your eyes, give rise to an experience that you have internally. So for example, it is not true that grass is green itself. The greenness has to do with the relation between you and the grass. It is true that blood is red in itself. It is not true that the sky is blue in itself. All colors have to do with the interaction between you and the world.

To me that was shock. It was a shock not merely to discover that about the world. Look at the world, and look at the color, it is in the way it looks. There's no red in there. Reflects the wavelengths, but the red has to do with how my brain and my body is structured, and we were all close enough, and so that we pretty much see it in the same way, with the exception of some husbands and wives in some cases. Now what's interesting about this for semantics is that the traditional theory of meaning and truth was based on the assumption that symbols are related to world. Sentences like *the chalk is yellow* is true in case that the chalk is in the set of yellow things in the world, but there isn't the set of yellow things in the world, then the classical theory of semantics must be wrong. This is also important because of what was called the correspondence theory of truth. All the Anglo-American philosophy is based on the correspondence theory of truth. It says that if you take a sentence, the sentence is true, like *the chalk is white* just in case you map the objects onto the world, the properties onto the world, and if the sentence fits the world, then it is true, and it doesn't, it isn't. But if it fits the world independent of you and independent of any people, that cannot be true. Just from what we know about color, it cannot be true in general. That is, your brains, your bodies take part in meaning, take part in understanding, in ideas.

Now, if you step back from the point of view of today, we are now thirty years later, a lot of neural sciences happened, we've learned a huge amount. And if you are a neural scientist today, that seems completely obvious. After all, anything you can understand, you can only understand through your brains. And brains are highly structured, and you are only able to understand what the structure of the brain will permit you to understand. So it makes sense from the point of view of current neural science. But in 1975, this was revolutionary. It said that the theory of meaning that we've had for two thousand and five hundred years did not work, that the theory of what truth is, the theory of truth was false. Difficult to say that the theory, the very theory, the very understanding of what truth is or isn't true. That is a major, major thing to understand. Since then, what we've found is that this is normal, that everything works like color in this regard, and we'll go through some more examples. That was the first of the interesting lectures I heard in the summer of 1975.

Now the second one was just as revolutionary, and seems revolutionary in the similar way. That was a lecture given by Eleanor Rosch. Eleanor Rosch was the person who first discovered the prototype theory, and we'll talk about that in a little while. But in that summer of 1975, she gave her first lecture on what she called basic level objects. Now basic level objects are things like bottles, chairs, tables, pieces of chalk, very simple objects. But, a given object can describe it as a physical object; I can describe it as a chair and I can describe it as a chair with a back and no arms. You know there are certain kinds of chairs and I can describe them in all kinds of ways. What she found was that there was a certain level of description, a level of categorization. That was cognitively more basic than other cases.

For example, if you close your eyes, you can get a mental image of a chair. Now, close your eyes and try to get a mental image of a generalized piece of furniture, not a chair, not a table, no particular kind, just a general piece of furniture, and you can't do it. There is no mental image above the level of chair. Chair is the highest level of categorization, in which you can get a mental image. It turns out also it's the highest level of categorization, in which you do something with your body in interacting with the chair. You have motor programs for interacting with the table or you're sitting in the chair, motor programs for turning on lamps, but no motor programs for dealing with all and only the furniture. Nothing that is to do with your body for all and only the furniture. That

173

doesn't happen. So what she pointed out was a very special kind of category, basic level category. Notice the same is true for something like a "car". You can get a mental image of a car, you do certain things with the car, you drive it, you shift, etc. , or you press the paddles. There're certain things that you do with your body for all and only furniture. That doesn't happen.

So what she pointed out was this is a very special kind of categorization, and it was a category, basic level category. Notice the same is true for something like a "car". You can get a mental image of a car, you do certain things with the car, you drive it, you shift, etc. , or you press the paddles. There're certain things that you do with your body with the car, but not with respective vehicles which include cars, buses, trains and boats. There is no general mental image of all vehicles. It's like furniture, too high a level. So the basic level is the level defined by mental imagery, gestalt perception where you could see something at a distance and see its general shape, motor programs, and also it turns out most of your information about categories comes at the basic level. It's very information rich. You know a lot about chairs and cars, much less about vehicles. That isn't true about the rest. So in general, what Rosch concluded from this was something important. Basic level categories are defined by your bodily interactions with the world. That is the ability to have gestalt perception, form a mental image and interact physically with your body. They are interactive categories and as such, the basic level which is cognitively real, and part of your mental structure is not out there in the world by itself; it is in your interactions with the world, with your body. And that means that semantics has to be embodied, just as we saw in the case of color. Color semantics has to be embodied; basic level semantics has to be embodied. You have to take your body into account, you can't have a purely abstract mathematical theory of it.

Now the third lecture that was important that summer was given by Leonard Talmy. Leonard Talmy was just finishing his Ph. D at Berkeley, and he had been studying spatial relations in languages around the world. By spatial relations in English, I mean, things like propositions *in*, *through*, *by*, *across*, *above*, *below*, etc. , all of those, and Chinese has other verbs for spatial relations. Different languages have different ways of expressing spatial relations. For example, in Mixtec, which is an OtoManguean language of central Mexico, in Mixtec, all spatial relations are given by body part metaphors. So if you want to say something like the cow is standing on the hill, they have no word for "on". You would say the cow is standing the hill's head. You project the head onto the hill, you see the head, and the cow's standing on the hill's head. Now for each body part like the head or the arm, there's a corresponding space, for the head is above, for the space is here, and for the arm is here.

And we now know from neural science something very important. It's been discovered that these associated spaces are represented physically in the brain. There is what is called a pari personal space. When we get to the third day of lectures, I'll give you some, I will do some power points and slides of all the data analysis. Let's say if you take this portion of the face, there're certain neurons that fire when touch the portion of the face over here. So you see something there, certain neurons fire; and if touch that, the same neurons fire. That is, the body is set up to identify spaces close to body parts, and this is reflected in Mixtec, so if you say something like the airplane is flying over the hill, it's the airplane is flying the hill's head, with the head but it's the space associated above here. So it's a metonymy of the head for the space associated with the head, the pari personal space. And that's how Mixtec comes into work. Now let me give you another example in Mixtec. If you want to say something like the cat is sitting on the top of the house, what you say is the cat is sitting the house's animal back, animal back like the back of a horse or a cow. They have a word for animal back which is horizontal. So there is no word for "on" and you say the cat is sitting the house's animal back. Supposed you want to say the cat is sitting under the tree, you say the cat is sitting the tree's foot, in the arena near where you put the projector of the body onto the tree and you project the foot. So Mixtec works by body part projections and English has some of these. We have things like in back of me, in front of me, and so on. We have a back and a front that you project. So we have part of this in English, too.

Now in other languages, you also have many others—I won't go into that for another minute. What Leonard Talmy discovered was this. First, when you look across many languages and all the spatial terms, they do not line up. They are just different. They combine and they just take different aspects of space. They look strangely and wildly different. Why? You can decompose those terms into spatial primitives that are the same across languages. So one of the primitives has to do with containment, being inside a certain bounded region, for the word like "in", inside versus outside. Another primitive has to do with contact. A word like "on", if I say the chalk is on the desk, here is the chalk, it's in contact with the desk, if I remove it from contact, it's no longer "on" the desk. "On" requires contact, and it also requires in the central sense being above and it has to be supported by the desk. Now you get up the painting on the wall, and there is not above, but it is supported by the wall and in contact with the wall. So support and contact are crucial for the central senses of "on" and usually in the most practical cases, it's above, like this sort of "on".

Now all languages appear to have primitives like contact, support, verticality—above and below, in and out —that is containment; they also have a source, a path and a goal for *from*, *along*, *to*, and so on. What Talmy did was to start to break down these primitives, and he broke them down into many dozens of them, not that many dozens, but there are a number of them. He found that there were two classes of primitives, some were topological. So containment is a topological property which means that you can take a container. The same is true for path. If I have a source, I have a goal, and I have a path. It doesn't matter if the path is wiggly, if it's long, if it's short, it's still a path. Those are topological cases. Then there are orientations cases like *up*, *down*, *front*, *back*. Those are the orientations given by the body, and then some orientations are outside. There are languages where you identify things as being north of something else or west of something else. So there are external orientations and there are bodily orientations, but they are all orientations cases.

And finally there are what he called force dynamic cases. These are cases like "against" where you are pushing against and there is a resistance. And he identified in language sixteen types of force dynamic interactions. So support is one, and being against, pushing against with resistance is another, and pushing with no resistance is the third, and you know there are cases where you block something, you come in and you create the resistance. He went through all these

176

cases and showed that all of the spatial relations could be given in terms of one of the two classes. Sometimes there are two classes at once. So for example, if something is in a bank vault, it is both protected from the outside, there are force dynamics, and it's also contained spatially, so you can have two at once. We recall these image schemas or force dynamics schemas, and every preposition or spatial relation term is a combination, a binding together of these various schemas. So for example, if I have something like "through". "Through" means you start outside, you go inside and you go outside again. So "through" has a sort of scenario where you begin outside and go inside and then outside. There is a source, a path and a goal, and you put them together. It's complex, but it is made of two schemas, a source path goal schema and a container schema which are two image schemas. "Into" is made up of schemas like that (see figure 1), "out of" is made up of schemas like that (see figure 2) where you start in and you go out. The idea is that these things can be combined, and different languages combine them in different ways, and then there can be variations on them which are very interesting. There are what I called radial categories of these complex schemas, so something like "over"—this is the central sense of "over", where let's say you have a hill or may be a bridge, or something like that, where this goes over that. It can be flying above it, it can be in contact with it, you could drive over the hill, fly over the hill; it's above and across. So it goes across something, across the middle line, you have a path like that, and it's above it. It is putting together several image schemas at once to get that "over" (see figure 3). But there's another "over", where there's nothing moving, you just have that (see figure 4). So the helicopter lands, it's no longer "over", and it's "on" the hill. But if it's moving, it can still be going over the hill, but it has to go from one side to the other. Now you can have another version. So this is another path of "over". Now suppose that you are standing here, and there is a building over here, and this is a possible path over the hill to that building. Then you can say the house is over the hill from me, from where I am. There is a possible path, so that's another variation on this "over", at the end of the possible path to something. Now this is a very productive variation. It's a general rule of English at least, where, for example, you can say "he walked across the street", it's a path, or "he lives across the street", you actually have to walk a potential path to where he lives. So you have a street, you can walk across the street, or you are here, he's there, and there is a potential path to go across the street (see figure 6), and he lives at the end of that path, you say "he lives across the street". So the word "across" can attach itself to something that means like this or something systematical related. Similarly the word "through". You could say "he walked through the doorway", or "the main office is at the end of path through the doorway". So basically, there are relationships, systematical relationships that link the central senses of propositions to non-central senses, to other senses. And "over" is interesting because there are over one hundred senses of "over".

In *Women, Fire and Dangerous Things*, which I happen to bring here, at the end of the case study two, in there you know you have, this is a diagram of sixty senses of "over" and how they are related to each other, with examples, you know, of various types of "over", and so on. Now I won't go through all of them, but the point is this: spatial relations differ from language to language, and they are very complicated, and so you might say how does anyone ever learn them? The idea is you learn primitives. You have primitives like source path goal, containers, contact, support, etc. you have maybe fifty to a hundred primitives like these, and you can put them together in lots of different ways in different languages, and then given that, there is a word that expresses some complex of primitives, if there is word expressing a bunch of primitives put together in a certain way, then that word cab be extended to a related set of primitives in some systematic way. There is a system behind this.

Now why is that interesting? Many of these primitives have to do with the body, there are bodily orientations; they have to do with force which has to do with the way your muscle work. They have to do with force which has to do with a cognitive topology which has something to do with the human mind constructs. So if I say there are bees, a bunch of bees swarming in the garden, there needn't be any fence around the bees. The "IN" container is in your mind, you're understanding the container around the bees. We once had a bunch of bees swarming in our garden and we understood this very well. Ten thousand bees once descended upon our garden, and sat coy the tree for a while. Then they started buzzing around, ten thousand bees. You could see the bees buzzing but they are in a contained area, and they are in the garden. Now this is important first because the primitives are embodied, and that is how it is possible for you to learn them. We'll talk in a little while about how they are embodied. We won't say how, we just say they happen to be somewhere. There is a theory about how they are embodied. But right now we know that they are embodied in some way and all these complex terms can be decomposed into simple primitives. Now this is extremely striking in certain languages of North-west Mexico. Eugene Casad is a linguist who has worked on Cora, C-O-R-A. Cora is a language of North-west Mexico. Cora is a very interesting language. Cora has a system of 137 spatial relations, but none are prepositions. None of them are postpositions, none are body part metaphors, and none are cases. Where are they? How does Cora do spatial relations? Cora uses deictic locative pronouns. English has two, "here" and "there". Cora has 137 deictic locative pronouns. Gene Casad who did the field work on it worked on it worked on this language for thirteen years before he found out anything about the system and when he found it out, he understood it in terms of this decomposition.

Let me give you some feel for how Cora works. There is a system in Cora, something like this, a system of morphemes where there are two parts to a morpheme and the first part of the morpheme indicates how close something is. Is it very close to you? Is it a medium distance or is it far away? So you are here and it is there or here, wherever. The question is how close it is. If it is, for example, the medium distance you use "m", the second part has to do with whether it is in your line of sight, seen in your field of vision, inside versus outside. Here you have "u" and here you have "a". the third part of the morpheme has to do with whether the objects is on the slope, on the top or on the bottom of the slope. If it is on the slope, you say "h", so "muh" means over there at medium distance, inside of the line of sight on the slope. "Mah" means over there at far distance on the slope. I'm sorry, over there outside the field of vision is medium distance. If I remember correctly, if it is down here, it is a long vowel. So if you say "ma:" with a long vowel, then it is medium distance outside the field of vision on the bottom of the slope, and so on. You get the general idea and the rest of this fills in. I cannot remember exactly which one is where.

This is a real language and has a system working, meh, u, a, ya.... It has this system. And the system is phoneme by phoneme with these image schemas. The image schemas are part of the universal system. The way they put together is not part of the universal system. Now this says first with respect to spatial relations, if you look at the words they all look different. If you can break it down to the image schemas, then you see the universal. (...) This is something again embodied, it is not something you can do in formal semantics. You think about the system, you say how would you do any of this in terms of set theory. It is hopeless. This is why you need cognitive linguistics. You need something that has to do with the way you are embodied, the way your mind is embodied, the way you interact with the world. That is part of what cognitive linguistics is about. And when you see this, you begin to see the systematicity in language that you just don't see in standard semantics.

Now why should this exist? Where do image schemas come from? We have only the beginning of an answer but it is a very interesting beginning of an answer. There is a book by Terry Reigier called *The Human Semantics Potential*, and in this book Regier goes over the results of his doctoral dissertation. Regier is a cognitive scientist trained in computer science, cognitive psychology, cognitive linguistics and neural computation. He has done all of that work. He was the first cognitive scientist graduate from Berkeley. He did all of those things. What he discovered was this: there are certain parts of the brain that have the right nerve structure so that applying principles of neural computations to them, they will compute the image schemas. So for example, there is part of the brain back here, which has topographic maps.

What is a topographic map? Let me give you an example on how topographic maps were discovered. We know, for example, there was an experiment done also at Berkeley in the same laboratory where the color work was done, in which they took monkeys and had removed the back of the scalp to be able to register, you know exactly what was firing and where and so on. And they had a target set up. The target looks like a couple of circles and then an axis through the target.

These are black and white. They gave the monkey curare which paralyze the eyes, so there were no eye movements, so that the monkey looking at the target would see the target. He was still, and his eyes were still and the brain will be firing and where there was something dark, certain neurons would fire and where there was light, neurons would not be firing.

What does firing mean? It means that certain chemicals pass out the neuron. So what did they did was that they injected a radioactive version of the chemicals that passed out of the neuron so that as the neuron was fired they got refilled with the radioactive version. So whenever this was firing after about half an hour, it was all radioactive. Then they sacrificed the monkey, they killed the monkey, took that part of the brain out that was radioactive and put it onto a photographic plate and put it in a refrigerator for two months to develop the photographic plate. When they took out the photographic plate after two months, they had a piece of this, and in that piece, they could see things that look like this. That is, these lines were deformed in a systematic way. That could be predictable systematically, that you could see the extra lines but they were sort of twisted around because the brain isn't flat and it was twisted, folded and what you have in the brain is a copy of what is on the retina in V one, primary visual cortex. That is a topographic map.

There are other types of topographic maps for your body, appear for your motor system. So there is a part of your brain appears and fires when you speak and move your mouth. There is another part over here when you move your arms and there is another part when you move your legs, and they are laid out in some systematic linear order so that the part that fires when you move that finger. So you have topographic organizations in the brain. Now what Regier did was the following. He said somehow the brain has to compute, let's say, inside and outside. How could the brain compute inside and outside for any arbitrary figure? That is I gave the figure like that, it has inside and outside. I give it a triangle, I give it a five-side figure. They could be any sides, in any place. It has to be able to tell this is inside and that's the outside. How could a brain do that? And he said: Look, Let's put together something we know about the visual system of the brain. Here are the some things. We know that the brain in the primary visual cortex comes in layers, and inside the layer you have neurons that are connected to each other. Lots of neuron connections. This is connected. These are connected all over these places. Lots of connections. We also know that the connections can be excitatory that they can stimulate the other neurons to fire or inhibitory that they can stop others from firing. So this fires the other excitatory connection and the next one will be stopped. We also know that there are layers of neurons. Let's assume this is another layer underneath that one and that, there are connections across the corresponding parts of the layers. So, this is connected to here and that is connected to there. This one in the corner is connected to here. And I think this is underneath that. That is, it is connected. Here is one layer. Here is another layer, lots of connections to whatever is sort of in the area, not one to one but little connections come in group of connections, but very close cross this.

Now some of these are inhibitory, going from one layer to another, and these can be excitatory or inhibitory within. We also know that there are some layers with their spreading of activation or inhibition from the outside to the inside. How do we know this? There is a great experiment done by Professor Roman Candron at UCSD which shows this is in an interesting way. In the eye, the back of the eye, the nerve that connects the eye comes in and every one of us has a little blind spot in the back of our retina. We have a tiny blind spot where the nerves come in. we don't see the blind spot, our brain feel the blind spot, and the question is how do they feel it? What is the mechanism? So what he did was this. He got a little target where this is green on the outside and yellow on the inside. And he set it up so that when you flash this, you could sort of monitor people's eye movements. And just as it was going right, your eyes were going right by it, this would flash on, so this would just go inside the blind spot of the opposite nerve. Yellow part, the outside would be green. That is, this part of the brain connected to that part of the eye retina is filling in from outside to inside. It's the green, the detectors from where we experience as green are moving form from outside to inside, filling in that inner part in our brains. So we know they are spreading in that direction.

So Regier put this information together, and he said there is another piece he put. He said look, if you see a shape, you see an object with an interesting shape like this bottle. I hold up this bottle. See it, it is a shape. The way that you tell is a shape, one way is that your brain computes the differences in shading between this and the background, and computes the outline of this. So there is a part of the brain that computes this in a lower level of vision at the very beginning of the visual system. So he said let us suppose, since we have that, that we have a topographic map that picks out the shape (let's say, the shape is this). And suppose we want to ask the question "Is the circle inside the triangle or is the circle outside the triangle? " For the triangle we know that this shape is picked out. Now let's assume then that this map with this shape is picked out, and these are all, this means that all along here there are active neurons. These are active, more active than the ones in the back. These are highly active neurons. Let's assume that there is another connection between here and here. Every neuron here and here, with this neuron in this map inhibits the neuron in this map, so there are inhibitory connections. This inhibits this. So this fires tends to make this not fire. Now let's suppose here you have activation flowing from outside to inside. Well, if these are firing and then inhibit, each of those what you will get is an inhibited triangle over here. And if these fire from outside to inside, then you get activity here and then it hits the inhibited part and stops, and you will get no activity inside the triangle. That is, this neural mechanism will distinguish interiors from exteriors for any shape at all, any size at all and any location at all. That is, this is the way to compute the image schema for a container.

So what he said was this. The human brain has the right structure. Think of it this way. If I were God, I created people, I created people with all this apparatus, and I wanted to make image schemas. How would I wire up the brain to do it? If I wired up the brain in this way, I will get a container schema computed in this fashion. Now we don't know that this is true. This is a computational model. And we do not know that this really happens. We do know that every piece of it happens and we know that somehow the brain has to do it and it has to do it in a place where this is possible, and the place that has the topographic map structure is back here. And this is the kind of computational structure that would work this out. Now that is part of Regier's book. He then did the same sort of thing for orientation structures and so on. And what he did then was he did a computational model where he asked the computer to try to learn new cases from all. That is, he retained the computer. Let's see. OK. This is above the triangle. This is below. That's next tot triangle, and so on. For different trainings of figures, he takes squares, and so on, and he would give them extra cases when he retrained them and say this, when you see this, this is above and another one is not, but not for many cases and on different figures. And then he gave it a new figure, and he said: "Is this in or out? " And virtually in one hundred percent of the cases, he would predict, it was either the correct answer. So we know that if the brain works this way, and it has that possibility and has to work somehow sort of like this, you can get image schemas. What was very interesting thing about this is this is an embodied mechanism and has to be a mechanism. That is, it gave you some idea of how it is possible to have a spatial relation, a primitive spatial relation. Now I can go through the cases for how we get over, and under and through, and so on. But for "through" you put together a source and a path and goal, and there you put two of them together. What is done is something quite remarkable. He's allowed us to take the first step in understanding how a physician brain can give rise to a concept, an idea, and how that concept like containment will allow us to get image schemas for the various languages. So they can be then fitted together and when they are simultaneously activated, then you get something like through, you will have a path through a container, or into, or you have a path that starts outside and moves into the container. So what he did in his thesis was show how you could put these things together and get the results of this sort.

Now let's stop for a moment and consider where we are. We have come very far from the idea that meaning is in the relationship between symbols and sets in the world. Meaning is in your brain. Meaning has to do with things like this. Meaning components arise because your brain has a certain structure. If it did not have that structure, we wouldn't have the image-schema that we have. That is very important. And all of a sudden, we see an enormous shift in the understanding of what meaning is. It is no longer in the relationship between words and some structure in the world. It has to do with our bodies, our brain. That is with the locus of meaning and how we interact with the world. Meaning comes out of our interactions with our bodies. So that is the fundamental theory of meaning within cognitive linguistics, and that's how that arises. And then we'll got through other kinds of examples in a while. Now what I would like to do is take another five minutes or ten minutes to go through one more phenomena and then I will let you take a break because you need one. We are blowing your mind fairly well so far but let me go one step further.

Back in 1975, in the summer, I heard a fourth lecture and that was very important. And that was the first lecture by Charles Fillmore on frame semantics. What Fillmore did was ask a very deep question. Fillmore had been reading the literature on semantic fields in European linguistics. A semantic field is a set of related words. So I give you the words "knife", "fork", "spoon". They are a set of related words or I give you words like "Monday", "Tuesday", "Wednesday", "Thursday" and they are a set of related words or I give you words like "to sell", "to buy", "cost", "price", "goods". Those are related words. And you can tell when words are not related. For example, if I give you the words "Monday", "Tuesday", "apple", "Thursday", which one doesn't fit, you know which one doesn't fit. Fillmore asked how can you characterize the meaning relationships among sets of related words? Is there a theory of how this works? And what he showed was that there is such a theory. It's a theory of what he called semantic frames. And in a frame, there are a couple of things. There are what he called semantic roles. These are elements of a frame, and there are relationships at a time, and there might be sequences, which he called also scenarios. So for example, suppose we take the set of words "buy", "sell", "cost", "price", "goods", we say what is the frame for that. Well, we have four roles "buyer", "seller", "goods", "money". Now and there is a scenario. The scenario has two parts. And in the first part, the buyer has the money, the seller has the goods, the buyer wants the goods, the seller wants the money. In the second part, they exchange the money for the goods, that is, the seller gives the goods to the buyer and the buyer gives the money to the seller. And in the third part, the buyer has the goods and the seller has the money. OK? Every commercial event works like that. That is called a commercial event frame, and words like "buy", "sell", "goods", "price", "cost", and so on all those commercial event words are defined relative to this frame. So the frame has roles. It has scenario over time and it has relationships at each point in the scenario. At least that. Some frames have slightly different structures, but that's a very common frame structure. Now notice that a word like "sell" or "buy" uses other ideas. It uses the idea of possession. Perhaps they use the idea of desire. Those are more primitive ideas. And as you go through the system of frames, you get more and more primitive ideas and where did they end in the body, in possession, in desire and in things of that sort. That is, the system of frames is based on the body. Now also you will find there are image schemas here. For example, if I say these are transferred, that the buyer transfers the money to the seller. What does that mean? There is a source, a path and goal. It means there is a force, the buyer is exerting the force on the money, moving it to the seller. So there is a force dynamic schema and a source-path-goal schema as part of this. Frames use image schema structure inside the frame, so that the frames start with embodied elements, put them together in this way and build up more and more complicated ones. You can't account for this in logic. There are no frames of semantics and no embodied frames of semantics in the theories of logic. They do not exist. OK, so this is the fourth example that I encountered in the summer of 1975.

Lecture Two   Cognitive Semantics: The Basic mechanism of Thought (2)

There is a classical theory of categories that again comes from Aristotle and it says that a category is defined by a set of features, a set of necessary and sufficient conditions. That is a list of properties and that everything is either in a category or out of a category. And that the defining features are what are called the essence of this category. This is a classical theory. It has been around for over 2500 years and it doesn't work. Unfortunately, it would be nice if it works, but it is not true.

First, there are many concepts that are graded that have degrees like "tall". You can be, you know, I am short, other people are tall. And there are words called hedges that are changing the degree of tallness, so you can say, "he is pretty tall, somewhat tall, very tall, not very tall, and so on". And these hedges depend upon the category being defined by gradations. So when a category is defined by gradations, it is not something that you can either in or out. You can be tall to some degree, or rich to some degree. What that means is that the classical theory just doesn't work for any category like that. You need some theory of graded categories. And in these cases, there are categories, for example, if you take something like tall, there are some people who are just obviously tall. Yao is tall, right? No question, No. 1 tall. So it is not the case that everything is between zero and one—something is very tall and some people are not tall. So that one problem with that is that you need to extend the theory of categories to include graded categories.

But, in addition, they were discovered in the 1970s by a woman named Eleanor Rosch, a very famous professor, one of my colleagues at Berkeley, phenomenon called prototypes. And she discovered that there are cases where there are gradations of membership in a category even if the category does have straight boundaries, there are better and worse examples of the category. She did some famous experiments, a set of about 15 experiments. Let me give you an example of one. She said, look, if you have a notion of a bird, some birds are more birdlike than the other birds, so a penguin is not a very birdlike bird. And so what she did was this. She set up an experiment where she would test time reactions. So in the reaction time experiment, you flash on the sentence. And you are supposed to push the button "true" or "false", no problem. It comes on and says "a sparrow is a bird,"—"true"; it comes on "a chicken is a bird", you go "true". "A pelican is a bird", you go "true", and so on. and they measured the time and what they find is that there is a gradation of times, and this gradation of times fits the judgment of how close something is to a typical bird. So a typical bird might be a little song bird like a sparrow. In America we have robins and other song birds. But a small song bird is more of a typical bird. A vulture is not a typical bird. A bat is not a bird at all, but it is sort of like a bird. And what you find is that even though there are birds and non-birds, there is a boundary of the category that really isn't bird but it it's like a bird in some ways. Even though there is a boundary, there is a degree of membership, a degree to which something is like a typical case. So you have a notion of a typical case of bird and degrees to which something is like a typical case. So gradedness can combine with typicality.

Now typicality is actually used in reasoning. So this is a famous experiment in which, let me give you an example. A duck is not quite a typical bird, right? It is atypical, sort of in the middle. The experiment went like this. They had given subjects a bunch of questions, and one question said there is a certain island where all of the sparrows got an illness. Would you expect the ducks to get that illness, OK? Most people said "Yes". Then there is another set of subjects who got the question there is a certain island where all the ducks got a certain illness and would you expect the sparrows to get that illness, Ok? Many fewer people said "Yes". That is the influence goes from the typical to the non-typical but not from the non-typical to the typical. So you reason, based on the scales of typicality. So that is reasoning goes from typical to non-typical and that is one of the functions of typical cases.

Now, further study by linguists showed that there are more kinds of prototypes. For example, there is an ideal case prototype that is different from a typical case prototype. It is easy to see, think of the difference between all the women and the audience. What is the difference between a typical husband and an ideal husband? Are they the same? Very different. You have different prototypes and you reason about them differently, OK? For example, if you are looking for a husband, you might rate people based on your ideal and you rate them on an ideal case. However, what do you think about typical cases? If you meet somebody who has just married to someone, what would you expect about their husbands to be like? To be more like a typical husband. Given no other information, it's like that.

And the same thing is like buying a car. Suppose you want to buy a used car, an old car, OK? There is a typical old car, an ideal old car, and a terrible old car. The terrible old car has a special name in English. There are two

188

names: one name is a "lemon", there is another that is a "Junker", either, you know, are nightmare cases. You have, for categories that are very important, typical prototypes, ideal prototypes, and nightmare prototypes. There is actual a word in English for the nightmare cases and this is an expression "from hell"—the used car from hell, the boyfriend from hell. These are the nightmare cases. You judge people, when you go to buy a car; you want to avoid the nightmare case, look for the ideal case and expect the typical case, OK. Try to judge this.

So what happens is that you have in, when you are learning an important category, you learn a very complicated structure in that category—you learn typical cases, ideal cases, nightmare cases and you use them for different kinds of reasoning. You think about them and you use them for different kinds of reasoning. You think about them and reason about them for different purposes. And this is normal for just about every important category we have. Now this fact contradicts Aristotle's view of categories. Aristotle said: "In a category, all members of the category are equal. There are all the same: they either have the essence or they don't have the essence; they have the defining properties or they don't". That is the end of the story. It is a false story. Most categories are characterized in this way. Now it turned out that there are other categories. These are categories that can be defined instantaneously. I can make up a category and you will be able to think giving your knowledge about all of these things, you will be able to compose a structure like this. For example, suppose I make up a category—things you take on a picnic, right? You don't take a bear on a picnic or an elephant on a picnic. You might take a little dog on a picnic, probably not a cat, you know, and so on. There are things you will take on a picnic, you will take a bottle of tea on a picnic, you know, and so on. You are given certain examples, you know what you will take on a picnic: what would be typical or what would be ideal for a picnic or what would be disasters for a picnic. You could make this up immediately for a new category if you have the right knowledge.

Now there are other kinds of prototypes that are very important. These are the very special case prototypes. There are cases that are called salient exemplars, a terrible technical term that only a psychologist could make up. This is

a. . . . Let me give you an example. Take the category "terrorist attack", OK? The salient exemplar would be "9. 11", right? It is the most famous the one that would come to mind immediately and what happens with salient exemplars is very interesting. People's judge probabilities are based on salient exemplars. So we had a terrorist attack in America on 9. 11 and now that has become a salient exemplar of terrorist attack. As a result, all of the people in America, people worry about 9. 11 type attacks. In the middle of cornfields in Iowa, people worry about terrorist crashing airplanes into their houses. I mean, completely irrational, there is no probability that this will happen. In the middle of Ohio, in the Midwest, thousands of miles from any interesting big city, any important city, people want to have mask to protect them from biological warfare. So what happens is that the salient exemplar increases the probability that people will understand their lives in terms of that exemplar. People reason use the probability judgments based on that. And this has been studied a great deal. So those are some of the cases of prototypes.

Now there is another really, really important case of prototypes, and that is, what we call radial categories—central cases and non-central cases. Take the category "mother"—simple category "mother". Now a "mother" is defined by many frames. We talk yesterday about frame semantics and the notion "mother" is defined by many frames. One frame is the birth frame—the person here is the mother, the other person is the child, the baby, so the mother and the child. That is one frame, but there are other frames. For example, the marriage frame—the wife of your father is your mother; there is another frame, there is a frame of genetic inheritance—female who you half your genes from is your mother; OK, there is a nurturance frame—the woman who raised you is your mother, we call it a nurturance frame. Now normally all of these frames come together. So if you say "my mother is coming to visit me", you expected to be the person who give birth to you, the person who raised you and the wife of your father, right? But the word is more complicated than that, right? There are stepmothers, and stepmothers didn't give birth to you, you don't get genetic trace from them but they raised you. There are. . . . Now that we have the possibility of egg implantation, and so on, there can be a notion of a birth mother

190

that is not the genetic mother. So you can have a genetic mother, the person you get egg from and the birth mother, the person who gives birth to you who may not be the person who raises you. You may hire someone to be a birth mother, then she hands over the child and then you have a nurturant mother. So there are different kinds if you separate, you can separate these things out. And we now have in English, because of the technology expressions not only like step-mother, but birth mother, genetic mother and surrogate mother. A surrogate mother is somebody who is paid to give birth to the child even though she may not contribute the egg and may not raise the child. She just gives birth.

Now what is interesting about this is the following. Normally when you apply an adjective to a category, all the properties of the category hold plus the properties of the adjective. So if you say "he is a rich man"—he is a man and he is also rich or "she is an intelligent woman"—she is a woman and she is also intelligent. But if you say "she is a birth mother", she doesn't have all the properties of a mother, she only gives birth. Right? That is you have fewer of the frame's hold, not all of the frames. So this is what we call a radial category. In the central case, think about a wheel with spokes. In the central case all of the frames hold—you know you have birth, genetic, nurturance, and so on. And then with certain modifiers, you can pick up one of these properties or one of these frames or two and they can go out from the center. And you can have various concepts of mothers, a lot of them, from generated center with various possibilities and with specialized words like *birth* and *surrogate* to tell you which of the possibilities they are. This does nat fit the ordinary theory of modification. The ordinary theory of adjective modification says that adjective just adds a property to the noun whereas in these cases they in fact are some track models. They pick out some models and ignore others. So it is a very important thing to notice how that works and to notice that the category mother is not an Aristotelian category, it is a radial category.

Now we will talk about other radial categories in a while, but I want to just get it started to give you the idea there are such things. They are extremely important. Now there is another kind of prototype, a last one I will talk about. This is a frame-based prototype. So for example, think of the prototype of the thought of word of bachelor, what is the frame for the word bachelor? Normally a word like bachelor in English refers to a male of marriageable age, who is not married and is eligible to be married. So a male eligible to be married, who is not married, is the usual case. Now those properties form a frame for bachelor. But now there are tricky cases. Suppose you think of an Arab sheikh, who has only two wives but can have four. Is he an eligible bachelor? He is eligible to be married. You know, it's not so clear. That is, this is a variant on the frame. In some respect he is a bachelor and in some way he is not. He is not clearly a bachelor but he is a variant on the frame because the frame was not made up for Arab sheiks. OK?

Take another example "the pope". Is the pope a bachelor? Well, he has not been married. But you know he is really eligible to be married. Oh, not really, possibly he could quit the church to get married but it is sort of odd to call the pope a bachelor. But in some ways he is a bachelor, so there is another in-between case. So what you have is gradations based on the variations on the frame. And the reason is the frames don't always fit reality. Frames are cases that are made up their idealized or what we called idealized cognitive models. They are made up and they are mental models but they don't fit reality. And we have words and we can ask questions: Is he a bachelor or is he not a bachelor? And that question presupposes a straight division. But the straight division is false in terms of reality. The straight division may be defined by fitting the frame completely or not fitting it completely. But when you try to fit a frame to reality, it may only hold partially. And that gives you another kind of prototype. Every frame defines a prototypical case whatever it is. And non-prototypical cases are cases that are partly fit the frame.

So, that is the story of prototypes. There are many types. There is not just one. You use them in reasoning, in categorization, and so on. And they are very important for many, many things. Why is this philosophically important? It is philosophically important because classical semantics, formal semantics, if you go to.... If you take a course in formal logic or what is called formal semantics, it will assume that the property of a category is defined by a set, a set of things, but a set is defined.... It is something that is, we remember, in a set or out of a set but there is no prototype properties. Sets do not have properties. Sets don't have any of the properties we just discussed, so that a set theoretical semantics which is what most of the books on semantics are in a generative tradition and in generative tradition they use formal semantics. They can't account for any of the phenomena we just discussed. None of them. They are not discussed in textbooks on formal semantics because they can not be handled by formal semantics. So this is an extremely important thing. If you go out and you look at many linguistics departments, they all have courses of semantics and there will be formal semantics, logic semantics and they will miss all of the cognitive phenomena we just discussed. One of the reasons why I became a cognitive linguist was in order to discuss this phenomenon. OK, let's move on.

I want to tell you a little about how I started working on conceptual metaphor. This is a true story. In 1978, I was teaching an undergraduate seminar with five students. At the time I was interested in what was called an art form in America called performance art and I was giving the undergraduates a seminar in "performance art and linguistics" and then there we went to through various topics, reading papers on those topics. And on the day that we were to read paper on metaphor. It was a very cold rainy day, we all sat around a little table and there were five students. And one woman in the class came in a little bit late. And it was raining, so she was all wet and she was crying. We tried not to notice that she was crying, which was difficult because she was sitting at the table right here, right here. So we went on with the class, and I said "Well, OK, on page so and so, professor so and so claims the following. What do you think of this?" I got to look around the room and then looked at her and she says: "I can not do this today. I have got a metaphor problem with my boyfriend. " And she looks around and she says "maybe you can help. "

This was in Berkeley in 1970s. We said "of course". And we formed a group, for group therapy, and we said, "Ok, tell us your problem. " She said "Well, on the way to class, my boyfriend... I was walking with my boyfriend, and he said something that upset me. He said that our relationship had hit a dead-end street, a dead-end street". And she said "I don't really understand this very well. You know maybe you can help me get, understand it. " So we said, "Look, if it's hit a dead-end street, you can't keep going the way you have been going. You may have to turn back. " And then we realized that English have a lot of expressions in which love was seen as a kind of journey. So for example, you could say of a love relationship. "It has been a long bumpy road. " You could say things like "We are going in different directions. We are at the cross roads in the relationship. " You could say "The marriage is on the rocks. It is off the track. We are spinning our wheels, even an airplane image, "We may have the bail out". You know, take a parachute. Now, as you know, by the way, being a linguistics professor, I difficultly wrote down all of these expressions and made a list. And I said, Jean, this is an interesting list, you know. Is there a generalization here? And we looked at this list and we see "Well, in every case, love is seen as a journey. The lovers are the travelers. " What is the love relationship? The love relationship is the vehicle; sometimes it is a car, sometimes a boat when you are on the rocks, a train when you are off the track, a plane when you are bailing out, you know, but some kind of vehicle. So love relationship is vehicle. Write down: love relationship-vehicle. What about this journey where you are going? Well, there is, you have common life goals and the common life goals are the destinations that you are trying to reach in this journey—common destinations. Write down "common life goals – destinations. And what about this.... Why do you keep "hitting dead-end street and spinning your wheels"? These are difficulties in the journey. So it turns out that difficulties in the love relationship are difficulties in the journey. That is, they are impediments to travel, things that keep you from getting where you want to go, so "you spin your wheels and you go on rocks, etc...." So you write these down and they are completely systematic. They look like almost a mathematical mapping. OK? Gee, that is very interesting. We have this generalization that looks like a mathematical mapping about these different expressions. And the woman says, "I don't care about your generalization. My boyfriend is breaking up with me. " She said, "He is thinking in terms of this metaphor. " So I said, "That is interesting. How can you think in terms of metaphor? " I mean the classical theory of metaphor doesn't talk about thinking in terms of metaphor. How does this work? So we looked at a case. We said "ok,

194

let's suppose you take something like ' we are spinning our wheels in this relationship. ' " What we know about "spinning the wheels" is that it is an image. This image is there is a car and wheels are turning. Is the car moving? The car is not moving. It is stuck. It stuck in the. . . . In America the term "spin your wheel" applies to a case when your car is not moving. It stuck in ice or sand or snow or something like that. The wheels dig in it and the more you turn, the more they dig in. so in this case, what you have is the vehicle is not moving. You put a lot of energy into getting it moving. You try to rock the car, move it or get the wheels going, and so on. And you feel frustrated. Now, what about in this relationship? When you say "we are spinning our wheels in this relationship", it means the relationship is not going anywhere. No progress towards common life goals. Secondly, it means you put in a lot of energy; you want to go to somewhere. You are putting energy into it and you feel frustrated. That is the reasoning you do about love. Why is this the mathematical mapping. . . vehicles and relationship and so on. So the idea is that to understand the use of dead-end street, which means that you can't keep going in the way you have been going, you have to something else, either give up the relationship or turn and go in some other direction. Ok, you have to do something else. That is the inference. It is said for a reason. It is said for that reason. Now this, by the way, she did not make up with her boyfriend. But she found somebody else later on, she got a job, she got a Ph. D, she got married to a very nice man and she is fine. In fact, she is the chairman of the department.

Now, what is interesting about this is the following. First, when I went to high school, I learned a definition of metaphor, and it came from Aristotle. Aristotle, back to 2500 years ago, said that metaphor is a matter of words; it is a word used not in its normal sense but in an unusual abnormal sense. Secondly, that it is based on similarity that is use mainly in poetry or rhetoric, in special rhetoric situations and that it is not the usual kind of language, it is not the typical language at all. But it is useful to see similarities. Ok. It turns out that he was wrong. First of all, all of these expressions we saw are cases with a metaphor is not in the words. There are a lot of different words: spinning your wheels, being off the track, going in different directions. . . a lot of different words. The generalization, the metaphorical generalization is the mapping, is the relationship between love and travel, which is that travelers map onto lovers, that vehicles map onto relationships, that destinations map onto common life goals, that impediments to travel map onto difficulties. That is the general of all the expressions and that is what the conceptual metaphor is. And it is that mapping that allows you to reason about love using reasoning about travel. It allows you to reason about one domain "love" in terms of another familiar domain when you understand the reasoning patterns. Ok? Notice that love and travel are not similar in themselves. The metaphor is not based on similarity. It is not in the words. It is in the concepts. And I notice in each case you have a frame, a frame of traveling being mapped onto love. In each case you have two domains, a complex structure given by a frame and mapping of more than one element onto another point. That is what conceptual metaphor is.

Now then you will ask how does this work on poetry, and so on. We will get to that in a while. Notice why Aristotle gave the definition he gave. He had to. Aristotle was the inventor of logic. And his logic assumes that the logic of the mind was the logic of the world and the categories were defined by essences and that if you had a word, and that word fits categories, and that if the word did not fit its usual category, the only explanation he could give is in terms of similarities of properties. That's all he had. So he was forced to give that definition. And that is false. He gave an incorrect theory. Now notice the issue of definition. Definitions are not the issue here. Aristotle actually gave a theory of a phenomenon. He observed that people use the things he called metaphors. And what he did was give a theory. He said, "It occurs in this kind of language. It is about words. It is based on similarity. " That is a theory. That theory came to be taken as a definition. But it isn't. it was a theory. And it was an incorrect theory. It appears now that we have looked at not just the data on love but thousands of other metaphors, that they all work, that they involve mappings from one domain to the other. It is a different theory. And we will go through more of that today. But it is important that if someone says I learned the definition of the term metaphor when I was in high school—and this does not fit it. That is wrong. You didn't learn the definition. You learned the theory, and it was a false theory.

Now, why is this important? First, in terms of philosophy and semantics, it is vitally important. If the meaning is taken as the relationship that you find in formal semantics between symbols and the world, there is no room for metaphor, because metaphor is in your mind. Where are those mappings? They are not just out there in the world. You know, it's not in the world independent of people that love is a journey. It is the way people understand it. The metaphors, those mappings are in your mind. They are not in the world. And that means to understand the meaning of expressions like "We are spinning our wheels in this relationship" or "we are going in different directions" or "it is a long bumpy road." If you want to understand those, you cannot do it in the classical theory of formal semantics. You just can not. It doesn't work, because the classical theory is disembodied. It is just in the relationship between the words and the world. It has nothing to do with cognition. Now Aristotle also claimed that metaphor was special on poetic. That was not ordinary everyday English. It is a common English expression to say something like "we are going in different directions", "it has been a long bumpy road." That's not poetic. You don't have to be a poet to say this. It is not political rhetoric or anything like that. It's normal discourse. So metaphor is a normal mode of thought, as we will see, completely normal, in some cases, even universal, but normal.

Next, it is important because of what is called distinction between literal meaning and non-literal meaning. There is a tradition in semantics of what is called literal meaning. And literal meaning is based on the old theory of meaning where the words are supposed to fit the world literally. That literal meaning has to do with the way words conventionally in your language are taken to fit the world and anything else who is a matter of rhetoric, indirect speech, and so on. So if you use an indirect act, if I say something like "it is cold in here," to mean "close the window", I am not just being literal about it, I mean close the window. So that's taken as non-normal, not quite literal meaning.

However, the distinction between literal meaning and non-literal meaning breaks down in the case of metaphor, conceptual metaphor. That is, and the reason is this. The other part of the notion of the literal meaning besides fitting the world is that is ordinary everyday language. So the idea is that everyday language fits the world. Here we have ordinary everyday language, which is metaphorical. It doesn't just fit to the objective world; it has something to do with your mind. But then there is a further question: Can a metaphor be appropriate? Is it appropriate? And this is the question in fact that a student brought up. One of the reactions when we figured all these things out was about the "dead-end street". It was "Jean, I really want you to go into the relationship to go into another dimension, like the fifth dimension". You know, that is, she didn't want that metaphor to hold. She thought the metaphor was inappropriate. But there are people for whom the relationship is a matter of finding common life goals and reaching them and then this metaphor might be appropriate for them. It might not be appropriate for someone else. So metaphors can be appropriate or not. And when they are appropriate, then we can say that certain sentences are true or false. That is, "it can be a long bumpy road". It could be true that you are going in different directions if you both understand the relationship in that way. So what we are going to see is that metaphors can be appropriate or not appropriate that they may be true or false, or false in other cases. They may be just not fit the world. ... You know there are sort of false metaphors. And this is a whole new domain of semantics: the notion of literal meaning. If you ask: Is this literally true? Is it literal to say: "It has been a long bumpy road in this relationship? " Well, it is an ordinary everyday expression. It may be true but it doesn't quite fit an objective world but it does fit the world and the world the way the lovers understand it and that is perfectly reasonable that may be sufficient for it to be appropriate. So the issues brought up by the theory of conceptual metaphor are way beyond the issues brought up by formal semantics. They are different questions. You have to think about meaning in a different way. And you can't accept the old philosophy. You can't accept the correspondence theory of truth that says truth is the relationship between the words and the world, because it doesn't work that way for metaphor. It can be true but you have to got think it very carefully of what it means for metaphor to be true or not true on inactive or not appropriate, and so on. so our semantics becomes much more interesting, much more complicated, but entirely different than it was before.

Now let's take some other cases. After I discovered this, I started looking for other cases, I asked, hoe many of these are there? And we now have one. You know, they can't just be 10. They have got to be a lot of them. How many? So far we have found hundreds. We suspect they are thousands. They are just all over. As soon as you started to notice them, they are everywhere. So what I like to do now is try to give you some sense of how common these are and then some sense of their properties. For example, there is a general metaphor that *more is up and less is down.* Prices rise. They fall. They skyrocket and so on. So *more is up and less is down.* And if you take a copy of *Metaphors We live By*, and you go through in here in any one of these early chapters, there is a long list of up and down metaphors. So here we go. Lots of *up and down metaphors*: *Happy is up; sad is down. So I am feeling up today. My spirits rose. I am depressed. He is really low. He fell into a depression. That boosted my spirits. So happy is up; sad is down.* Why is happy up and sad down? Because there is a physical basis of this. When you feel happy, you are smiling and you feel erective, your muscles are up, and so on.

That is true around the world. When you feel depressed-drooping, there is a reason for this. It has been observed by Paul Agmen, who studies the physiology of emotions that this is true in all cultures around the world: the human universal about the emotions and the body. And when you have this correlation, you will learn happy is up and sad is down. Conscious is up; unconscious is down. You day: get up, wake up, I am up already. He rises early in the morning. He dropped off to sleep. He is under hypnosis. He sank into a coma. So conscious is up; unconscious is down. Health and life are up; sickness and death are down: He is at the peak of health. Lazarus rose from the dead. He is in top shape. He fell ill. He is sinking fast. He came down with the flu. He is declining. He dropped dead. He may not fall, he dropped dead, OK? Physical, having control is up; under control is down. So I am on the top of the situation. He is in a superior position. He is at the height of his power. He is in the high command. He is in the upper echelon. His power rise; he is under control. He fell from power. His power rise; he is under control. He fell from power. His power is on the decline. He is my social inferior. He is a low man on the totem pole, and so on. So you get lots and lots of these. I won't go through all of them in there, but like *good is up*; *bad is down*. Things are looking up. We hit a peak last year, but it has been downhill ever since. Things are at an all-time low and so on. *Good is up*; *bad is down*.

Now one of the things that you learn from these right away is that there are many metaphors and metaphors are in the conceptual system, and a single word like up can be used for different metaphors, and that the word can be metaphorically ambiguous. So let me give you an example. If I say, I have a sentence like *It is an all downhill from here* in English. *It is an all downhill from here*, it is ambiguous. It could mean things are just going to get worse and worse. Or this is another metaphor. I will go over in a while. That is one in which actions are motions and ease of action in ease of motion and going down. So you could say, for example, how is your dissertation going. You say "Well, it is an up-hill climb" meaning "it is hard". Or you could say "it is all downhill from here" meaning "it is easy". So "it is all downhill from here" could either use the idea that *Action is motion and down-hill motion is easier that up-hill motion*, or it could mean *Good is up*; *bad is down* and they could have almost opposite meanings. So the metaphor is not in the words. The metaphor is not in the sentence. The metaphor is in the conceptual mapping on which the sentence is based. That is a very important thing to learn. The metaphor is not in the words. "People are thinking of the thing. " That is a metaphorical sentence as if the sense of metaphor is in the words of sentence. The words of the sentence evoke an understanding, evoke a conceptual understanding. That conceptual understanding itself can be metaphorical. And a metaphorical sentence evokes a metaphorical understanding. Now these are totally different ideas from the Aristotelian notion. They are completely different from what you have learned in formal semantics. In order to think about metaphorical semantics you have to change your brain. You have to forget a lot of things you were taught. For example, metaphor is in the word.

So let that sink in for a minute, and then I will talk about some other cases. First, there are lots and lots of examples. And some of the most profound examples are very deep. They have to do with the most basic concepts that we have. Take the notion of time. It turns out that there are various metaphors for time, not just in English but in many languages. Some of them appear to be universal. Some are universal. But let me give you an example of this. There is a metaphor for time in which times are moving objects that are going this way. The future is ahead; the past is behind. Now in Chinese, sometimes it is up and down. We will talk about that in a minute. In English, it is not. In English, it is "the future is ahead; the past is behind". And you don't think about the past is being up which you might in Chinese. So languages differ with respect to these.

Not only that. There are languages where *the future is behind, and the past is ahead*. It is very interesting. There is a.... My colleague Rafael Nunez has been studying language in the Andes mountains in Peru and Chile. There he finds languages in which the past is ahead because you can see what has happened and the future is behind because you cannot see it. And so when they say things like, you know, "it happened long ago", they point ahead. There are lots of video tapes of people talking "this happened two years ago, and these happened long ago. " They go further into the future ahead. But in English, the future is ahead; the past is behind. So we have expressions like "let's put that all behind this. Look what is ahead of us. " It is forward looking. Now given that "the future is ahead and the past is behind", you then have further metaphors: times and events. Events are associated with times. Times can be coming toward you. So you used to say things like "Christmas is coming! It's coming up on me. Christmas is here. Christmas has past. Christmas is behind us now. " So you can see this is going this way. Not only that. Relative times can work the same way. Think of two times coming towards one. Which one precedes the other? Thanksgiving precedes Christmas. Thanksgiving comes first. Christmas follows. So you can see that, as you go along, as times go along, the language fits it too. Now in this case, there is a figure-ground distinction. I am the ground. Right? I am the observer. The times are the figures. They are moving relative to the ground. They are moving relative to me. That is another metaphor for time where figure and ground are reversed. It is called figure-ground reversals or duals. There is one in which time is a landscape, it's a path on the ground, you are moving along time. Time is a point on the ground. I am moving and the points on the ground are the ground. I am the figure. So you can talk about things like "being on time, being within a certain amount of time as if there is an area. " You could also talk about, you can say "not only Christmas is coming up on us, but we are coming up on Christmas, we are approaching Christmas". So they are two different metaphor—either the Christmas is approaching us or we are approaching Christmas—depending upon which metaphor you see. Same words "approach" and "come up on", same words with the opposite subject and object, you know, but different metaphors. Not only that. You can have metaphorical ambiguity with these two metaphors. Let me give you an example. Suppose we will schedule the meeting on Wednesday. We will have a meeting on Wednesday. Someone says "let's move the meeting ahead two days. " When is the meeting? How many people say Monday? How many people say Friday? Nobody wants to be a volunteer. It turns out it is ambiguous. She is moving to Stanford next year. She did a set of experiments to show that this metaphor is psychologically real. The first thing she did was in the laboratory. She had little movies in which she would show either things coming towards you or had a camera showing you moving ahead with you holding the camera and see what happen when you are moving ahead. And she will show you a little film clip and then she would ask the question. She would say: Is there a meeting scheduled on Wednesday, you know, the meeting has been moved ahead. When is the meeting? And if you have time, things moving towards you spatially in this field, you get one answer. It you have you moving forward, you get another answer. So if you are moving forward, the answer is Friday; this is moving forward, the answer is Monday.

Then she did a clever experiment. She went to San Francisco Airport, where there were planes coming in and people waiting for the planes. She asked the people on the planes and the people waiting for the planes. So for the people waiting for the planes, you say "Ok, there is a meeting scheduled for Wednesday, we got to move to it ahead. You know, when is the meeting?" and as for the people coming on the planes, they just came off the planes and she asked them at the moment they came off the planes the same question. People coming off the planes said "Friday" and the other people said "Monday".

This is a real fact. It really happens. Metaphors are part of cognition, the part of the way you think, and the part of the way you reason. You reason in terms of metaphors. And the words are guides of metaphors and imperfect guides, because they can be ambiguous. So that's the next lesson we will learn. They are real. They guide your reasoning. We think in terms of them and the words lead you to this mode of thought. But the mode of thought isn't in the words. The meaning is not in the words.

Now what I like to do next is give you a sense of the complexity of the system. And the way is embodied. So what I like to do is taking some examples from W*omen*, *Fire and Dangerous Things*, a monster's book. This is from a study of "anger". Zoltan Kovecses, a great Hungary linguist. I will tell you about Zoltan. Zoltan is a wonderful person. And he decided about 15 years ago, more than 15, maybe 20 years ago, he wanted to study emotions. But he got on to it in an interesting way. As a linguist in Hungary, he was.... During the communist period in Hungary when the Russians were controlling Hungary, it was very hard to earn a living. So as a professor, professor's salaries were very, very low, so he had to do other work. Luckily he had other skills. One skill he had was that he was a championship water polo player. He is, you know, a huge man, very strong. He was on the European Championship water polo player, and he was a hero, a national hero in Hungary for water polo. I would around Budapest with him and all the women would throw themselves at his feet. He was recognized everywhere. Then he also knew English very well, so he would dub movies that were translated into Hungarian. But even then he couldn't earn much of a living there, so he had another profession, which was to make up idiom dictionaries. And he tried to make an idiom dictionary of English and while he was on the letter "A", he got to the word "anger". And he came upon a long, long list of idioms and they look like this, see, "He lost his cool. She was looking daggers at me. I almost burst a blood vessel. " These all mean that you got angry. "He was foaming at the mouth. You are making my blood boil. He is wrestling with his anger. He is on a short fuse. He is just letting off steam. Don't get a hernia. Keep a grip on yourself. Don't fly off the handle.

When I told him, he blew up. He channeled his anger into something construc-tive. He was red with anger. He was blue in the face. He appeased his anger. He was doing a slow burn. She kept bugging me", and so on. He came up with 300 of these in English and decided to apply for a grant to do research on this with me, because he has read *Metaphors We Live By*. He didn't tell me. He just showed in my office one day and said: I want to study "anger". I looked up, "OK".

Zoltan, being a professional athlete, was very disciplined. He wanted to ac-count for every single idiom. And he would show up in my house early in the morning, time to study body idioms. And this article took us 9 months to do to figure out the system. It is not easy to do this research. It took us two people 9 months. When you get into the system and you finally feel beginning to see it. What you discovered is that it is embodied. It turns out that at the same time I happened to be reading the work of Paul Agmen, who is a friend of mine, who is the world's expert on the physiology of emotions. And he had done some stud-ies the previous year on the physiology of "anger" as well as "fear" and some others metaphors. When you get angry, your actual skin temperature rises 4/10 of a degree, Fahrenheit. When you get angry, your blood pressure goes up. Your heartbeat rate increases. When you get angry, you don't see as clearly as you otherwise would. Your perception is made less good. And when you get an-gry, it is likely harder to control your body in fine order movements. Those are acts of the physiology of anger. When you get, for example, when you get afraid, your temperature goes down about half a degree. That is why you are fro-zen with fear. The metaphors are based on the body. And the way it works is this. By the way, there is also a system of metonymies, so with metonymy, so with metonymies, you have the. . . . I haven't talked about metonymy yet. So let me stop and talk a little about metonymy and then come to metonymies and met-aphor cases.

If you go to frame semantics, we look at a frame. Suppose you think of the frame semantics for a restaurant. You go into a restaurant, and they seat you at a table. And the waitress or waiter comes over and gives you a menu, and you order some food. And there is the food you have, you know, you eat the food,

204

you pay it, and so on. The roles are customer, waitress or waiter, the dish you ordered, that is your food, the money you pay, and so on. And there is a scenario for doing this. Now in America one waitress can say to another waitress: "the hamburger left without pay. Or here the "Bao Zi's left without pay", or "Table six left with pay" because the table is part of this. That is one part of a frame for reference. Given what you know, it is implicit unconscious knowledge that you have about your own physiology of "Anger". You can have metonymies for being angry like "don't get hot under the collar" means "don't get angry". Or "he is a hothead" means "he get angry easily" and so on. Or the thing about "don't burst the blood vessel" means the blood pressure is going up, so the increasing of blood pressure stands for the anger. So there are a whole lot of cases like that. "She is red with anger, scarlet with rage." Or agitation "she is shaking with anger." "He is hopping mad". In English we have an expression "hopping mad" is that bong, bong bong. He is agitated that he is hopping. "He was quivering with rage. He is all worked up", and so on. And he is upset. These are metonymies of the body bodily state for the anger state. Now or things like "she was blind with rage" because she can't see it well. "He was so mad that he couldn't see straight." Right? That is to say he could see accurately. So you have a metonymy there.

Now in addition to this, there are metaphors. And there is a whole system of metaphors for anger. Here is how they work. There is one metaphor that "anger is heat". That is, metaphor has two special cases, two framings for "heat". That is, in one framing for heat, the heat is like a fluid in a container. Think of the soup in a pot or something in a furnace-oil in a furnace or something, in which you have a closed container and fluid and the container is being heated and the fluid is being heated. That is why you can say "He made my blood boil." OK? "Or he is letting off steam." So "blow off steam" means the stems is coming out and it is likely to explode. If you keep it in, it will explode. That means "getting very angry with someone, losing control". So "exploding" is losing control. Now when you look at this, you have stages in heating container. You heat a liquid and you can let it simmer and slow if you wish to cook soup. You put it on the low heat and it simmers. So "he has been simmering for a long time. " So it is a low level of anger for a long time. Or if someone is very angry, you can say, "simmer down, get less angry". You can "let him stew", which is low simmer for a long time. Somebody is angry—"let him stew. Let him cool for a long time. " Now when the intensity of the heat, you put liquid in the container, you have more and more heat, it starts to get boiling. When it boils, the liquid goes up. So you get things like "his anger welled up inside him. He could feel his gorge rising. We got a rise out of him. His anger kept building up inside him. He was in a towering rage. " So there is something going up. When you heat liquid intensely, it produces steam, so "he got all streamed up. He was fuming, letting off steam. " Now if you close the container, you close the pot, you heat it up, you can have things like "he became to start to burst. " So you can be bursting with anger. You could say "I could barely contain my rage. I couldn't keep it in any longer. " If you try to keep this pot closed, and it's boiling and boiling and it can explode. And so you can say "he exploded with anger. He blew up. He had an outburst. " And then there are special cases. So one special case is from a car, from a piston. "He blew a gasket". A gasket is a little ring around the top of the piston, so if it gets too much pressure, the ring bursts. So "he blew a gasket". Volcano: "she erupted". Electricity: "I blew a fuse". Explosives: "She is on a short fuse". Bomb: "That really set me off". These are kinds of explosions, and then you have an explosion of this little pot with liquid in it, and the liquid comes out, so "his anger finally came out" and things like "smoke was pouring out of the ears". So what you have is a very rich understanding of the heating of the liquid in a container. And that maps onto being angry. And there are stages of heating and reasoning about anger. That's one case, just of "anger is heat. "

But there is another case of "anger is heat" and that is fire. And it is a different metaphor. It has different languages and there's different frames for fire. So think about the frames for fire. You have a thing that is burning—"wood", let's say. And as the wood burns, it gets consumed, the wood disappears: consumed as it burns. So someone can be "consumed with anger". And the cause of the fire is the cause of the anger. So those can be inflammatory remarks. Things that are inflammatory means causing fire. You can inflame the situation, make people more angry. And many, many others: "his sincere apology adds fuel to the fire. " Make the other person more angry. And you could say "Boy, I am burned up. He has been smoldering for days", and so on. so here you have a general metaphor, metaphors occurring at certain levels, a general metaphor "anger is heat", that is motivated by the physiology.

Then you have two special cases, two frames about heat. One frame for heat is the liquid in the container being heated; the other is fire. Two different frames. They map, both mapped anger but they are different metaphors because they are different mappings. And then each of them gives rise to language: one has things like "You made my blood boil", the other is "I am consumed with anger". On the fire one, "he is letting off steam" in the other one—different conceptual mappings. The language is assorted by each of them and then you reason differently, depending on them. And one you get you explode, and the other one you can set people on fire, you can spread the fire. Both are dangerous but in different ways. Now those are not the only metaphors for anger. There are others. So let me try to give you a sense of the range. I won't go through in full detail. But anger can be seen as insanity. "He is mad. "—the word mad means insane. "When I just touched them, he went crazy". "One more complaint, he is going to berserk". "He went out of his mind". "he goes bonkers". "He is in an insane rage". "If anything else goes wrong, I will get hysterical". Anger is insanity. "When my mother finds out, she will have a fit". "He is fit to be tied". "He is going to throw a tantrum". And then you get a violent frustrated behavior—you know, insane behavior standing for anger. "He is tearing his hair out". "He is heading against the wall". "Climbing the walls". Insane behavior stands for anger. Then you have another one. "Anger can be an opponent", that you struggle against, because people try to control their anger. So in that case, you can be "struggling with your anger, battling your anger, fighting back your anger, wrestling with your anger, you can be seized by anger, you can take control of your anger, surrender to your anger, yield to your anger, be overcome by anger, appease your anger", and so on.

Then there is "Anger is a dangerous animal". "He has a ferocious temper, a fierce temper". "It is dangerous to arouse, wake up his anger. " "He has a monstrous temper". My favorite is "he unleashed his anger" : he took the leash off that he got; he unleashed his anger. "His anger is insatiable" : he would eat up people. And things like you have a wonderful one for China—it is a dragon image : "he was breathing fire". Now and in general also you get things like that "He was bristling with anger. He's got mu hackles up. " That is, when you have a dangerous animal that is dangerous, their hair stands on it. So you get "bristling with anger, baring his teeth, ruffling his feathers, snapping, growling, snarling, animal behavior".

Now what do we learn from these? First, for an important concept, like anger, you don't just have one metaphor; you have a system of metaphors. And the system, you have levels. You can have a level of "anger is heat" the two special cases, which are different mappings and therefore different metaphors. "Anger is heat" is based on the physiology, but the frame of heating something in a container is not. That is a special frame, a special kind of use of heat. So given something that isn't directly based on the physiology, you can extend that to something that isn't directly based on the physiology. What about "anger is insanity"? Why? Because what marks insanity is "loss of control" and that is part of being angry, loss of control. What are other cases of "loss of control"? "Wild animals, animals going wild" and so on. So what you find and also if you're trying to stay in control, that is, in "wrestling with your anger", like fighting someone. What you find is that the metaphor system is therefore purpose. I mean it is therefore reason. I am going to talk about that in a minute. In fact, let me do that now. One of the metaphors that we found in *Metaphors We Live By* was the theories of buildings. So you have things like "he laid the foundation for that theory. " Or "that theory has weak foundations. " Or "the theory is built on solid facts. What is the ground for that theory? Is it built on solid ground? The theory can crumble. You can prop up your theory", and so on. now when you actually look at this in detail, it turns that certain parts of the building are mapped on the theories : the ground, the foundation, the walls, anything that holds up the wall, the buttresses, you can buttress your theory; buttress holds up the walls and that is all. There is no paint in the theory. You don't have electricity, electric lights of your theory. You don't have the plumping of your theory, the floor of your theory. Look around the building, most of the things aren't there. The air-conditioning of your theory, nothing.

Now why is that is so small? Why there only something is mapped and not others? It's the fact that works this way. And what the theories have to do with building? Why should theories have anything to do at all with buildings? These are the questions asked by a student of mine Joe Grady, who wrote a very interesting dissertation based on observations like this. And what he discovered was the following. There really are other more basic metaphors than theories of building that the theory of building metaphor is made up of. He discovered that there are what we called primary or primitive metaphors, and that the primitive metaphors, the primary ones, are all based in physical, in actual experience and that they can be put together in various ways. And when you put them together, it becomes less obvious what the experience is. Let me explain. When you looked at theories of buildings, you looked the words used like crumble and foundation and so on. He found the same words we used in other metaphors. There is a metaphor that "a society is a building" and the society has to have a strong foundation or weak foundation. It can crumble. You can try to prop up the society or fix the foundation of the society, the same words for society. Why should you have the same words for societies and theories? It seems strange. He got the idea for the answer from a speech by the first George Bush during the Gulf Was in 1991. In that speech, Bush got up there. There is the other bush, and said of Saddam Hussein's invasion. He said: this will not stand. Used the word "stand". "This will not stand" means "this will not persist". This is a metaphor that says that "persisting over time" is standing erect. And you can see why? It is like flowers come out of the ground, they persist over time and they stand erect and they die and they go into the ground or trees or buildings themselves and so on, people. Things that are persisting over time, typically standing erect. When they ceased persisting over time, they died. So that is one part. There is another metaphor he noticed which is that an organizational structure is a physical structure. You understand an organization in terms of the physical structure and that makes sense because if you look at an object and you examine it, you see the way of it is organized by looking at the physical structure. So the physical structure is the organizational structure if revealed by the physical structure. Now given those two metaphors, what happens when you put them together? You bind them together and you get an organizational structure that persist over time is physical structure that remains erect, remains tall. He stands up. Now what is an organizational structure that persist over time? One, a society; two, a theory. Physical structure that remains erect is a building. So what you have is a whole structure of basic metaphors that have been fixed together as pieces like building blocks to make other metaphors. And you have a general metaphor that a physical structure that remains erect. I am sorry, an organizational structure that persists over time is a physical structure that remains erect and then special cases are societies and buildings.

What that means is that the conceptual structure of metaphor is being put together in blocks just all other conceptual structures is being put together. Conceptual structure means taking pieces and putting them together, combining them and you combine the frames. So similarly, you can have primitive metaphors and you can combine them into bigger metaphors. Now this work was done in 1997 by Grady. And by coincidence, there were two other dissertations done by students at Berkeley in 1997 on metaphor. One was by Grady's best friend Christopher Johnson and he studied metaphor acquisition by children. And here is what he found. He found that. . . . Here is the way he went about it. He said, you know, it is hard to study this but he said "we have a vast number of computer archives of all the records of child language acquisition that have been done by researchers". Let's take a metaphor like "knowing is seeing" (I see what you are getting at, it is clear to me, and so on). Let's take that metaphor "knowing is seeing" and then do something interesting. Let us look up the word "see" for all children at each age and find out what they would say at each age with the word "see", what the sentences were, then they discovered a generalization. The first sentences are all non-metaphorical, literal "see, Daddy!" then there is a stage in which "knowing" and "seeing" come together and the grammar of "seeing", of "knowing" fits the word "see". So you can say, "See Dad come in. See what I spilled". So knowing and seeing come together. Then there is a further stage of metaphor "see what I mean". What he says is that this is premised condition where knowing the target domain and the source domain of the metaphor occur together in the child experience. And that is necessary for later metaphor. So that is his finding.

Now the third dissertation explains the first two. The third one was a dissertation by Sri Narayanan. He did much more than this but part of the dissertation had to do with a neural theory of metaphor. He worked on neural computation and he worked on a very difficult problem. I will tell you later on what his problem was. But part of it required setting up a computational model of how metaphor works. And in this, he observes first that the source and target domains for basic metaphors that we have like "more is up" are in different parts of the brain. Quantity is computed in one part of the brain where you compute number. And verticality is computed in another part of the brain which has to do with both balance and vision, with those brought together. So the idea is verticality and number are in different parts of the brain. How would you get metaphor linking them? Well, if you experience why is "more is up" — "more is up" because every time you pour water into a glass, the level goes up; every time you put books down, the level goes up. That is, in general, putting more things means higher level. Every day of your life, it's correlation. You pour water into the glass, you see there is more water and it is higher. Two parts of your brain are activated together over and over again. When that happens, neural connections are formed between them. The way the mechanism, I won't go into mechanism, the mechanism has to do with straightening the synapses between those two parts of the brain. So the connections get formed, the slogan that the neuroscientists have is "neurons that fire together, wire together". They form strong connections. Those connections are the metaphorical mappings. So that when one part of the brain is activated, the corresponding part of the other one is activated. You know, verticality-quantity. They are the metaphors. The metaphors are physically there in your brain according to Narayana.

How does this explain the Christopher Johnson's results about acquisition? He says, "When knowing and seeing occur together, where this seeing activated and knowing activated, then you learn connections and then you get the metaphor. Then how does this explain Grady's observation about primitive meta-

211

phors, about primaries? Grady studied over a hundred different primaries. And what he found was, in every case when you had two experiences that came together in the life of a child, the life of everybody, what happened was that they formed primitive metaphors. So, for example, take the metaphors for "time" (where time is a moving object or you move over time) and in general what is "time" in your brain? Time has to do with the firing of neurons. Every forty times, every second, there is a pulse that goes through your brain, from the brain stem throughout to the rest of the brain. It times the rest of your brain. It arouses you like a clock to your brain. And everything else is timed relative to that. Time has to do with the relationship between an event and other regular events. For example, the sun going around regularly, or water dripping regularly or watch ticking regularly. That is one event relative to another event gives you time. Then when that happens in the brain and you see someone moving towards you. You notice the passing of time or when you are moving relatively to something else. So what's going on there is everybody is going to understand time as moving object or time as you moving relative to someone else because everyone has the same experiences.

What about anger? Anger is heat or anger is activation around the world, or anger is an increase of pressure inside. You have a, for example, Chinese has an expression of "having too much Qi" for anger. That is too much internal energy. So what happens is that no people noticed from the physiology that the physiology corresponds to the state of anger and you get metaphors linking them. You get neural connections linking them. So the idea here is that the universal metaphors are the metaphors that arise mostly in childhood, maybe not all in childhood, but mostly in childhood just by living in the world. They don't require language; they are pre-linguistic. That the experiences are bringing together the source and target domains of the primitives, of the primitive metaphors only, of these primitives give rise to neural connections for those metaphors and create them and then a language like "can come along", like "see what I mean" or "he is boiling mad". What is interesting about this is that this sets up a system of hundreds of primitive metaphors that you learn automatically just by going around the world everyday, living your life as a child, happily doing whatever children do, you are going to learn hundreds of metaphors. We will go through more of them this afternoon.

Then, but those are not only the simple primitives, then they fit together into larger ones like "theories are buildings". "Theories are buildings" are not learned in that way. That is a more complicated, elaborate one and what is learned in that way is things that persist over time over time is standing erect because all the children go around seeing flowers and trees and people persisting over time and standing erect. What is learned is that organizational structure is physical structure because all kids are always looking at them, examining them and looking at the way they are organized. As a child goes around, his or her everyday life constantly different parts of the brain are regularly activated together. When they regularly activated together they are going to learn the neural connections between them, which are the metaphors. And that is how metaphor systems get established. But only systems of the primaries and then culture on top of that allows you to put the primaries together to form larger and larger more complicated metaphors, which we will discuss in very great detail this afternoon. So I'm going to stop here.

Lecture Three   The Neural Theory of Language

This is not easy even for me.

What I would like to do this morning. This is going to be a very different lecture. I usually never use Powerpoint, but this is necessary, as you will see. So I apologize for the Powerpoint. I've talked a little bit about neural science as we go along. I want to give you some ideas of what it means for language to be embodied from the point of view of the brain. And we've also talked about embodiment from another point of view, the point of view of interactions in the world and social interactions, and so on.

So, what the questions we had earlier had to do with Mark Johnson's discussion of embodiment of image schemas in terms of functioning in the world with your body, and that's correct, that is part of that embodiment. We also talked about Terry Regier's study of image schemas and its embodiment in the brain. These are not two different notions of embodiment. They are the same, but that is not obvious.

So, what I'm going to do today is tell you why they are the same in detail. I want to do a few more things. I want to talk about what it means several concept; what mental simulation is, what it means to have a theory of meaning that has to do that is embodied could also be about the world. Those are important questions I want to go through all of that. I also want to talk about the semantics of grammar. And what kinds of conceptual grammar and how one can get a theory of what those concepts are.

So, this is a paper done jointly with Vittorio Gallese of the University of Parma in Italy. He is one of the discoverers of mirror neurons which I'll discuss in a while, and all the neuron science data is from his research group along with professor Rizzolatti in Parma. So I did not do neural science. I'm a linguist. But I worked with him and we've worked on this together. What we found in going through his data is that there are a lot of phenomena that were never written up in the scientific journals because they did not know what they meant. And what we are going to do is go through them here and show what some of these things mean for linguistics.

So, let's continue. This is the Neural Theory of Language Group at Berkeley, by Jerry Feldman, Srini Narayanan, Lokendra Shastri, and Nancy Chang. Here are certain assumptions about everyone concepts, maybe one or two people don't, but most people accept them. One is that concepts are the elements of reason, that if you are reasoning, reasoning is a complex process and concepts are the elements of reason. By the way, if anybody wants this, I can make the overheads available to professor Li, and so you don't have to take notes. You could just ask him and how he could send them to you, get a list, and they are yours. So, if you don't feel like scribbling, don't worry.

Also, concepts agree to constitute the meanings of words and linguistic expressions. Now, there is a traditional theory of concepts, and that traditional theory we will say doesn't work, but here it is. The traditional theory says that reason and language are what distinguish human beings from other animals, and concepts, which are the elements of reason, therefore only use human-specific brain mechanisms, that is the brain mechanisms that people have that other animals do not. That reason therefore is separate from perception and action, since animals have perception and action, and reason does not make direct use of sensory-motor system, since animals have a sensory-motor system, they can see and hear and move, and so on. So, concepts are "disembodied" in this sense, that is, they do not have to do with perception and action in the world in the traditional theory. That's what that says.

Now, we claim something very different. That human concepts are embodied, that many concepts make direct use of the sensory-motor capacities of our body-brain system. We will say exactly what that means in a while, that many of these capacities are also represented present in human primates, that is, in monkeys. And one example, the concept of grasping, will be dicussed in detail. We will take that example because it has been studied ectensively the actiuons of monkeys.

We are going to talk about what we call amodality. The traditional theory implicitly claims that even action concepts like grasp did not make use of the sensory-motor system. As a concept, according to the traditional theory, *grasp* must be embodied. Thus the traditional theory claims that the concept *grasp* is amodal. Modality has to do or modality, something like vision or action or hearing or smell, those are modalities. The claim is that concepts have nothing to do with the bodily modalities: vision, action, smell, moving your body, and so on, that they are amodal. Since the concept of *grasp* is a concept, it therefore must be modality-free even if the concepts designates an action-doing this, even if it designates an action in a specific modality, namely, using the hand, ok? So, that is the traditional claim. Now, there are certain properties that concepts are generally agreed to have. Not everyone agrees on this but almost everyone does.

One, they are universal in the following sense. They characterize all particular instances. So for example, the concept of *grasping* is the same no matter who the agent is, what the patient is or how the grasping is done. Ok, that is what it means by universal. It is a general concept for *grasping* that works for all the kinds of grasping. No matter who the agent is or what the patient is or how it is done, that's what universality means, ok?

Secondly, the concept is stable, all concepts are stable, they don't change. The concept of grasping is not going to be different tomorrow than it is today. Secondly, concepts are internally structured. So, we know, for example, that grasping has a structure to it. You start out by opening your hand, reaching for something, closing your hand, and so on. so, concepts are internally structured. They are compositional. Compositional means you can fit them together. For example, take the concept of a bottle and the concept of *grasping*, you can fit them together to get a concept of *grasping a bottle*. Inferentially, they give rise to inferences. For example, if I grasped for the bottle, then I reached for the bottle; if I haven't reached for the bottle, then I haven't grasped the bottle. Ok? Simple inferences. There sre relations among concepts. They may be related by hyponymy, antonymy, etc. So, for example, the concept of grasping is more general than the concept of grasping with a full hand or grasping with the finger or grasping with the mouth, ok? There is a hierarchy that is what hyponyms are about. Concepts are meaningful, that is, they have meaning. They are not just ramdom symbols or something like that. Concepts have to mean something and concepts are independent of the words used to express them, and that's very important. Why? Because different languages can express the same concepts in different words, and the words can change over time. So, those are the genral properties. Now, concepts can be either " concrete" , that is sensory-motor concept like grasp, or abstract, not sensory-motor concept like *grasping an idea* which means understanding an idea, that is an abstract, not a concrete, not a sensory-motor concept. So you have both kinds.

And what we are going to do in this talk is introduce some basic ideas for making sense of concept from the neural science. Instead of amodality, that is not known perception, hearing or use of the body, we are going to talk about multimodality, where you have multiple uses of your sensory-motor system, of using the body and perceiving and hearing and yelling feedback from touch, and so on. We are going to talk about the idea of functional clusters. These are high level notions and they function as conceptual units. I'll explain later with each of these. We'll talk about the idea of simulation, that is, this is going to be necessary for meaningfulness and contextual inference. And then we are goignt to talk

216

about the idea of parameters, that is, these govern semantic simulations, simulation of what you doing, understanding it. And they characterize inference and they link to language. So, those are the ideas that we are going to be going through shortly.

Multimodality first. The action of grasping is not amodal. It's not that, you know, the action as opposed to the concept. The action is multimodal because I can both do it and see it. So I'm using both perception both motor program that one modality and multimodality and the visional modality. So it is multi-modal. And we are going to argue that that allows for universality. We don't know it yet, but you'll see it.

Functional clusters. These form higher-level units we'll talk about what they are, what they mean. They are clusters of neurons. They have internal relational structure required by concepts, so we are going to show that. I'm going to show that there are two types: local clusters and network clusters. You will see what those mean as we go along. Multi-modality is realized in the brain through network clusters, and these are in the brain parallel networks between the parietal and premotor cortexes. That is parietal cortex back here and premotor up here. There are connections between them and we will see that leads to multi-modality. Network clusters are formed by interconnected local clusters of neurons and these are canonical and mirror neurons, and we will see what they are momentarily.

To understand simulation, to get the meaning of grasp, we must at least be able to imagine ourselves or someone else grasping an object. Now this is very important. Let's stop for a minute and think about the theory of meaning. What does it take to understand the meaning of the word grasp? You have to at least be able to imagine yourself or someone else grasping anything, if you can't imagine it, you do not inderstand the concept of grasp. Ok? So that's the point. We are going to base the theory of meaning on the theory of imagination and we are going to claim that imagination is done by neural simulation, and I'll explain exactly what that is. The conceptual of grasping that grasping is an action and we make it into a concept that we can reason about and have a language. The conceptualization of grasping via simulation therefore requires the use of the same functional clusters in the action and perception of grasping, and we will see this momentarily.

Now, all of this is based on a set of results in neural science. We know that there are visual imagination uses the same neural substrate as vision. Let me explain what that means. There is a part of the brain that is active when you actually see something. If I'm looking at this bottle, imagine looking at that bottle, some of the same neural system is active, that is, imagining seeing uses the same neural system as actually seeing. The same is true for movement. If I go to pick up the bottle, a certain part of my brain in the motor system is active. How do we know this? We know this via FMRI research, that is, we study what is actually going on in the brain. Now, since you can understand a concrete conceot like grasping only if you can imagine doing it or observing it, the capacity for mental simulation, that is the capacity for imagining it, for carrying it ir actually doing it. Thus action and observation together provide the basis for meaningfulness in the neural theory of language. So this is where we are going.

Now, in order to do this at all, we need a very important concept of a neural parameter, very different from the concept of the grammatical parameter. In neural parameter, all actions, perceptions and simulations make use of parameters and their values, and neural parameterization is pervasive, all we'll tell you what they are. The action of reaching for an object, suppose I'm reaching for this bottle, makes use of the parameter of direction, so one part of reaching is direction. Parameters like a part of dimension, a feature. Ok? One parameter is direction. It aso makes use of the parameter of force. If I'm reaching for something, I can do it very gently or I can do it forcefully or with medium force. Those are parameters, and they are governed in actions by certain clusters of neurons in the neuron system, and that has been discovered, it is part of what we know about neural science.

The same parameter values that characterize the internal structure of actions and simulations of actions also characterize the internal structure of action concepts. Let me say that slowly. That's the crucial part of this. We are going to claim that if you look at the parameters that characterizing acting and perceiving the neural parameters, we are going to see that those same parameters, that is, the same clusters of neurons are characterizing the internal structure of the concept as well as the action and the perception. That is the basic claim that we are going to making.

Now, let me stop for a minute and talk about the neural theory of language. That is going to be crucial in all of this. That theory uses the computational modeling mechanisms. It uses what is called connectionism, not PDF connectionism. Let me explain the difference very briefly. PDF connectionism parallel distributed processing connectionism to each other in all kinds of ways, but just every possible way. And then you put constraints on it, that is you give it an input and if it makes a mistake, you see, one of the things it does is they categorize something as being, let's say, grasping or not grasping; or a word, if it is a word, bad or is not the word *bad*. Now, you put in something the word *bad* and you say it is bad or not, it may make a mistake. You put in the word cat and you may say is the cat bad or not, and well, you'd get it right or make a mistake, and you can feedback the equivalent of the answer through the system— the neural system. It is the way mathematically to do this. And what that does is learn all kinds of information in this bunch of neurons. But, because everything is connected to everything else, you get lots of interference between the concepts and circuits like this can not control motor action, can not do vision, can not do language and so on for most linguistic tasks. There are some taskes where people claim they might be able to do something in language, but for most they cannot.

Structural connectionism has to do with the actual kinds of structures that you find in your brains. The PDF structures are very rarely found in brains— there are some parts of the brain you have things like this but most parts you did not. Structural connectionism takes the structures of brains, neural structures and what it does is make mathematical models of them. So, it says if you have a neuron and it fires, let's call that firing value the amount of, let's say, chemical going down the axon. Let's give that number, you have maybe a thousand inputs to that neuron, each with a certain amount of chemical, let's give them numbers, and there are multiples effects in the synapses, so let's multiply those by other numbers, add them up and if you get enough, it fores and goes down and goes to the next neuron. So with models like that, you can make mathematical

models of neuron firing: neuron by neuron by neuron. . . spreading out in spreading activation, you know, for each neuron spreads to a thousand others and
gets a thousand inputs, and models like that have been constructed, and one of
those things that people do in our group is then model, how such systems work.

Now, that doesn't mean that we have made a full model of the brain or anything like that. What we intend to do is to make higher-level models of clusters
of neurons and we will talk about those. These are called localist models, and in
them the units are not individual neurons but whole clusters, we will talk about
clusters momentarily.

Now, localism allows the neuron theory to characterize precise computations, that should say exactly what each neuron is doing as they did in actions
and inferences, not what each neuron but what each cluster is doing. And because it uses functional clusters, it is not subject to a certain objection called the
grandmother-cell objection. So let me tell you about the grandmother-cell objection. There was an earlier theory in which you have structured connectionism
one neuron at a time, and people said that's ridiculous for language, because
neurons die. And imagine the neuron for your grandmother: if the neuron for
your grandmother would die, you would no longer know who your grandmother
was. That just doesn't happen, right? So that's silly. But however, if you have
clusters of neurons between ten and a hundred and fifty neurons for each concept
and those have been discovered and forty-nine left. They do the same job. So
that's not a problem with this kind of system.

Now, the advantages of structure connectionism are these: structure connectionism operates on structures of the sort found in real brains. From the
structure connectionism's perspective, the inferential structure of the brain and
its organizational in terms of functional clusters. Let me say that again. The inferential structure of concept, the way we can reason with concepts, the possible
forms of reasoning, follow from the network structure of the brain, the way that
the neurons are set up in clusters. That's what we will be arguing, and that's
what the theory says.

Now, structured connectionism comes with various mechanisms. One is dynamic, that is, it operates over time, a dynamic simulation mechanism that

220

adapts parameter values to situations. So in a given situation you might be picking up this bottle with a small force, or you might be doing it in this direction or in that direction. So it allows you to adapt the situations. It is a neuron binding theory. What is neuron binding? Neuron bindoing, in the traditional sense, has to do with, when two things occur in different parts of the brain, there is a mechanoism for identifying them and having them be understood as the same entity. For example, suppose you look at a blue chair, now there is part of the brain that computes the structure of a chair, the image of a chair. So, somehow when you see a blue chair, you have something in one part your brain doing the clor blue, and another part of the brain saying this is a mental image of a chair and it fits that. But you have to be able to link them up, so there is a single object of blue chair. The name for this process is neuron binding, and there are certain theories of how it works. Right now the most prominent theory is that when the blueness and the chairness are firing in sequencing together, then you understand that as being the same object. We do not know that this is true. It is the best current theory we know that such thingds do occur, but we don't know that it is the right theory. It could be a different way. There could be some other mechanism, but there are some mechanisms for binding. We know the properties for binding, but we are not sure of the exact mechanism.

So what we have is a model for binding that assures that you have simultaneous firing. If that is wrong, we could construct a different model to try to fit those other facts. We also have spreading activation throughout the network with, what is called, a probabilistic inference mechanism. Here is how that works: probabilistic means that the values are between one and zero. It's not just firing and not firing. If you have a cluster of neurons, let's suppose you have a hundred neurons in there, maybe only eighty of them are firing and twenty of them are not. So if that's the case we have them, say, firing point eight out of one. So if 85% are firing, is point eight five. But the amount of firing is probabilistic in that the values between zero and one, and the model has a probabilistic computational mechanism for putting probabilities together to get new ones.

So to gather all of these mechanisms, which is a lot of work. That's what these guys are doing at the Computer Science Institute. These jointly allow for modeling of both sensory-motor simulations and inference. Ok, those are the mechanisms that are used.

In the neural theory of now, by the way, you don't have to worry about this because there are other people doing this work. At least I don't have to worry a-bout this, because there are very smart people working on it. There are also fixed structures we call schemas, sometimes frames: image schemas and frames about schemas. A schema that structures an action has an internal structure that consists, just as frames do, of roles, parameters and phases. A role, the agent—me, the patient—the bottle, the action—grasping, or maybe other sub-actions like reaching, opening the hand, cosing the hand, tightening the hand, lifting the arm, moving the elbow towards your mouth, those are roles. Phases: in the first phase, you open the hand and reach out; in the second phase, you grasp, which means you close your hand around and tighten it, then you might, third phase, lifted use it in some way. Those are phases. The parameters are: force, direction and various other parameters. Ok, now, that's what a schema is. That's how we characterize the structure of frames.

The idea of multimodality, functional clusters, simultaneous and parame-ters, those four ideas are going to allow us to link the neural theory, structural connectionism to neuroscience. We are trying to link the actual neural modeling of the computation to what the neural scientists are found and I will show you how to do it.

So, let's look at the neuroscience evidence. In the sensory-motor system, the neuroscience evidence allows us to characterize these aspects of concepts: universality; semantic role structure, what is called aspectual linguistics at it is the phases of an action, and parameter structure. And here is how it works in grasping. We are going to say that universality is achieved by multimodality. That is when multimodality functional clusters are in action, like grasping, fire, when grasping is performed, observed, imagined, inferred or heard, any of those things, when that happens, we are going to say that there are certain neu-ron clusters that are firing. The grasping can be of any type, done by any agent, on any object, in any manner and in any location, when this happens, you get

222

universality. So, if you can show that there is multimodality for some functional cluster, then we are also showing that that functional cluster can play the conceptual role of universality for the given concept.

So, in addition, there is multimodel integration. The premotor cortex as a whole. Let me stop for a minute and tell you about the premotor cortex. If I perform an action, like lifting up this bottle and grasping it, two different parts of the brain are active at least. One is the motor cortex up here, where neurons that fire control individual movements, for example, this and this, opening and closing the elbow, opening and closing the hand, turning individual movements; moving the arm forward, moving the arm up, moving the arm down, going like that, like that, like that. Those are the kinds of movements controlled by the motor cortex. Ok? Very simple. The motor cortex does not allow for the integrated movement for a choreography. Think of the brain as a choreographer telling each of the individual neurons here how to perform a dance. First you got to move your hand out, you got to do this and you got to do that. The choreographer is the premotor cortex. It has connections to the motor cortex, and what it does is it somehow—in a way we'll tell you in a minute. What it does, say, is first to do and when, and how much force they have and parameters they have. The way it does it is as the following. There is a circuit with neurons connected to each other, that fires in sequence, connecting all of these neurons to that in the motor cortex, and if this one fires, when this fires, it says because of the connections to here it says "move your arm like that"; the next one fires and it says "move it forewars"; the next one fires and says "tighten it"; the next one fires and says "lift this". Now, how does it say it? It says it because the neurons in the sequence of in the sort of string of neurons: here, here... they have connections to the part of brain here that do all of these things. So when the first oen fires, there's a connection to the motor cortex that says, "ah, it is connected to this thing, go do that"; the next one fires, "it's connected to another thing that activates the part that does that". Ok, that's the mechanism. This mechanism has been first modeled by Sri Narayanan, the same guy who did the same neural theory of metaphor in his thesis. They are related work.

It turns out that the circuits that do this characterize the phases of actions.

What comes first, second, third, and they also characterize aspect in natural language, that is, what is aspect about. It says some actions iterate. It's a loop, you can type and type and type and type; other actions like walking, go on and on and on... there is no final state. Things that have a final state, like jumping, you jump and it's over, and so on. That is, these circuits may have end points and they may not have end points, they may have loops. And then they indicate purpose. How does a circuit indicate purpose? It has a test for whether the purpose has been carried out. For example, here the purpose is having this thing in your hand and being able to control it. That is your purpose. So each point you check, do I have it in my mind? No. Do I have it in my hand? No. Do I have it in my hand? Well, yes, but I can't control it. Do I have it in my hand and can control it? Yes. That is your check and when that condition is met, then, the purpose is met. Ok? So, that is the idea behind this whole system, and it's completely worked out. It's not only been program. It's a program in so detailed and there is new program and system that has been invented to do it and so on.

Ok, now, so that's the modeling part of this. The premotor cortex that choreographs these things is not a uniform field, means it is not the case that every neuron in there does the same kind of thing. There are functionally distinct areas that do different things, and each of the premotor areas is reciprocally connected, that means, connected both ways, with distinct regions of the posterior-back here, parietal cortex. So this is connected to this in three different ways. The premotor cortex is part of the theories of parallel functional networks. By parallel we mean that this parallel is to this is parallel to that.

Now, multimotor integration. The cortical premotor areas, namey over here, are endowed with sensory properties and that is very interesting. Because you have connections between the parietal cortex, the parietal cortex gets sensory information, gets information from the eyes, from the ears, from touch, and so on, has sensory information, right? If there are connections both ways between the motor premotor cortex and the parietal cortex, then, neurons in the premotor cortex are going to get information from the parietal cortex. They are going to have sensory properties and respond to visual sematosensory in duditory stimuli as well as choreographing actions. So, that these parietal areas which are traditionally considered to process presensory information also gain information from the motor areas because the connections are going both ways. So, if you are doing something, there is also information going what you can see, what you can hear and so on, what you can touch, the information about touch. So, you get information going both ways what that means is you are integrating various modalities, you are integrating movement with seeing, hearing, touching. What the group which Vittorio's group in Parma has done is therefore looked at the various parts of the premotor cortex and isolated all it's different functional regions. They work somewhat differently. And we are particularly going to be concerned. We're going to be concerned with F4, F5 and this little ridge over here.

Now, here are the various parietal networks from various points of view. These are networks that go like this, and so on. And you could see what are they and where they are. And then we're going to go through one by one. In area F5, there are three classes of neurons that have been found in monkeys. With the monkeys, they actually take off the monkey's skull and they probe and they find these things. There are motor general purpose neurons, and then there are visual-motor neurons which are called canonical amd mirror neurons.

So, let's start with the general purpose neurons. There are three types that that proup has found for the moinkey: grasping neurons, holding neurons and manipulating neurons. And the kind of task they gave the monkey is grasping an object. You know whatever kind of object it is, getting a peanut and twisting it, and holding an object, getting something like this and holding onto it. And they train the monkey to do each of these three things and then they feed it if it does it right, and so on, and train it for a long time and then they get to do this. Now, in F5, let's look what's going on here. These drawings are what are called histograms. They show the firing of individual neurons. Som you have a neuron and you can see that is firing right here. And this line in the middle is where is doing the thing that you are interested in. So, here is one firing pattern, and here is another firing pattern, and so on. And what happens? Let's see in A. here is a firing pattern when the monkey, for this particular neuron, here is one particular neuron, grasps something with its mouth, goes and picks it up with its

225

mouth. The neuron fires in the premotor cortex. Here is where it grasps with the controlatoral hand, that is, lefty, the left hand. Ok, so goes the grasp with the left hand, the firing pattern. Notice that the same neuron is firing. Ok? The amount of firing and whether it's exactly the same doesn't matter much. It's the sort of regular. It's the appropriate amount that matters. Here is the ipsilateral hand, the same hand, namely, the right hand. And it's firing here. That is this neuron fiures only when the monkey grasp and it doesn't matter how. Can do it with its mouth or either hand. This is for a general grasping of any kind, at the level of individual neurons, and there's a group of neurons, maybe fifty to a hundred or something like that. I don't have the actual numbers here, but there is a whole bunch of them that work just like this.

Now, think about it, that is kind of interesting, because it's firing for grasping any kind at all, but what is actually doing is something different with its mouth and with its arms. So, what we know from general purpose neurons; what do they achieve in theories of concepts; partially universality, their firing corre-lates with a goal-oriented action of a general type, regardless of effectors, that is arm or mouth, or manner, that's how you do it. That's what you do it like this or like that.

Now, goal-oriented, it turns out that this firing only occurs if the animal actually gets the object. If it just moves its hands like this, nothing happens with the neuron. The neuron doesn't fire just for moving like this or movements with the mouth, it actually has to get the object. So it says it has achieved the goal.

Now, let's look at another part of F5c and its connection to the PF part of the parietal cortex. There you have circuits that contain what are called mirror neurons. Now, mirror neurons are extremely important. This is a big deal for many reasons. So, here's where we have to pay attention. If you don't remember any thing from this lecture about mirror neurons, remember mirroe neurons. Mirror neurons fire, discharge, they fire when either the monkey performs one of the number of actions like grasping or holding or twisting the peanut or when the monkey sees another individual, another monkey or the experimenter doing the same action. Ok? Monkey see menkey do. It is because there is a connection

226

between the motor part, the premotor's part that controls action, and the parietal cortex that controls vision, because the connection go both ways. The monkey has over its life-time, these neurons have been tuned, the connections have been tuned in such a way that they fire when either the monkey sees someone else do the action or the monkey does the action.

This has also been found in human beings. So, let me stop for a minute with this story and take a little story on the side and tell you why this is incredibly important. This is the basis for us for imitation, for learning how to do something. You go and study marshal arts and the master says, "look at me do this" and you go and do this. Right? Now the master says "do this" and you go and do this. Not so easy the first time, but we have to practice.

Now, the idea is because of the mirror neurons that this is possible, first. Secondly, it has to do with being able to tell what someone else is emotionally feeling. Why? The reason is that when you have a certain emotion, it can show in your body, so if you are angry, you can see it in people's faces. People are happy, right? People are depressed, right? In certain many cases, you can see that because the muscles in the face and body reflect what someone is feeling. So, if you can see what someone else's muscles are doing, and if that connects to your muscles, toi the neurons that control your muscles, you don't have to be doing the same thing although little children often do. You don't have to be doing the same thing, but that is going to be connected to your emotional system. That is the physiology of emotions, so you will be able to feel what someone else feels, sort of do a kind of mind readg, and this makes that possible. The name for this is empathy. Tha mirror neurons provide for empathy and there exist both monkeys and people which means we evolve to have empathy with other beings. Evolution allowed us to connect with other people and to have empathy with them, and that is an extremely important thing to know, because the traditional theories of evolution said we only evolve to pursue our own goals, to achieve our own purposes for self interest, and that's not true. We evolve naturally to connect with other people and to have empathy. That is a very important part of human nature. So that's where this eventually will go in terms of moral theory. This changes all of moral theory.

Now, let's get back to the circuit, which gives rise to these mirror neurons. Now, so here is where the mirror neurons are, and let me show you how they work, and here is the evidence for them. Over here, if I remember all this correctly, you have the firing when the monkey sees the experiment picking up something, grasping something; and then, over here you have the firing whn the monkey does it himself, and you see the same firing. Now, if here you see the same neuron firing in the monkey grasping something, but if the experimenter takes an instrument, like a pair of pliers, not its hands and grasp the entity, there is no firing, because it is not the same action, even though the same effect has been carried out. So you got to really do it with your hand. Ok, very important. Here is what happens in the dark. The monkey can't see anything but is does it in the dark. The neuron fires. So what you have here — these are other similar cases where the monkey is doing something else. If the monkey is doing another action, some other thing, not just picking something up, but doing something totally different action, no firing. He sees somebody else doing the different action, here, no firing, right? So, basically, it's only when tha you get the fire.

Now, that is an over simple fire story. Here is the complicated story. 30% of the neurons work like that—that is, the neurons fire only when you have exactly the same action going on. But there is what is called category loosening and that is really interesting. And let me escape for a minute and get exactly what's here. In A and B, you have observed grasping. The monkey is seeing, here is the neuron, there the monkey is seeing grasping. And here is the grasping with the precision grip like that; here is the grasping with the whole hand. Here in C, you get the precision grip. You get a firing with the precision grip when he sees or observe somebody else doing this. But when the monkey sees somebody else doing this grip, nothing happens. Right? Over here, the monkey does either grip, it fires. Monkey sees this one, it fires; he sees the other one, nothing happens. Now, this is wild and interesting, why?

This is a special case of grasping. There are two special cases. That neuron fires when the monkey does any kind of grasping, but when he sees only one kind of grasping; there is another set of neurons that do the reserve. When the monkey sees one kind of grasping, while it's the prototypical grasping from the monkey, this is the prototype from the monkeys, but when he does, only one. So, what that means is that the sub-case, the sub-category of precision grasping, is linked in these neurons to the general notion of grasping, that is hierarchical structure in semantics. Linking the general kind of grasping to the special case is present at the single neuron level. That is pretty wild. If you think about it, we have a hierarchy of concepts, right? More general, more specific. That is replicated at the single neuron level, neuron by neuron, is the set of neurons that just do that. To me, this is astonishing. When they first found that they didn't publish it because they had no idea what it meant. They didn't talk to a linguist, they said, "ah!".

With the precision grip, PJ is for this grip here. Look, when the experimenter grasp and the object. This is at the grasping. You also get a firing when you release the object. Right? That is, there is a neuron that fires in phases. It computes the aspect of grasping, the central part and the final part. There is other neurons which fire in the beginning parts when you are going to. That is, there are neurons that fire controlling the phases of the action, and you can find them one by one.

Here, the experimenter grasps and releases the objects with the right hand. This is the left hand, same thing. Now, this is an interesting case. Here the experimenter grasps with a whole hand (WH), and releases it with the left hand, and notice that you are getting firing at the end, but not much. This is mainly for the right hand. Here you get the monkey grasping the object with the right hand in this neuron, and you get nothing here. That is, you can both fire with releasing the object, and here is neuron that fires when the experimenter is going through a phase, but only when the monkey is doing the central action. So, it's linking my central action with all your phases.

Here, the experimenter presents the object with the left hand. Nothing happens when the experimenter just presents the object, it's not grasping, so no firing. And here when the monkey grasps with whole hand. This is with this grip. This is the whole hand. So when the monkey is grasping, this is for any kind of grasping you will get firing here now. But, with observation, with either of the grasping you get aspect. You will get at two stages: here and release. So, there is a link between the central concept of grasping and whole structure, the phases of grasping. This is kind of nice in this experiment what you see in A, is a full vision, the monkey can see the experimenter did no block, the experimenter just doing like this, no firing. The purpose has to be carried out. Over here, in B, the experimenter is reaching over here. The monkey is hidden, but the experimenter is reaching and has begun the action and then goes and grasps it, and during the phase in which it would be carried out, it's done. I think that is the monkey of the experimenter. And here you have hidden mimicking, no action. Nothing.

So, (I'm sorry, I got this wrong) This is the monkey, the monkey is going and going like this, and you get firing over here, and you get the firing when this is carried out, ok, when the purpose is done. So, this is for purposeful grasping, that is, when the purpose is carried out, done. And even if the monkey can't seize it with its own hand, if it is carried out, done, firing. If it is just this, no firing in either case. So, you have to get the purpose.

So, like humans, monkey can infer the goal of an action even when the visual (oh, I got it wrong), even if you can not see it, you can infer the action. Now, these are the cases where there is sound. And what you'll find here is that there are certain things like when when you break a peanut, you can hear it, or you grasp a certain kind of ring, you can hear the metal, and so on. And here you have the firing. Here are two different neurons—three and four. Here is the firing. Let's first look at Three: vision and sound. Ok, the monkey can both see and hear, mo problem. Here the monkey can see, but no sound, so you get firing again.

Here the monkey can't see it, but can hear the sound, so as soon as the sound comes, it hears the sound and the action is her, then you get this neuron firing, but not because you can see it, and so on. So, what's interesting here is the firing anticipates the action. It's anticipatory when he sees it. He says that he is going to break that peanut, so it's going to start the fire. But with sound you can't see it, there is no anticipation, no firing. So, that says anticipation of an action is built into its neurons. And this is what the actual modal neuron does is when you actually doing it. Ok, that's what's happening.

The same sort of thing goes on here. This thing is with peanut breaking and paper ripping, and so on. Vision and sound, you get this with peanut breaking, if you only have vision, and no sound, this neuron is not firing. If you have just sound, it's firing, and you have modal-neurons. So this neuron is toned to both, doing and hearing, but not seeing. So, to give you some sense of the richness, or what's in the brain, this is an interesting case. Here you have in the blue: food action, hand action, mouth action. This is with a human being, and it turns out that there are two cases. One were some bodies in the FMRI, and they are asked to either perform an action with mimicking, that is they pretend that they are kicking an object, but there is no object there—do this but there is no object. As soon as you are grasping, here in the yellow, but no object. So you see that happening. Assume that you are grasping something with your mouth, you are biting, here, but no apple. Here they give an object, and what you see is a region in the parietal cortex parallel to where the activation is for full hand and mouth is done. And this could be done with the same object like the apple. So the activity for understanding and representing an object in the brain depends upon what you're doing with it. Ok, this is a very interesting part.

Now, how do mirror neurons work? Is this magic? No, it is not magic. They work by simulation. When the subject, the monkey or you, observes another individual doing an action, like grasping. The subject, we claim, is simulating the same action, that is, the subject's brain is carrying out what he sees. I see you going to lift that and I'm carrying out automatically because my parietal cortex is getting the visual information. It's connected to the motor cortex which can imagine using the same neurons, carrying this out. I see this. I'm imagining what you are doing unconsciously. I may not know it, but my brain is imagining what you are doing and what you are going to do. And that is why you get the idea of someone starting at the monkey, say, starting to see the peanut twisted and you see the activation. So, the idea is that when you see something happening, normally, you understand it. If I see someone picking this up, I can understand it because the connections in my brain simulating doing it. I'm automatically because the connections in my brain simulating doing it. And that is what understanding is, and that's the basis of a theory of meaning. That is the basis of what is called simulation semantics. That is why we've gone through all of this to show you what a neural theory of meaning is. And what is going on here is: since the subject observes another individual doing action, the subject is simulating the same action, since action and simulation use the same neural substrate, that would explain what the same neurons are firing during action observation and during action execution.

Now, what did we know from mirror neurons? We get partial universality because they code an action regardless of agent, patient, modality, that is, you get partial role structure, why? They code an agent and a purpose role. Let me explain why. If you think about it, these neurons, when you see something, they have someone else, some other agent doing something. They also fire when you do it. The same neurons therefore identify you with the other agent, right? And what they do, in order to do that they are picking out an agent role, a grasper roel. So, these neurons have the function of picking out a grasper of separating. Think of it this way. They separate the dancer from the dance. You know the line from Yeats—how can you tell the dancer from the dance? You have a brain and mirror neurons and that's how. That is they, because you can feel yourself dance and you could identify yourself with the dancer, you are separating out the dancer from the dance, and the grasper from the grasping. Also, they distinguish purposeful action where you actually get the object from just moving your hands. So they distinguish a role of purpose from nonpurposeful action.

Now, so they also achieve category tightening and loosening its hierarchical structure, and some limited prototype structure—this is a prototype *grasping*. And you find out that this occurs as a prototype in some of these neurons. Now, here is where that circuitry is. Here is the next group. We are going to F5ab, next circuit. This links the premotor area at F5ab to the parietal area AIP. And these are interesting things. These are called canonical neurons. Let me try to give you a feel for what these neurons do. These neurons fire when you either performing an action on an object or you see the object you can perform it on, right? I can do it if I see the bottle or I grasp the bottle, the same neurons are

232

firing. Now, that's fairly wild. It says transforms in intrinsic physical features of objects, shapes and size, the things that you can grasp, into hand motor programs required to act on them. And the things that are looked at are manipulating objects, grasping, holding and tearing apart. So these are canonical neurons. They are located along this ridge.

And here is how this works. You have the monkey grasping a ring, and this neuron fires, but it's grasping a plate, a cube, a cone, a sphere, a cylinder, nothing. Here you may get a little bit firing because of the similarity of shape with a ring, but not much. Here, you have a similar case, again, firing with the ring, but not all of these things. This has to do with what happens in the dark. Don't worry about it, it's complex.

So, how do the canonical neurons work? Again, by simulation. The sight of a graspable object triggers the simulation of grasping. The reason for that is that you have connections between the parietal cortex and F5, but they are different connections. You are linking the patient of an action to the action, that's what this does: it links the patient of the action to the action. So they achieve partial universality. They code regardless of patient, manner or action. They code a patient role and a purpose role. They only fire when you actually get the purpose, and they fire in the presence of an appropriate patient for a given action. So, what you get so far is the coding of a whole lot of conceptual structure.

Now, let's got to the third circuit. This one links area of F4 and VIP in parietal. Let me explain briefly about this. There is a notion called peri-personal space. Let me explain what that is. Take my check. If I touch my check, there will be certain neurons firing. If I see something coming towards my check and doesn't touch it, the same neurons will fire. The same thing, my arm, you got to grasp my arm, you haven't touched it yet, the same neurons are going to fire as if you are touching it, ok? So, what happens here is, that's what it all says. Here is the palces where it works, and the actions are head turning for looking at what's going on. This is reaching with the arm and controlling it. And here is the monkey, here is the monkey's face and its peri-personal space, so, any entry, any of this again has firing in this area. The same is touching any of this area. And if you put something into this region around it, it is the same as if you touch the corresponding place. The same here.

Now, here is the neuron firing. You have the monkey in this region and what you are doing here is showing what happens when you put something into space at various angles here, here, here, and so on, and you see the amount of firing varying. The maximum firing is right next to the check. And this is the region in which you get any firing at all. Here is how this works in another experiment. We have something, the monkey is looking up here and something is coming not here but towards the chin, I mean, coming toward where he's looking the same thing, and you get some firing. Here let's see what is going on, here, the monkey is looking here—I'm a little confused. Let me escape, ok, in ENG, the neuron for the chin. This responds when you touch the chin, something is coming towards the chin, the monkey is looking at it, it responds. If the monkey is, um, if this is coming towards the eye, the one for the chin doesn't respond. Here this is coming towards the mouth, not the chin, the mouth, thank you. It's putting something in the mouth. Now, her eit says the chin, but it's probably the mouth.

Now, I need to get back out of this... here, you have the similar thing. This is a neuron that fires when you touch here. If you have a probe like this going towards here, then it fires. But, if I move over a bit, over the central line, I go towards here, not towards here, no firing. Here again, even if the monkey is looking away, I go towards here, firing; if I go over a little bit, no firing.

So, how does that work, again by simulation. The sight or sound of a possible target—you see something coming towards your chin, and there is a connection between the touching of the chin and seeing the area that allows you to see it. It's going to be the same as if you actually touched it because you are anticipating it. You are simulating this action and you are simulating that it's going to hit the chin.

So, these achieve partial universality, doesn't matter what the patient is, and they also code location of an action because your location is where you've been touched or where something is moving. These are the experiments. All right, then, what does this mean? The premotor and the parietal areas, rather than having separate and independent functions, are neutrally integrated, not only to control action, but to serve the function of constructing an integrated representation of actions, together with objects acted on and locations toward which the actions are directed. In these circuits, sensory inputs are transformed in order to accomplish not only motor but also cognitive tasks, like space perception and action understanding.

Theyhave phases and there are other experiments that go through more examples of how phases work. And jointly, they characterize stability. The same neurons where functionally doing the same things day after day. They can cover all the particular cases, and they have internal structure, they get semantic roles: agent, patient, purpose and location: they have aspectual structure phases; they are meaningful, because you can simulate and understand them; and of course, with the monkeys, they have independence of linguistic expression.

In summary, these things would work in the neural—now, let's go to the neural theory of language, and I'll stop, ignore this line for a moment. Remember what narayanan did about coordination actions. You have the premotor cortex connections to the motor cortex. I'm going to grasp this thing: the first neuron fires, I do this; the second neuron fires, I open my hand; the third one, I go like that; the fourth one, I go like that, and so on, because of the connections. Notice tha tall of thes things are in different places. You have to have another circuit connecting them, which is what Narayanan is modeling. You have to have another circuit, putting on all these things together on top of it, and that's what Narayanan circuitry does in part, it pulls all of these together. That's model. It's not discovered in neuroscience. And it tells you what to do at what stance. So it integrates things, and that allows you not only to do things in sequence but alos to infer the other things if you are understanding this, if you are simulating this, you can say, "oh, he is doing this and this, he is about to grasp". That is, you can make predictions, you can infer actions, you can do reasoning about this. And because you can link up the patient with the action, and the agent with the action, it does some compositionality. So, basically, if you put Narayanan's work together with this work, what you get is a theory of the concept of grasping as a meaningful concept. You get a theory of the meaning of the word grasp. Not just the action, the meaning.

Now, notice what we've done. For at least one concept, grasp, a physical concept, functional clusters, as characterized in the sensory-motor system and as models using structured connectionist binding and inference mechanisms, have all the necessary properties for concepts, not just actions, not just perceptions, but concepts.

Now, we have a neural version of Ockham's Razor. Ockham's Razor says, "Don't postulate anything more than you have to. " Under the traditional theory, action concepts have to be disembodied, that is in the traditional theory, there would have to be another set of circuits to do all of this stuff for the concepts in addition to what is doing for the actions and the perceptions. Nut here we show that if you have just what they are for the actions on the perceptions, you get everything you need for the concepts, because the same neural sub-structure is giving you imagination, it allows you to simulate in your imagination. Because of that, you would have to duplicate all these apparatus in order to get, in the traditional theory, to get concepts. In this theory, you don't have to do that. It just follows from what is going on in the sensory-motor system. So, how does this work? What follows from this?

Now we start moving faster. We are getting into the linguistics. For each type of action, you have a fixed schema, consisting of certain parameters: roel parameters, like agent and patient; phase parameters, like initial, middle, and the final state; manner parameters, like degree of force and direction. These are all represented down to the neural level. A grasping from the point of view of linguistics, if you are doing linguistic semantics, and you are doing what a frame semantics would do, here is what you would need: the roles: agent, action, patient, location; the manners: force, type of grip, effect of use; the initial state: the object is located in peri-personal space, if your grasp is close enough to the Starting transition, you reach with a direction toward the object, you know, toward the object location, opening your hand. Central transition: you close your hand with force, how much forces of the function of fragility and how much the patient is with; the goal condition is that the effector, the hand encloses the object with the manner, a grip determioned by parameter values, situated conditions; a final state: the agent doesn't control the object. That's what a linguistic description of grasping has to have, and that's what the concept of grasping is. To do reasoning about grasping, that's what you need; and that is what you get in the sensory-motor system, without any special other parts. That is, it says the concept of grasping, the concept, it's a concept, not just an action—is embodied.

So, what this does is fit the grasp schema to the neuroscience of grasping in each way, that is, each schema parameter is a functional cluster, each parameter value is either a firing pattern over a functional cluster, or some neuron binding to a functional cluster as when the agent is bound to an actor in context. And then ther is what Nayaanan calls an executing schema or an x-schema. This is the chin that fires for this one and this one and this oen. It executes an action. It's a neural circuit connecting the parameters of the fixed schemas so that they can dynamically coordinate the firing over time and adapt the values to inputs from context. And note, the same neurons that are defining the fixed schema are neurons subject to dynamic, that is, defining the fixed schema for grasp. We have a set of neurons that define once and for all what it means to grasp this here, here, and here, but because there is a dynamic circuit connecting them, right? They can be activated by the executing schema during performance, observation and imagination. Schemas are not like logical conditions. They run bodies and that's what's interesting about this. Schemas are not abstract things here. They run bodies, and they do it as well as they can, in the real time adjusting to real conditions.

Now, how does this view of concepts differ from the traditional one? One, there are no necessary and sufficient conditions. That is, they are probabilistic. Things can fire or not. They can do it this way, they can do it and just do it a little bit differently the next time, and so on. That is the way they are probalilistic. There isn't an abstract representation. This is how you do it, it's just in your body. There isn't another representation of concept outside the body. There is no symbols. It is not symbolic. It's no symbols for the concept. It is just the neurons running in your body. So, here is why it is nit a necessary condition. Ther are degrees; there are variations, extensions, and so on.

Here is why it is not representational, because you conceptualize the world on the basis of how you experience it. We saw color is not in the world, nor its heat, it's not a representation of the world. It's what's going on in your body. Since our experience is a function of our body, brain and physical and social environment, so are our concepts and so on. So, that's important, those are directly physical; they are not representations of something else.

And there are no symbols. We can write down a symbol, like final state if we are writing it down, but that's our way of writing or symbolizing what is going on in the brain. There is no symbols in the brain. So in the theory of meaning, ther is nothing symbolic. Meaningfulness and meaningfulness of concepts does not require symbols in the brain—the brain does not symbol things. Now, when we write down symbols like purpose or agent, that means we are representing a functional cluster of neuron.

This says language is not modular. Right? You have connections between the modulars mean: this is premotor module, this is parietal module. Jere they are working together, constantly. They are multi-modal, they are not modular. Many concepts which are part of language are inherently multi-modal, and they exploit the pre-existing multi-modal character of the sensory-motor system. Concepts are exploiting the system of doing and observing the sensory-motor system, and they use the same system for conceptualizing.

What about abstract concepts? Right? Some are about motion; some are less concrete, like freedom. Conceptual metaphor accounts for some of this. That is virtually all abstract concepts have conventional metaphorical conceptualizations like grasping an idea. So, we have metaphorical mappings from concrete to abstract domains. , that is neural connections, to charactering the meanings of a vast number of so called abstract concepts. A vast number of abstract concepts are characterized metaphorically, not all, which we will come to in a minute, but a lot of them.

Now, what are conceptual metaphors? They are, a swe said yesterday, connectionist maps, they are direct connections, and therefore, we claim that the sensory-motor system is directly engaged in abstract reasoning. When you are talking about grasping an idea, you are understanding your mind as grasping, you are activating the grasp schema in simulating it.

238

Now, what's important? Remember the difference between imagining grasping, which can be done unconsciously or consciously, and actually doing it or seeing it. When you do it, there is a connection from the brain and the motor-cortex to your body; but when you imagine doing it, that connection is inhibited in the brain system, so your body doesn't do it, you just imagine it. Ok. Here is the understanding of grasping and notice the reasoning patterns about ordinary grasping work for metaphoirical grasping. So, you can begin to grasp an idea but not quoite get a hold of just like you can begin to grasp an object but not quite get hold of it. If you fail to grasp an idea, it can go right by you, or over your head just like a moving object. If you grasp some idea, you can turn it over in your mind like your can turn ovewr an object. And you can't hold onto an idea before you grasp it. So the inferences are the same. They are the same inferential structure just mapped over by metaphor. And inferences are going on in the sensory-motor system. They are going on in the physical grasping, when you imagine that and then you map onto ideas. That's what it means, that's how the invariance principle works. It is because you are actually using the sensory-motor system, that the sensory-motor system structure is used in metaphor. So, that's what I just said, it's used metaphorically.

Now, I want to finish up with some new work. These are—I want to introduce the concept of a Cog. Let me try to explain what a Cog is. It's crucial for abstract reasoning and for grammar and for many other things. Let's go back to the premotor versus the motor cortex. Ok, motor, premotor. Whenever we perform a complex motor movement, like picking up a glass and talk a drink, two parts of the brain are activated: premotor and motor. The motor cortex, as neural emsembles that control "motor synergies". The synergy is a simple action like this or that, right? Like opening or closing the hand, flexing or extending the elbow, turning the wrist and so on. Complex motor schemas are carried out in the premotor cortex. Now, let us call the motor primary, like that's what it's called, primary motro cortex right here, because it's directly connected to the body. Ok, what we called primary is directly connected to the body. Let's call the premotor cortex secondary, because it has connections to the primary cortex that controls the action. So let us call that primary and that secondary.

Now, what the schema that controls actions. This is what the executing schema, what the Narayanan called the controller X-schema, which controls action: first do this, and then do this, and then do this. What he discovered is that that characterizes aspect in the languages of the world. In his dissertation he also showed that this can compute the logic of aspect abstractly. That is we just look at this schema, it computes the logic of aspects. How does it show this, by what miracle would this done?

Here is how it works. He took the notion of aspect, which is first you have the beginning of an action, then the middle of it, it might reiterate, it mingth extend a long time / short time; it might be a purpose satisfied in the final state, and so on. And what it showed was that for about sixty different actions, the same structure appeared. So, you have lots of different actions, but all of them: start, have a middle part, reiterate or continu, may have a purpose or not, may have a final state or not. If they have a final state, then they are perfective; if they have none, they are imperfective. So, when you look at it, it basically computes aspect. He then said how could you show tha the same circuitry that can move your body or can recognize that? And that's why he set up his neural theory of metaphor. He said let us take a set of metaphors about abstract domain, international economics. He then went to the business section of the New York Times, and the Wall Street Journal, an the Economist, and collected sentences that used physical verbs, like push and pull and fall and run and so on, and he got thousands of the examples, right, in about, you know, three seconds on the computer. Then, he took about thirty of these examples and worked them out in this. Let me give you some of these examples. France dell into a recession and Germany pulled it out. Another one. India is stumbling towards the liberalization of its economy. So, what he did was then figure out what metaphors they were linking the physical actions to the economics. We worked tha tout like a linguist with a little help from his friends. And then he asked, could the same circuitry that can move the body do the reasoning about economics correctly, using the part about falling into a recession, pulling out, stumbling and so on. And he showed that it could for thirty cases—enough to make it look real. That is the same circuitry that can move your body, can do reasoning, which is just

240

what we would expect, if concepts we defined in the way we hace just sugges-
ted.

This is the controller x-schema and the initial phase, starting phase, etc;
pre-central, central phase and so on. This is how aspect works. So this is the
kind what you had for actions and it's also for aspect in natural language. And
this is the kind what he used to call Petri Nets. He changed them, and so on.
And here are the properties of them, but we've already talked about them.

Now, what's interesting about this is that aspect shows up in the grammar of
every language in the world. Every language has ways to indicate that an action
is about to start, that is either long or short, that has duration or it's instantane-
ous, that is finished or not. Every language can say those things in its grammar.
So, the semantics of aspect, which it could carry this out is part of the semantics
of grammar in every language of the world. So, this controller x-schema that
Narayanan made up is part of the semantics of grammar; and where is it located? It is located in the premotor cortex in the secondary structure. Aspect by itself can fit any action. They fit an action and how it is concerned to the motor
cortex to carry out the action so that if you don't have any connections, if you in-
habit all the connections in the motor cortex and just run the controller schema
itself, not seeing what it controls, you get the logic of aspect, pure aspect.
What this says is that the concept of aspects, all the aspectual concepts, come
out of Narayanan's model of the controller x-schema in the secondary structure—
the premotor cortex.

So, here we have one case in which a secondary structure is showing up as
the meaning of something in universal grammar. Let us call that a Cog. Are
there other Cogs? Are there other cases where something that's in grammar has to
be computed in the brain by a secondary structure with connections to primary
structures? And the answer appears to be yes, that all grammatical meaning appears to work this way. Think of the primitive image schema-containers, sourse-
path-goal, contact, rotation, front-back, up-down, all the primary force dynamic schemas. Take for example the container schema, which presumably is computed in the visual cortex according to Reigier and in certain ways. It computes
a generalized container but can fit any shape at all, as we saw. And where does

241

it get the shapes? By connection to the parietal cortex where information about shape is registered. So it is a secondary structure that can fit any shape. It can fit the bottle, the room, the building, any shape at all. But that information about shape and size is given elsewhere in the parietal cortex. So, that means that the part of the brain that computes the container schema is also secondary. And that is true for anything, something that computes generalized—source, path and goal for any particular one is going to be linked to, as going to be in the secondary structure in the brain linked to the primary ones: particular number for a minute. There is part of the brain that computes numbers. It can tell one from two, from three and so on. That part of the brain can also tell pne bell and the sound from two bells, from three bells, or one tree from two trees, from three trees—either vision or sound. That is, it is in the secondary structure that can be linked eith vision or sound which are primary. A number shows up in the grammar of every language, so it looks as if, and here is a cog hypothesis, that the meaning of grammatical concepts, the concepts that show up in grammar, are the concepts computed by secondary structures in the brain. That's the hypothesis. The concepts that show up in grammar around the world are exactly the concepts computed by the secondary structures in the brain. I do not know if this is true. It is a hypothesis, and it is a plausible one, but it is the hypothesis to direct future research.

Now, one more thing. I've done two more studies with respect to cog. I have a book on the cognitive structure of mathematics called *Where Mathematics Comes From*. The book was with Narayanan. It's a nine hundred page book going through everything from addition to subtraction up through higher mathematics, calculus, you know, it has all inds of stuff from higher mathematics, showing that mathematics is metaphorical in full detail. Now, the metaphors that we found in mathematics, let me give you an example of what that would be. Think about the number line. You have a line, and you have a longer line, zero, one, two, three, etc. in the number line, there is a metaphor: numbers are points on the line. It is only a metaphor. In set theory, numbers are sets: zero is the empty set, one is the set containing the empty set and so on. That is a different metaphor. Mathematics is based on metaphor. Mathematics is baded on meta-

242

phors going from one branch of mathematics to another. Very very common. That's how mathematics is built up. When you look at the details of these metaphors, they are all cog to cog metaphors, like lines and numbers, and the's why mathematics can apply to anything. That's because if the meaning of—think about the meaning of grammar. A concept built into grammar can apply to any concept at all, any particular concept that is in the grammar of the sentence, any special case they can apply to, via links from the secondary to primary structures. The same is true of mathematics. Mathematics is abstract. What makes it abstract is that is the find over secondary structures that can then be linked to any corresponding to primary structures. I have another paper as long as this one about srt, and form in art. I looked at art criticism, and it turns out that in art criticism, as done by certain art critiques in the seventies who looked at these things of this sort, the structure of a painting is basically image schema structure. You can show this is the center, this is the contained region, here you have motion from here to here. Here you have a force applied in this direction, and so on. So, it looks like image schemas are structuring art, and image schemas are all cogs, they are all secondary structures. So, it looks like structure in general, in human cognition is coming out of secondary structures in the brain, which then apply to, and why the reason of abstract, they can apply to that.

Now, the very last thing in this lecture. It is the nature of cog, and so on. one more. Let's think about language acquisition, because that is the major place where cogs are important. We know from the work at the Max Plank Institute that when children learn grammar, they learn it one verb at a time. They learn the construction for a verb at a time. They learn the construction for a verb like *give*. I give him a book or something like that. They learn a different grammar for a verb like *fall* or a verb like *hit*. So they learn these grammatical constructions one verb at a time and then they could generalize the new cases. The question is what is generalization? And it's used to be thought that generalization is kind of induction, you get a new structure that is somehow by magic imposed.

Now, this theory, the theory of cogs says something different about generalization. It says that the secondary structure is already there in the primary structure. That is id I'm giving you something, like this, I have in the secondary structure a source, a path and a goal, and I have a force dynamics, and an agent, a patient, and an object that I move in. and then I have the particular thing, if I'm handing you the bottle, I have connections to the fact that this looks like a bottle, has a shape like a bottle, that I'm doing it, that you are the patient, you are the indirect object and so on—you are the recipient. So there is already in the structure of giving an abstract structure in the secondary part of the brain, in the premotor cortex controlling the action. The generaliuzation is already there in the special case, and what you learn is to inhibit the special case, and what you learn is to inhibit the special case, the connections to the special case, so that you can then have connections to new cases. So generalization is not learning something new. It is inhibiting connections to the old special cases. When you do that, you are making connections to new special cases, but you already know the generalization, because they are part of the special cases. That something that's true of the neural system of the human brain. It's not something that abstractly true of a mathematical system—nit's certainly not true in a mathematical system. So if you try to understand language acquisition in terms of an abstract mathematical system, you will never reach this conclusion. But if you do it in terms of neural system, you do.

Thank you!

Bibliography

Aijmer, K. 1996. *Conversational Routines in Spoken Discourse* [M]. London: Longman.

Bateson, G. 1972. *Steps to an Ecology of Mind* [M]. New York: Ballantine.

Beauvais, P. 1986. A Speech Act Theory of Metadiscourse [J]. *Written Communication*, (61).

Blakemore, D. 1987. *Semantic Constraints on Relevance* [M]. Oxford: Blackwell.

Blakemore, D. 1992. *Understanding Utterances* [M]. Oxford: Basil Blackwell.

Bligh, D. A. 2000. *What's the Use of Lectures?* [M]. San Francisco Jossey Publishers.

Brown, G. & G. Yule. 1983. *Discourse Analysis* [M]. Cambridge: Cambridge University Press.

Chafe, W. 1986. Evidentiality in English Conversation and Academic Writing [A]. In Chafe and Nicholas (eds.). *Evidentiality: The Linguistic Coding of Epistemology* [C]. Norwood, NJ. Ablex.

Chaudron, C. & J. R. Richards. 1986. The Effect of Discourse Markers on the Comprehension of Lectures [J]. *Applied Linguistics*, (7): 113 – 127.

Cheng, X. G. & M/ S. 1997. Steffensen. Metadiscourse: A Technique for Improving Student Writing [J]. *Research in the Teaching of English*, 30 (2): 149 – 181.

Colom, G. C. & Williams, J. M. 1985. Perceiving Structure in Professional Prose: a Multiple Determined Experience [A]. In Odell & D. Groswami (eds.). *Writing in Nonacademic Setings* [C]. New York: Guiford.

Conley, T. M. 1983. *Interpersonal Communication* [M]. Urbana-Champaign: University of Illinois Press.

Craig, R. T. & A. L. Sanusi. 2000. 'I'm Just Saying···' Discourse Markers of Standpoint Continuity[J]. *Argumentation*, (14): 425 – 445.

Crismore, A. 1989. *Talking with Readers: Metadiscourse as Rhetorical Act* [M]. New York: Peter Lang.

Crismore, A. 1992. Metadiscourse and Discourse Processes: Interaction and Issues[J]. *Discourse Processes*, (13): 191 – 205.

Crismore, A. & R. Farnsworth. 1990. Metadiscourse in Popular and Professional Science Discourse [A]. In: W. Nash (ed.). *The Writing Scholar: Studies in Academic Discourse*[C]. Newbury Park, CA: Sage.

Crismore, A. & Vande Kopple. 1988. Readers' Learning from Prose: the Effects of Hedges [J]. *Written Communication*, (5): 184 – 202.

Crismore, A.; Markkanen, R. & M. S. Steffenson. 1993. Metadiscourse in Persuasive Writing: A Study of Texts written by American and Finnish University Students[J]. *Written Communication*, 10 (1): 39 – 71.

Crompton, P. 1997. Hedging in Academic Writing: Some Ttheoretical Aspects [J]. *English for Specific Purposes*, 16(4): 271 – 289.

Dahl, T. 2004. Textual Metadiscourse in Research Articles: a Marker of National Cultural or of Academic Discipline[J]. *Journal of Pragmatics*, (36): 1807 – 1825.

DeCarrico, C. & J. R. Nattinger. 1988. Lexical Phrases for the Comprehension of Academic lectures [J]. *English for Specific Purposes*, (7): 91 – 102.

Dillion, G. 1981. *Constructing Texts: Elements of a Theory of Composition and style* [M]. Bloomington, IN: Indiana University Press.

Brown, P & S. Levinson. 1987. *Politeness: Some Universals in Language Usage* [M]. Cambridge: Cambridge University Press.

Eoyang, M. 1987. *Functional Perspective on Textual Linguistics*[M]. Norwood, NJ: Ablex.

Fairclough, N. 1992. *Discourse and Social Change*[M]. Cambridge: Polity Press.

Flower, L. 1987. *Problem-solving Strategies for Writing*[M]. New York: Harcourt.

Flowerdew, J. & L. Miller. 1977. The Teaching of Academic Listening Comprehension and the Question of Authenticity [J]. *English for Specific Purposes*, 16 (1): 27 – 46.

Fraser, Bruce. 1998. *Contrastive discourse markers in English* [A]. In Jucker & Ziv (eds.). *Discourse Markers* [C]. John Benjamins Publishing Company: 301 – 326.

Geisler, C. 1994. *Academic Literacy and the Nature of Expertise in Interpretive Anthropology* [M]. Mawah, NJ: Lawrence Erlbaum.

Gilbert, G. N. & M. Mulkay. 1984. *Opening Pandora's Box: A Sociological Analysis of Scientific Discourse* [M]. Cambridge: Cambridge University Press.

Goffman, E. 1967. *Interactional Ritual: Essays on Face-to-face Behavior* [M]. New York: Doubleday.

Goffman, E. 1974. *Forms of Talk* [M]. Philadelphia: University of Pennsylvania Press.

Goffman, E. 1967. *Interactional Ritual: Essays on Face-to-face Behavior* [M]. New York: Doubleday.

Goutsos, D. 1997. *Modeling Discourse Topic* [M]. New Jersey: Ablex Publishing Corporation, Norwood.

Grab, W. & R. Kaplan. 1996. *Theory and Practice of Writing* [M].. Harlow: Longman.

Gutt, E. -A. 1990. *Translation and Relevance: Cognition and Context* [M]. Oxford: Blackwell.

Halliday, M. A. K. 1973. *Explorations in the Functions of Language* [M]. London: Edward Arnold.

Halliday, M. A. K. & R. Hasan. 1976. *Cohesion in English* [M]. London: Longman.

Halliday, M. A. K. 1994. *An Introduction to Functional Grammar* [M]. London: Edward Arnold.

Hansen, C. 1994. *Topic Identification in Lecture Discourse* [A]. In Flowerdew (ed). *Academic Listening Research Perspective* [C]. Cambridge, New York: Cambridge University Press.

Harris, Z. 1970. *Papers in Structural and Transformational Linguistics* [M]. Reidel, Holland: Dordrecht.

Harris, R. A. 1991. Rhetoric of Science[J]. *College English*, 53 (3), 282 – 307.

Hopper, R. 1981. The Taken for Granted [J]. Human Communications research, 7:195 – 211.

Hyland, K. 2000. Disci*plinary Discourse*: *Social Interactions in Academic Writing*[M]. London: Longman.

Hyland, K. 1996. Writing without Conviction? Hedging in Science Research Articles[J]. *Applied Linguistics*, 17(4): 433454.

Hyland, K. 1998a. Persuasion and context: The Pragmatics of Academic Metadiscourse[J]. *Journal of Pragmatics*, (30):437 – 455.

Hyland, K. 1998b. Exploring Corporate Rhetoric: Metadiscourse in the CEO's Letter[J]. *Journal of Business Communication*, 35(2):224 – 45.

Hyland, K. 2000. *Disciplinary Discourses* [M]. London: Pearson.

Hyland, K. & P. Tse. 2004. Metadiscourse in Acdemic Writing: A Reappraisal [J]. *Applied Linguistics*, 25(2): 156 – 177.

Hyland, K. 2005. *Metadiscourse*: *Exploring Interaction in Writing*[M]. London and New York: Continuum.

Ifantidou, E. 2005. The Semantics and Pragmatics of Metadiscourse[J]. *Journal of Pragmatics*, 37: 1325 – 1353.

Ifantidou, E. 2001. *Evidentials and Relevance*[M]. Amsterdam/Philadelphia: John Benjamins Publishing Company.

Intaraprawat, P. 1988. Metadiscourse in Native English Speakers and ESL Students' Persuasive Essays[D]. Unpublished Doctoral Dissertation. Normal, IL: Illinois State University.

Ifantidou, E. 2001. Evidential Adverbs and Relevance [J], *Lingua*, (90): 65 – 90.

Ifantidou, E. 2005. The Semantics and Pragmatics of Metadiscourse[J]. *Journal of Pragmatics*, (37): 1325 – 1353.

Jacobson, R. 1960. Closing Statements: Linguistics and Poetics[A]. In T. Sebeok (ed.). *Style in Language* [C]. Cambridge, MA: MIT Press.

Jucker, A. H. 1993. The Discourse Marker *Well*: A Relevance-theoretical Account[J]. *Journal of Pragmatics*, (19):435 –452.

Jung, E. H. 2006. Misunderstanding of Academic Monologues by Non-native Speakers of English [J]. *Journal of Pragmatics*, (38): 1928 – 1942.

Keller, E. 1979. Gambits: Conversational Strategy Signals [J]. *Journal of pragmatics*, (3): 219 – 238.

Khuwaileh, A. A. 1999. The Role of Chunks, Phrases, and Body Language in Understanding Academic Lectures[J]. *System*, (27): 249 – 260.

Lakoff, G. 1972. Hedges: A Study in Meaning Criteria and the Logic of Fuzzy Concepts[A]. In P. Peranteau, J. Levi, and G. Phares (eds). *Papers from the Eighth Regional Meeting*, *Chicago Linguistics Society*[C]. Chicago: Chicago Linguistics Society.

Lautamatti, L. 1978. Observations on the Development of the Topics in Simplified Discourse[A]. In V. Kohonen and N. E. Enkvist (eds.). *Text Linguistics*, *Cognitive Learning*, *and language Teaching*[C]. Turku, Finland: Abo University Press.

Leech, G. 1983. *Principles of Pragmatics*[M]. London: Longman.

Lindemann, S. & A. Mauranen. 2001. 'It's Just Real Messy': The Occurrence and Function of *Just* in a Corpus of Academic Speech [J]. *English for Specific Purposes*, (1): 459 – 476.

Longo, Bernadette. 1994. Current Research in Technical Communication: The Role of Metadiscourse in Persuasion [J]. *Technical Communication*, 4(2): 348 – 352.

Luukka, M. 1992. Metadiscourse in Academic Texts[A]. In Britt-Louise Gunnarsson, P. Linell and B. Nordberg (eds.). *Text and Talk in Professional Contexts*[C]. Lund: Universitetsbiblioteket.

Markkanen, Raija& H. S&tier. 1997. *Hedging and Discourse*: *Approaches to the Analysis of a Pragmatic Phenomenon in Academic Texts* [M]. Berlin: De Gruyter.

Mauranen, A. 1993. Contrastive ESP rhetoric: Metatext in Finnish-English Economics Texts [J]. *English for Specific Purposes*, (12): 3 – 22.

Mauranen, A. 1993. Contrastive ESP Rhetoric [J]. *English for Specific Purpo-*

ses, (12).

Meyer, B. J. F. 1975. *The Organization of Prose and its Effect on Memory*[M]. Amsterdam: North-Holland.

Murphy, D. F. & C. N. Candlin. 1979. Engineering Lecture Discourse and Listening Comprehension[A]. *Practical Papers in English Language Education*[C]. Lancaster Institute for English Language Education, University of Lancaster,

Myers, Greg. 1989. The Pragmatics of Politeness in Scientific Articles[J]. *Applied Linguistics*, (10): 11 – 35.

Nash, Walter. 1992. *An Uncommon Tongue* [M]. London: Routledge.

Palmer, F. R. 1986. *Mood and Modality*[M]. Cambridge: Cambridge University Press.

Pierce, C. 1996. *Collected Papers of Charles Sanders Pierce*[C]. Cambrifge: Harward University Press.

Rabin, C. 1986. The Discourse Status of Commentary[A]. In C. R. Cooper & S. Greenbaum (eds.). *Studying Writing*. Beverly Hills, CA: Sage.

Ragan, S. L. & R. Hopper. 1982. Alignment in the Job Interview [J]. *Journal of Applied Communication Research*, (9): 85 – 103.

Rahman, M. 2004. Aiding the Reader: The Use of Metalanguage Devices in Scientific Discourse [J]. *Nottingham Linguistic Circle*, (18):29 – 48 .

Rossiter, J. 1974. *Theories of Communication* [M]. Oxford: Oxford University Press.

Rounds, P. L. 1987. Characterizing Successful Classroom Discourse for NNS Teaching Assistant Training [J]. *TESOL Quarterly* 21. 4: 643 – 671.

Rouchota, Villy. 1998. *Procedural Meaning and Parenthetical Discourse Markers* [A]. In Jucker & Ziv. *Discourse Markers*[C]. John Benjiamins Publishing Company, 97 – 125.

Sangster, R. 1987. *Metadiscourse and its Categorization*[M]. Bloomington: Indianna University Press.

Schiffrin, D. 1980. Metatalk: Organizational and Evaluative Brackets in Discourse [J]. *Sociological Inquiry: Language and social Interaction*, (50): 199 – 236.

Schiffrin, D. 1987. *Discourse Markers* [M]. Cambridge: Cambridge University Press.

Simpson, Rita C. , Sarah L. Briggs, Janine Ovens, & John M. Swales. 1999. *The Michigan Corpus of Academic Spoken English* [M]. Ann Arbor, MI: The Regents of the University of Michigan.

Sinclair, J. M. & D. Brazil. 1982. *Teacher Talk* [M]. Oxford: Oxford University Press.

Skulstad, A. S. 2005. The Use of Metadiscourse in Introductory Sections of a New Genre [J]. *International Journal of Applied Linguistics*. Volume 15, (1).

Sperber, D. & D. Wilson. 1986/1995. *Relevance: Communication and Cognition* [M]. Oxford: Blackwell.

Steffensen, M. S. & Cheng, X. 1996. *Imaginative Aspects of Comprehension in First and Second Language* [M]. New York: Oxford University Press.

Swales, John. 1990. *Genre Analysis: English in Academic and Research Settings* [M]. Cambridge: Cambridge University Press.

Thomas, J. 1995. *Meaning in Interaction: an Introduction to Pragmatics* [M]. London: Longman.

Thompson, S. E. 2003. Text-structuring, Metadiscourse, Intonation and the Signaling of Organization in Academic Lectures [J]. *Journal of English for Academic Purposes*, (2): 5 – 20.

Tyler, A. 1992. Discourse Structure and the Perception of Incoherence in International Teaching Assistants' Spoken Discourse [J]. *TESOL Quarterly* 26, (4): 713 – 29.

Valero-Games, C. 1996. Contrastive ESP Rhetoric: Metatext in Spanish-English Economics Texts [J]. *English for Specific Purposes*, 15(4): 279 – 294.

Vande Kopple, W. J. 1985. Some Exploratory Discourse on Metadiscourse [J]. *College Composition and Communication*, (36): 82 – 93.

Vande Kopple, W. J. 1991. Themes, Thematic Progressions, and Some Implications for Understanding Discourse [J]. *Written Communication*, (8): 311 – 347.

Verschueren, J. 1999. *Understanding Pragmatics* [M]. Edward Arnold Ltd.

Watts, R. 1989. Taking the Pitcher to the 'Well': Native Speakers' Perception of Their Use of Discourse Markers in Conversation [J]. *Journal of Pragmatics*, (13):203 – 237.

Widdowson, H. 1990. *Aspects of Language Teaching*[M]. Oxford: Oxford University Press.

William, J. W. 1981. Literary Style: The Personal Voice [A]. In Shopen & Williams (eds). *Style and Variables in English*[C]. Cambridge: Mass Winthrop.

Williams, J. W. 1999. *Style: Towards Clarity and Grace*[M]. Chicago and London: The University of Chicago Press.

Wunderlich, D. 1979. *Foundations of Linguistics*[M]. Cambridge: Cambridge University Press.

Young, L. 1994. University Lectures: Macro-structure and Micro-features[A]. In Flowersew (ed.). *Academic Listening Research Perspective*[C]. Cambridge, NY: Cambridge University Press.

成晓光. 1999. 亚语言的理论与应用 [J]. 外语与外语教学. （9）: 4 – 7.

成晓光. 1997. 亚语言研究 [M]. 大连: 辽宁师范大学出版社.

戴炜栋, 束定芳 等. 1995. 英语常用衔接词例解词典 [Z]. 上海: 上海外语教育出版社.

何兆熊. 2000. 新编语用学概要 [M]. 上海: 上海外语教育出版社.

何自然. 1997. 语用学概论 [M]. 长沙: 湖南教育出版社.

胡春华. 2007. 微型学术讲座中元话语的关联阐释 [J]. 西安外国语大学学报, （4）.

胡春华. 2007. 汉语总是意合的吗？——英汉微型学术讲座中元话语探微 [J]. 华南热带农业大学学报, （3）.

胡春华. 2007. 从微型学术讲座中的元话语看外语教学的课堂实施 [J]. 中山大学学报论丛, （5）.

胡壮麟. 1994. 语篇的衔接与连贯 [M]. 上海: 上海外语教育出版社.

贾爱武. 1999. 语言课堂话语模式的分析与改进 [J]. 解放军外国语学院学报, （4）: 72 – 73.

李佐文. 2001. 论元话语对语境的构建和体现 [J]. 外国语, （3）:

44 – 50.

李佐文．2003．元话语：元认知的言语体现［J］．外语研究，（1）：27 – 30.

李彦文，姜迪．1999．英语演说辞精粹［Z］．北京：世界图书出版公司．

刘静．2005．边界轮与话语整体可理解性［J］．解放军外国语学院学报，（4）：6 – 11.

冉永平．2004.言语交际的顺应—关联性分析［J］．外语学刊，（2）：28 – 33

汤燕瑜，刘绍忠．2003．教师语言的语用分析［J］．外语与外语教学，（1）：19 – 23.

杨雪燕．2003．西方有关外语课堂过程研究综述［J］．外语教学，（3）：57 – 62.

杨平．2001．关联—顺应模式［J］．外国语，（6）：21 – 28.

徐海铭．2001．元语篇：跨文化视域下的理论与实证［M］．南京：东南大学出版社．

徐海铭，潘海燕．2005．元语篇的理论和实证研究综述［J］．外国语，（6）：54—61.

张炜，胡春华．2007.微型学术讲座中元话语的顺应论诠释［J］．语文学刊，（6）．